ELITE ATTACK FORCES

GERMAN ELITE FORCES

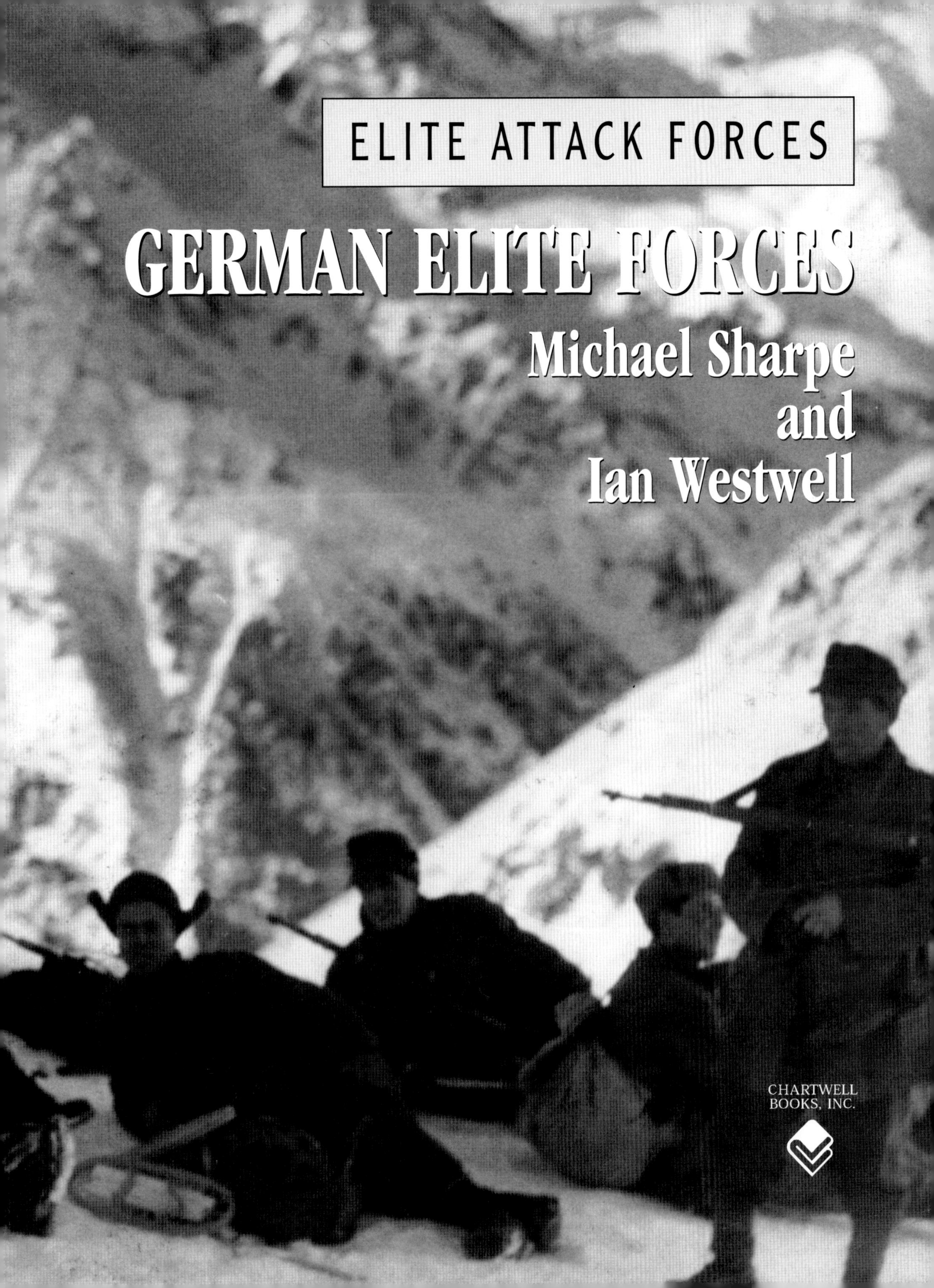

ELITE ATTACK FORCES

GERMAN ELITE FORCES

Michael Sharpe and Ian Westwell

CHARTWELL BOOKS, INC.

This edition published by 2007 by
CHARTWELL BOOKS, INC.
A Division of
BOOK SALES, INC.
114 Northfield Avenue
Edison, New Jersey 08837

ISBN 10: 0-7858-2325-5
ISBN 13: 978-0-7858-2325-4

© 2007 Compendium Publishing Ltd, 43 Frith Street, London, W1D 4SA
Previously published in the Spearhead series

Cataloging-in-Publication data is available from the Library of Congress

All rights reserved. No part of this publication may be reproduced, stored in a retrieval system or transmitted in any form or by any means, electronic, mechanical, photocopying, recording or otherwise without the prior permission of Compendium Publishing Ltd. All correspondence concerning the content of this volume should be addressed to Compendium Publishing Ltd

Printed in China through Printworks Int. Ltd

Acknowledgements
The photographs in this book were supplied by Chris Ellis, George Forty, and TRH Pictures. Artwork on pages 166-167 was by Jan Suermondt. Other illustrative material was provided by John Gresham.

Note: Website information provided in the Reference section was correct when provided by the author. The publisher can accept no responsibility for this information becoming incorrect.

Previous page: 5th Gebirgsjäger infantry company resting high in the mountains while on exercise in Austria.

Right: A 5th Gebirgsjäger trooper sighting for an MG42 gunner.

CONTENTS

5th GEBIRGSJÄGER DIVISION	5
Origins & History	6
Ready for War	9
In Action	15
Equipment, Markings & Camouflage	64
People	86
Assessment	90
Reference	92
BRANDENBURGERS	97
Origins & History	98
Ready for War	104
In Action	109
Insignia, Clothing & Equipment	158
People	172
Assessment	182
Reference	184
Glossary	188
Index	189

5th GEBIRGSJÄGER DIVISION
Hitler's mountain warfare specialists
Michael Sharpe

ORIGINS & HISTORY

From the earliest years of the Third Reich, the German military was expanded well beyond the limits placed on it by the hated Versailles 'diktat'. This expansion eventually embraced the small *Gebirgs*, or mountain, brigades within the newly organised Wehrmacht, so that at the outbreak of war there were three full *Gebirgsjäger* (mountain rifle) divisions on strength. As the war progressed further divisions were raised. By the end, Germany had fielded 19 Gebirgs divisions (11 army and 8 Waffen SS) and four *Hochgebirgs* (high mountain) battalions, although in fact, many of these were 'mountain' units in name only and, particularly within the Waffen SS, noticeably lacking in the skills of mountaincraft. The first SS mountain formation, 6th Gebirgs Division Nord, was formed in 1941 under the name Kampfgruppe Nord, but the standard of training was below that of the true mountain units and they suffered accordingly on the northern sector of the Eastern Front.

A most notable exception was the elite 5th Gebirgs Division, known also as the *Gamsbock* Division or *Sumpfjäger* Division, which was formed in the autumn of 1940 from the 100th Mountain Infantry Regiment of the 1st Gebirgs Division and elements of the 10th Infantry Division. After training in the Bavarian Alps, it first saw action during the spring of 1941 in the Balkans, where it helped crack the Metaxas defensive line and then conquer Greece. Within weeks of the successful Greek campaign, it became part of the German assault force launched against Crete. Again the unit distinguished itself, making a vital intervention at a crucial stage of the battle at Maleme and relieving the beleaguered Fallschirmjäger at Retimo.

From late summer 1941 to March 1942, the division was on occupation duty in Norway. In March 1942 it was sent to the Eastern Front, where it was attached to Army Group North and helped check the Soviet counteroffensive between Lake Ladoga and Novgorod. It remained on the Northern Front (as the northern sector of the Eastern Front is referred to here) and took part in the operations around Leningrad until the end of 1943.

In November, the 5th was withdrawn from the Russian Front and transferred to Italy under the control of the Tenth Army. It took part in the fighting retreat up the Italian mainland, distinguishing itself during the battles for the Gustav and Gothic Lines. Near the end of the war, after fighting on the Italo-French frontier, it surrendered to American forces in Turin in May 1945. During these and other actions the division established for itself an enduring reputation for bravery and professionalism that places it among the foremost units in military history.

ORIGINS OF THE GEBIRGSJÄGER

Although the origins of *Gebirgsjäger* (mountain soldier) in the German army can be traced back only to comparatively recent times, the experiences of commanders reaching as far back as Alexander the Great and Hannibal the Carthaginian (and more recently Napoleon) in trying to negotiate mountainous regions presaged the need for specialist mountain soldiers.

Below: Tough men doing a tough job: an artillery mule team on a mountain path. The last mule carries wicker mats and tarpaulins for emplacing the gun.

Until such time as these were available, mountainous regions were considered by strategists to be at best hostile and at worst impassable, and certainly unsuitable terrain in which to conduct military operations. Large bodies of conventional troops were vulnerable in mountain areas, as evinced by the experience of British troops on the Northwest Frontier of India in the late nineteenth century. Here a numerically inferior force composed of small bands of Afghan tribesmen, highly mobile and with expert knowledge of the terrain, resisted a statistically superior force for a considerable time. As knowledge of the terrain and mobility were key to the success of the small-scale guerrilla actions against the British in northern India, so they were in the mountain battles of subsequent wars.

From the mid-nineteenth century, the introduction of railway networks across Europe vastly increased the speed at which an army could advance. This in turn gave cause for defence planners to turn their attentions to vulnerable mountain regions, and prompted the organisation of mountain troops in certain European armies. In Italy, Alpine troops were trained for operations along Italy's northern border; in France, which has mountains on its frontiers with Spain, Germany and Italy, the Chasseurs Alpins were raised; and Austro-Hungary, with mountainous borders with Italy to the south and Russia to the east, created the Schutzen. The close alliance between the Austro-Hungarian Empire and the newly unified Germany meant that responsibility for the defence of Germany's mountain regions fell to the Austro-Hungarian Army and, at least for a time, its Schutzen largely negated a need for a large German mountain army.

Although mountain training and equipment in the Reichswehr were not standardised until 1914, several formations existed in nineteenth-century Germany that can be regarded as the forerunners of the Gebirgsjäger. These were the Bavarian Jäger battalions, the Schlettstädter Jäger of the Vosges Mountains, the Goslarer Jäger in the Harz Mountains, and reaching further back, the Saxon sharpshooters recruited from among forestry officials in 1809.

Above: The building block of the Gebirgsjäger – a smiling private in service dress.

ALPENKORPS

On 20 October 1914, shortly after the outbreak of the First World War, the Royal Bavarian war ministry gave the order to build up a unit of soldiers on skis, and on 21 November the 1st Bavarian Schneeschuhbataillon was constituted in Munich. This first true German mountain unit was followed in December by the 2nd, 3rd and 4th Schneeschuhbataillons, and in Württemberg and in Prussia further Schneeschuh

> **Order of Battle, Gebirgs Brigade, 1935**
> 98th Gebirgsjäger Regiment
> 99th Gebirgsjäger Regiment
> 100th Gebirgsjäger Regiment
> 79th Gebirgs Artillery Regiment

> **Order of Battle, 5th Gebirgsjäger Division October 1940**
> 85th Gebirgs Infantry Regiment
> 100th Gebirgs Artillery Regiment
> 95th Radfahr Abteilung
> 95th Gebirgs Panzerjäger
> 95th Gebirgs Pionier Abteilung
> 95th Gebirgs Nachrichten Abteilung

(snowshoe) units were raised. Half a year later these battalions had built the 3rd Jäger Regiment, which was attached to a newly formed German Alpenkorps.

The Alpenkorps drew men, mostly from the Württemberg and Bavarian armies, who were local to the mountains and, like their forebears, possessed the skills to conduct both offensive and defensive operations in this terrain. It was envisaged that they would also be employed as guides for the main body of the army, if compelled to pass over mountainous regions, or at times be called on to spearhead an assault. In general, however, there was a distinct shortage of men with Alpine knowledge in Germany, and mountaineering organisations were set up to create a pool of recruits with knowledge of rock climbing and survival skills.

In 1915, the Italian declaration of war against Austria triggered confrontations on the Alpine border between the two countries. With the need for skilled mountain troops now increasingly evident, the Alpenkorps was deployed from its base in Bavaria to Tirol in the Dolomites, on the southern part of the front. It was here that Erwin Rommel, then commander of a Württemburg Gebirgsjäger unit and later the legendary 'Desert Fox' of North Africa, won his 'Blue Max' (Pour le Mérite).

During the Great War, the Alpenkorps fought in Serbia in 1915 and in France at Verdun. In 1916 it was sent to the Romanian Carpathians. In 1917 it went to the Vosges, then again to Romania, and from there to the Alps for the Isonzo battles. In the final year of the war it fought in Flanders, at the River Somme and on the Bulgarian front. During the retreat through Hungary, it prevented the country's revolutionary regime from disarming it and reached German soil in good order.

Owing to the great success of the Alpenkorps in the First World War, the peacetime Reichswehr fought hard to retain its mountain troops. Despite the restriction to a 100,000 strong army imposed by the Versailles Treaty, several units were equipped with mountain gear and trained in mountain warfare in 1925, in the hope that these would form the basis of a future mountain fighting force. Recruits were at first drawn from the mountain-trained Bavarian State Police, and collectively these units were organised as the Gebirgs Brigade, the sole mountain unit at the time of the formation of the Wehrmacht in 1935. The brigade was initially commanded by Generalleutnant Ludwig Kübler and comprised the 98th, 99th and 100th Gebirgsjäger Regiments, in addition to the 79th Gebirgs Artillery Regiment. In August 1937 command of the brigade passed to General Hubert Lanz, and on 9 April 1938, it was formed into the 1st Gebirgs Division in Garmisch-Partenkirchen, Bavaria.

When mobilisation was ordered on 26 August 1939, the 1st Gebirgs Division had an establishment of three regiments, all based in and around Bad Reichenhall, while the four battalions of the 79th Gebirgs Artillery Regiment were located in the area of Garmisch-Partenkirchen. As the establishment of a Gebirgs division was two Jäger regiments, the 100th Regiment was deemed surplus to establishment, detached and, together with an artillery battalion from 79th Gebirgs Artillery Regiment, eventually formed the cadre of the 5th Gebirgs Division on 25 October 1940, in the Tirol region of Austria. The second regiment of the 5th Gebirgs was the former 85th Infantry Regiment, which became supernumerary when the 10th Infantry was upgraded to a Panzergrenadier division. The 10th Infantry also donated some of its artillery to the artillery regiment. Both Jäger regiments retained their original numbers, 85 and 100, although the artillery regiment was redesignated the 95th Gebirgs Artillery Regiment. Command was given to Generalmajor Julius Ringel, a veteran mountain soldier who had served in the First World War (and in the 3rd Austrian Mountain Division before this was amalgamated into the German Army, along with the rest of the Austrian Army, in 1938). The 5th Gebirgs Division was based in Salzburg, Austria, under *Wehrkreis* (war district) XVIII, although the personnel were predominantly from Bavaria.

READY FOR WAR

ROLE

The 5th Gebirgs Division was raised, trained and equipped in advance of the German campaign in Russia, in which it was envisaged that it would fight in its established role as mountain soldiers: that is, as specialist light infantry unburdened with equipment likely to impede rapid movement over difficult ground. Indeed, the terrain in which it was expected to operate dictated that the support elements available to traditional infantry divisions, such as heavy artillery, armoured vehicles or even tanks, more often than not were unavailable, even though in reality most of the battles in Russia were fought across lowland terrain. (Other 'mountain' divisions in fact spent so little time fighting in the mountains that the title seems somewhat inappropriate.) Although special weapons and vehicles were developed – lighter-calibre artillery and howitzers that could be disassembled and carried by pack mules, and lightweight cars – the Gebirgsjäger trained

Below: Mountain troops were expected to travel light, but adverse weather conditions, particularly at height, meant that they had to carry suitable clothing and equipment as well as their weapons. These soldiers are early in the war wearing greatcoats and comforters.

and fought principally as infantry assault formations.

In 1942 the German Army conducted exercises which demonstrated that standard infantry formations could operate successfully in the mountains, provided they were supported by specialist mountain troops. Although this seemed to obviate the need for the Gebirgsjäger, units continued to be raised until the end of the war. As a result of these exercises, between July 1942 and November 1943 some of the Gebirgstruppen, who had learned the skills of skiing and rock climbing from an early age, were creamed off to form specialist Hochgebirgs brigades. In total four battalions were raised, and it was intended that these would provide leadership for normal infantry regiments operating in mountainous terrain. Experience showed that there was no need for such units, and they were later stood down and absorbed into the standard Gebirgs divisions.

RECRUITING

Men for the 5th Gebirgs Division were recruited, at least initially, from the catchment area of Wehrkreis XVIII. This included the mountains of southern Bavaria, where an appreciation of Alpine terrain and the skills needed to fight and survive in it were instilled into young men from an early age. Later in the war, as manpower shortages began to bite, this and every other German division was forced to accept replacements of a lower calibre.

Above: Gebirgsjäger rifle section during training. Note that the section leader carries an MP38.

TRAINING

On arrival at the training depot, which for the Gebirgsjäger was at Garmisch-Partenkirchen in the shadow of the Zugspitz massif and the Waxenstein Mountain, the recruit was issued his equipment and assigned to his barracks. As was common practice in the German Army, whether he be a cook, truck driver, artilleryman or engineer, the recruit was required to train first and foremost in the skills of the infantry. Thus, Gebirgsjäger recruits had to endure basic training on the parade ground, in weapons drill and in other such standards of the military. As in most western armies (but unlike the Russians), the German soldier was trained and expected to be able to use any of the weapons he might come across and not just the one he was issued with. In times of need therefore the soldier could use rifle, heavy machinegun, the battalion mortars, battalion anti-tank guns or whatever weapon came to hand. Only after this training was completed were recruits allowed to specialise.

After about two weeks, the Oath of Allegiance was sworn. As with any other arm of the German army this was marked by a ceremony in which groups of six recruits would form a square on the parade ground and, with one hand on the Reich's War Flag (or in some cases a sword or a gun barrel draped with the regimental colours) and the other hand raised in a salute, would swear allegiance to God and country.

Later came more specialised instruction in rock climbing, cross-country skiing, compass marches, night marches and route marches. Great emphasis was placed on these as, not being part of a motorised formation, the Gebirgsjäger's main form of transportation was his own two feet.

The training syllabus was rooted in the knowledge that the mountain soldier in effect faces two dangers, the first being his enemy and the second his environment. Mountain areas can at times be inhospitable, subject to rapidly changing and hostile weather, rock slides and avalanches, often devoid of shelter, and unable to sustain the growth of plants and shrubs that would normally supplement the soldiers' rations. The troops were disciplined to conserve not just food but also ammunition, medical supplies and other material, as resupply would sometimes be difficult if not impossible. A serious wound could well result in death, as evacuation to a first aid post could take days, in some cases even weeks. Cover was often minimal. Whereas an infantryman on lower ground could dig a slit trench or dugout, mountain troops had no such a luxury. Rocks could sometimes be used to construct a 'sangar', like the ones that were used extensively during the battles for Monte Cassino, but the inside of these shelters could be lethal, with bullets and shells ricocheting around and splintering off razor-sharp lumps of rock.

Whenever Gebirgsjäger were employed, these and other hardships were commonplace. In Poland they undertook exhausting marches across vast plains. In Norway and Lapland they experienced the bitter Arctic weather; in the Balkans and Greece, the harsh and inhospitable mountains of Yugoslavia; the heat of the mountainous regions of Greece and Crete; and in Southern Russia the freezing conditions of the Caucasus Mountains. On many occasions they were involved in operations on normal terrain and proved themselves just as adept at fighting there. When used as conventional infantry, however, their specialist skills and training were wasted (a similar situation to that in which Fallschirmjäger troops found themselves), and the lack of fully motorised units within their divisional structure would often leave them at a disadvantage when employed in this role. The large volume of kit that they were expected to carry meant progress during an advance was slower than an equivalent motorised unit, and held many more dangers.

To cope with these demands, the Gebirgsjäger had above all to possess mental strength and physical stamina. These qualities were much in evidence among the ranks of the 5th Gebirgs Division and the best of the other mountain units, and a strong sense of camaraderie existed between them. During the later stages of the Second World War, men from other army formations were transferred to Gebirgs units to be trained as mountain troops but, although good soldiers, they could not develop the skills that seasoned Jäger had gained through years of experience from a very early age in their mountain towns and villages.

Above: Climbing – especially in Alpine conditions – is a skill that has to be learnt and practised assiduously. Early recruits came from Bavaria and many already possessed the basic climbing techniques that later recruits would need to learn.

ORGANISATION

The organisation of a Gebirgs Division followed the standard of the army. The division was composed of two Jäger regiments, each consisting of three Gebirgsjäger battalions and a headquarters group. In addition there was a regiment of artillery, and signals, engineer, semi-motorised reconnaissance, motorised anti-tank and medical units, as well as supply troops and administrative services.

The authorised strength of a typical mountain division was:
14,000 men
5,500–6,000 animals, including:
- 1,500 horses
- 4,300 pack animals
- 550 mountain horses

1,400 vehicles (including cars and motorcycles)
600 horse-drawn vehicles
13,000 rifles
2,200 pistols
500 machine pistols
416 light machine guns
66 light mortars

Below: The mountain troops were lucky with their commanders, such as the 'Hero of Narvik' General der Gebirgstruppen Eduard Dietl seen here during the operations in Norway.

44 medium mortars
75 anti-tank rifles
80 heavy machine guns
16 light infantry guns
24 light mountain guns
12 light mountain howitzers
12 heavy field howitzers
4 heavy infantry guns
39 anti-tank guns
12 light flak guns

Senior officers would often lead detachments that were usually no larger than battalion size (as this was realistically the largest force that could be deployed in mountain areas). The standard make-up of a battalion was 877 officers and men, organised into three Jäger companies, and usually one machine gun, one anti-tank and one heavy weapons company. Each Jäger company had an average complement of 147 men and was equipped with 12 machine guns, one anti-tank rifle and two 8 cm mortars (a little over 3 inches). Within the battalion, the German army had far fewer junior officers than other western armies (especially the Americans). This had the effect of encouraging senior NCOs and junior officers to assume more responsibility and thus show greater initiative than would be expected in other armies.

TACTICS

Unique guidelines governed the operations and tactical deployment of the Gebirgstruppen. Underpinning these guidelines was the knowledge that preparation and planning are vital to mountain warfare, and this was constantly stressed in their fighting manuals. Meticulous preparation was required, no matter how small the operation being undertaken, for the omission of even the smallest item of kit, or an error in navigational could prove fatal.

As most mountainous areas at the time lacked adequate road networks, consideration had to be given to not only troop movements but also to movement of supply trains and the transportation of heavy equipment. Avalanches also proved a real and constant threat to these movements. Thus careful map reading and weather forecasting were vital to enable troops to avoid dangerous areas or pass through with minimal risk. To minimise the threat of avalanches when traversing a slope, men were carefully spaced in columns at 30-yard intervals, and zigzagged lightly as they moved. Once one group had made it to safe ground, the next group could then move off. Vertical ascents or descents were not allowed due to the risk of dislodging snow.

Later in the war, the 5th Gebirgs troops often found themselves, like Fallschirmjäger

Above: A Gebirgsjäger company on a training march. The first five men are the MG08 machine gun crew carrying their weapon in sections.

Above: Another view of Dietl, here in the mountains with his staff officers. Note the usual variations in footware and puttees worn by mountain troops.

units, thrown into the line as ordinary infantry, far from their natural environment, and they frequently suffered as a result.

However, morale and esprit de corps in mountain troop units was almost universally very high, and commanders such as General der Gebirgstruppen Eduard Dietl, the 'Hero of Narvik', and 5th Gebirgs commander Julius 'Papa' Ringel were idolised by their men. When in their element – the high mountain peaks of Norway or the Caucasus – the Gebirgsjäger fought with an elan and determination that were second to none.

IN ACTION

On completion of training, the 5th Gebirgs Division was held in reserve at home for several months under XVIII Mountain Corps of the Second Army assigned to Army Group C. Then, in March 1941, it was posted to the Balkans to take part in the invasion of Greece: Operation 'Marita'. After the fall of Greece, it was landed on Crete, where it played a significant role in helping to secure the island from Allied forces that had been evacuated there. Following a spell of occupation duty on Crete, the division was posted back to Germany for rest and refitting. In March 1942, with the invasion of Russia already 10 months old, it was sent to the Eastern Front to take part in operations against Leningrad in the Volkhov region. Here it remained until November 1943, fulfilling the role of a 'fire brigade' for the Eighteenth Army, serving at various times on the Volkhov front, near Mga, near Schlüsselburg and on the Neva near Kolpino.

From the Eastern Front, the 5th Gebirgs Division was moved to Italy and in late 1943 arrived on the 'Gustav Line' near Cassino. It took part in the defensive battles up through Italy, encompassing actions on the Gustav Line at Cassino, and on the Gothic Line. Finally, late in the war, the division fought in the mountain region between France and Italy, before surrendering to US forces near Turin in May, 1945.

Order of battle, 5th Gebirgsjäger Division, 1 January 1941
I./,II./,III./ 85th Gebirgsjäger Regiment
I./,II./,III./ 100th Gebirgsjäger Regiment
I./,II./,III./,IV./ 95th Gebirgs Artillery Regiment
95th Aufklärungs (Battalion) Reconnaissance Abteilung
95th Panzerjäger (Anti-tank) Abteilung (motorised)
95th Gebirgs Pionier (Engineer) Battalion
95th Nachrichten (Signals) Abteilung
95th Nachschubtruppen (supply troops)

Main units
85th Gebirgsjäger Regiment
100th Gebirgsjäger Regiment
100th Gebirgs Artillery Regiment
95th Radfahr Abteilung
95th Gebirgs Panzerjäger Abteilung
95th Gebirgs Pionier Abteilung
95th Gebirgs Nachrichten Abteilung

POLAND AND FRANCE

100th Gebirgsjäger Regiment, which was transferred in autumn 1940 to the newly constituted 5th Gebirgs Division, had been heavily involved in the Polish campaign. Fighting in the Carpathian Mountains, the regiment captured the important Dukla Pass. The following spring it was committed to the crossings of the Maas River and later the Loire. Although predating the formation of the 5th Gebirgs Division, these actions provided vital combat experience for the tough battles in Greece.

MUSSOLINI AND GREECE

In the autumn of 1940, as Hitler consolidated his control over much of northwest Europe, Italian forces launched a surprise invasion of Greece to help satisfy Mussolini's ambitions for a Mediterranean empire to rival the one that his ally was building in northern Europe. The attack, which came from occupied Albania on 28 October, soon bogged down in torrential rain and mud before the stalwart defence put up by the Greek armies. Counterattacks launched between November and the New Year soon had the Italian armies on the back foot.

Mussolini's actions had been intended to impress his ally, but in fact had the opposite effect. In private, a deeply angered Hitler referred to the invasion as a 'regrettable blunder', and his suspicions regarding the effectiveness of the Italian military increased. The attack had only succeeded in driving the Greeks into an closer alliance with the

Above and Right: The first wholesale use of the Gebirgsjäger was during the Norway campaign when 3rd Gebirgsjäger under General Dietl performed to great effect. These two photographs of the campaign show: **(above)** the unit disembarking from a destroyer and **(right)** a signals section aboard a fishing boat at Narvik. Note the Edelweiss Gebirgsjäger badge on the right sleeve of the man at left. (See page 64 for more information on this.)

Left: DFS 230A glider carrying the 'combined operations' insignia for the Narvik campaign, incorporating a propeller for the Luftwaffe, an anchor for the Kriegsmarine and an Edelweiss for the Gebirgsjäger.

Below: Gebirgsjäger parade in Narvik after landing.

Above: Gebirgsjäger units made extensive use of animals – particularly pack animals – for artillery and transport. This supply column on the march is using some of the unit's authorised strength of 600 horse-drawn vehicles.

British, who honoured an earlier promise by landing troops on Crete and Lemnos, thus threatening Hitler's southern flank in advance of the invasion of Russia, and equally importantly, the vital Romanian oilfields. Hitler considered he had no choice but to send German forces to support the Italians, despite the setback to the timetable for the invasion of Russia, and ordered an invasion of Greece with a force of at least 10 divisions.

Operation 'Marita'

Planning for the invasion of Greece – Operation 'Marita' – at once began in earnest. This envisaged a limited move against eastern Thrace from Bulgaria, taking Salonika and the coast and pre-empting any attempt by the British to land behind the German advance into southern Russia. No further incursion was planned at this stage. However, these plans were upset by events in Yugoslavia where, in March 1941, a coup d'état against the pro-Axis regent installed a new government with an anti-German stance. Hitler now prepared another operation against Yugoslavia, codenamed '*Strafe*' (punishment), for the spring of 1941, to run concurrently with the attack on Greece. In the combined operation the Twelfth Army (Wilhelm List) was ordered to move on Greece, while the Second Army (M. F. von Weichs), Paul von Kleist's First Panzer Group and the Hungarian Third Army moved on Yugoslavia. The added burden actually produced a tactical advantage for the Greek operation. No longer would the German generals be restricted to a frontal assault on the formidable Metaxas Line along the Bulgarian–Greek frontier. They could now exploit the pathways into Greece that they had coveted from the start: the lightly defended passes leading from Yugoslavia.

For the operation the 5th Gebirgs Division was attached to XVIII Corps of the Twelfth Army, charged with penetrating the heavily defended 125-mile Metaxas Line that covered the Bulgarian border to the north and east of Salonika. In total, List's Twelfth Army numbered eight infantry divisions and the 2nd and 9th Panzer Divisions, divided among XL Panzer Corps (Georg Stumme), XVIII Mountain Corps (Franz Boehme), and XXX Corps (Otto Hartmann). They were faced by troops of the Greek Second Army (70,000 men) in the Metaxas Line, whose western flank was covered by the Yugoslav Fifth Army and the Greek 20th Infantry Division. To block an attempted thrust down the Aliakmon Valley west of Mount Olympus, the British had despatched an expeditionary force from North Africa under General Henry Maitland Wilson. This comprised some 75,000 men, including the 6th Australian Infantry Division, the 2nd New Zealand Division and the 1st Armoured Brigade, and could field some 100 tanks. The Australian 7th Division and a Polish brigade were intended for Greece as well, but were held back for North Africa, as Rommel was at that time advancing into Cyrenaica.

List's Operation 'Marita' is generally considered a masterpiece of military planning. Recognising the Yugoslav Fifth Army as the weak link in the Allied position, he struck out to the west at 05:15 on 6 April, before the Yugoslavs had time to complete mobilisation. As Weichs' Second Army thrust south into Yugoslavia from Austria, and Kleist's First Panzer Group pushed toward Belgrade from Bulgaria, Twelfth Army attacked Thrace, sending XL Corps westwards through the Vardar region toward Macedonia. On 7 April, the Kriva Pass and Skopje were taken after heavy fighting with the Yugoslav Third Army. But instead of heading for the Aliakmon Valley as the Allies anticipated, List then

ORDER OF BATTLE, 5th GEBIRGSJÄGER DIVISION, APRIL 1941

HQ
Staff Radio Support

- **95th Pionier Battalion**
  (Major Schatte)
  1/95th Pionier Company
  2/95th Pionier Company
  3/95th Pionier Company

- **95th Panzerjäger Battalion**
  (Major Bindermann)
  (37mm L/45 PAK 35/36)
  1/95th PzJäg Company
  2/95th PzJäg Company

- **95th Aufklärungs Battalion**
  (Major Graf Castell zu Castell)
  1/95th Aufkl Company
  2/95th Aufkl Company

- **95th Gebirgsjäger Artillery Regiment**
  (Oberstleutnant Wittmann)
  I/95th Art Battalion, Major von Sternbach
  (75mm L/19 GebG 36)
  II/95th Art Battalion, Major Raithel
  (105mm leFH)

- **85th Gebirgsjäger Regiment**
  (Oberst Krakau)
  I. 85th Battalion Gebirgsjäger Regiment
  (Major Dr Treck)
  1st Gebirgsjäger Company
  2nd Gebirgsjäger Company
  3rd Gebirgsjäger Company
  4th Gebirgsjäger Company
  5th Gebirgsjäger Company

- **100th Gebirgsjäger Regiment**
  (Oberst Utz)
  I/100th Gebirgsjäger Regiment
  (Major Schrank)
  1st Gebirgsjäger Company
  2nd Gebirgsjäger Company
  3rd Gebirgsjäger Company
  4th Gebirgsjäger Company
  5th Gebirgsjäger Company

  II. Battalion/100th Gebirgsjäger
  Regiment (Major Friedmann)
  6th Gebirgsjäger Company
  7th Gebirgsjäger Company
  8th Gebirgsjäger Company
  9th Gebirgsjäger Company
  10th Gebirgsjäger Company

- **55th Krad (motorcycle recce) Battalion**
  1/55th Krad Company
  2/55th Krad Company
  4/55th Krad Company

- **84th Flak Battalion**
  (20mm L113 AA Flak 38)
  1st Flak Company
  2nd Flak Company
  3rd Flak Company
  4th Flak Company

- **Light Convoy 1**
  III/100th Gebirgsjäger Regiment
  (Major Ehall)
  (37mm L/45 PAK 35/36)
  11th Gebirgsjäger Company
  12th Gebirgsjäger Company
  13th Gebirgsjäger Company
  14th Gebirgsjäger Company
  15th Gebirgsjäger Company

- **666 Pionier (Engineer) Battalion**
  1st Pionier Company
  2nd Pionier Company
  3rd Pionier Company
  4th Pionier Company
  3/7th Pionier

- **Light Convoy 2**
  II. 85th Battalion Gebirgsjäger Regiment
  (Major Esch)
  (37mm L45 PAK 35/36)
  6th Gebirgsjäger Company
  7th Gebirgsjäger Company
  8th Gebirgsjäger Company
  9th Gebirgsjäger Company
  (75mm L/19 GebG 36)
  10th Gebirgsjäger Company (MMG)

- **659th Pionier Battalion**
  1/659th Pionier Company
  2/659th Pionier Company
  3/659th Pionier Company
  4/659th Pionier Company

- **I./118th Artillery Battalion**
  (105mm leFH)

- **85th Flak Battalion** (20L113 AA FLAK 38)
  1st Flak Company
  2nd Flak Company
  3rd Flak Company
  4th Flak Company
  3/609th Motorised Flak (20L113 AA FLAK 38)

ordered XL Panzer Corps to attack through the strategically important Monastir Gap for Kozani, further west – the gateway into Greece on the open flank of the Allied line along the Vermion mountains and the Greek front in Albania.

The Metaxas Line

Meanwhile XXX Corps was moving on western Thrace and XVIII Mountain Corps preparing to assault the 'Metaxas' Line.

Beginning in April 1939, the Greek government had poured enormous sums of money into the construction of this system of defensive works in the mountains covering the Bulgarian border, which was named the Metaxas Line in honour of the then Prime Minister, Ioannis Metaxas. The defences consisted of heavily fortified concrete blockhouses, many of them interlinked by tunnels, and manned by first-rate Greek troops. In front of these were smaller outposts and weapons pits.

The German plan called for a frontal attack on this position, to be undertaken by one German infantry division and the reinforced 5th and 6th Gebirgs Divisions. In the days prior to the attack, the troops hauled ammunition and supplies from the Bulgarian town of Petrich up into their forward positions, sequestered on the wooded slopes below the enemy line. Observing the Gebirgsjäger at this task their comrades-in-arms began referring to them as the *Gamsbock* or 'mountain goats', a name that was enthusiastically adopted by the troops themselves. To support the infantry, artillery also had to be manhandled up the slopes.

By 05:00 on the morning of 6 April, the men of the 5th Gebirgs Division were poised for the attack. They had strapped rifles across their chests, and wire cutters, flare guns, entrenching tools and hand grenades hung from their belts. Shortly after 05:00 the gunners began to lay down a heavy preparation. Then flights of Ju87 Stukas approached to pound the ground positions, raising clouds of dust and grit that shrouded the mountaintops. While the bombs were still falling, the troops left the cover of the woods and scrambled up the snowy slopes that the Greeks had cleared of timber to provide their gunners with unrestricted fields of fire. Withering fire fell down on the advancing troops, proof that the large concrete and steel bunkers had largely withstood the barrage. Over the next few hours, in the face of extremely tough resistance from the Greek defenders, the mountain troops began to gouge holes in the line by clearing the trenches that flanked the bunkers. The engineers systematically blasted the casemates open with explosives or incinerated the defenders with flamethrowers aimed through the embrasures. Around midday the Greeks responded by calling in artillery fire on their own positions. Exposed on the slopes, the Gebirgsjäger huddled in the abandoned Greek trenches or burrowed into shell craters for protection. Through the afternoon and evening, the Greek troops emerged sporadically from their culverts in an effort to drive the Germans from the positions they had seized. But the men of the 5th Gebirgs Division were not about to give up their hard-won toeholds in the Metaxas Line. Bolstered

Below: Map showing the Metaxas Line and 5th Gebirgsjäger operations in the Balkans.

by reinforcements during the night, they attacked with renewed determination at dawn. Grappling up cliffs made slippery by the freezing rain, they blasted or burned the Greeks from one bunker after another.

Through the day, each carefully located nest of fortifications along the line of advance was gradually reduced through a combination of frontal and enveloping attacks, with tactical support from Luftwaffe aircraft. Using these methods the advanced units of the 5th Gebirgs Division, together with the reinforced 125th Infantry Regiment, finally penetrated the Metaxas Line on the evening of 7 April, pouring through large gaps in the line out onto the plain to the south. The savage contest cost the division 160 lives – nine more than the Wehrmacht had lost in the entire campaign in Yugoslavia.

Meanwhile the 6th Gebirgs Division crossed a 7,000-foot snow-covered mountain range and broke through the line at a point that had been considered inaccessible by the Greeks. The division reached the rail line to Salonika east of Lake Dojran on the evening of 7 April, and entered Kherson two days later.

After repelling several fierce counterattacks, the 5th Gebirgs Division moved on Neon Petritsi, and with this taken gained access to the important Rupul Gorge from the south. The 125th Infantry Regiment, which was attacking the gorge from the north, suffered such heavy casualties that it had to be withdrawn from further action after it had reached its objective.

Some of the fortresses in the line held out for days after the German attack divisions had bypassed them, and could not be reduced until heavy guns were brought up. However, in a deft move around the Metaxas Line, the 2nd Panzer Division motored west to the Yugoslav town of Strumica on 6 April, encountering little resistance on the way. The panzers then turned south towards the Greek border, brushed aside a Greek motorised infantry division near Lake Dojran, and took Salonika without a fight on 9 April. Coupled with the advance of XVIII Mountain Corps across the Metaxas Line, the armoured thrust succeeded in cutting off a large part of the Greek Second Army in Eastern Thrace and led to the collapse of Greek resistance east of the Vardar River. On 9 April the Greek Second Army surrendered unconditionally (the number of prisoners taken has never been established because the Germans released all Greek soldiers after disarming them). On the left wing, XXX Infantry Corps faced weaker opposition than west of the Nestos River, but had to overcome poor road conditions that delayed the movement of artillery and supplies. By the evening of 8 April, its attached 164th Infantry Division had captured Xanthi, while the 50th Infantry Division had advanced far beyond Komotini toward the Nestos, which both divisions reached on the next day.

Now only the newly formed Allied Group W, consisting of the British and Commonwealth forces and two inexperienced Greek divisions, stood in the way of the advance. In light of the capture of Salonika the group commander, Wilson, decided that a defence of Greece's northwest frontier was futile, and instead set up his main defensive line in a short arc extending westward from the Aegean coast near Mount Olympus to the Aliakmon River – a position that conceded northern Greece to the Germans but guarded the main approaches to Athens.

Stumme's XL Panzer Corps was even then poised at the northern end of the Monastir Gap, the strategic corridor from Yugoslavia to central Greece. On 10 April his lead units began to push through the narrows, and early the next morning ran into a 3,000-strong rearguard that Wilson had deployed on the panzer's route of advance in anticipation of the onslaught. Although eventually forced to withdraw, they succeeded in delaying the German advance, giving Wilson valuable time to establish his main line.

The rapid advance of XL Panzer Corps was now seriously jeopardising the position of the Greek First Army in Albania. However, it was not until 13 April that the first Greek elements began to pull back toward the Pindus Mountains. On the same day Stumme

Above: Mountain bivouac.

Above: General Ringel (second right) and a senior staff officer meet sympathetic fighters in Yugoslavia.

ordered the Leibstandarte Division and 73rd Infantry Division to the crossroads at Kastoria to stop the stream of retreating Greek troops, and the following 48 hours witnessed heavy fighting. On 19 April the 1st SS Regiment was ordered to advance southeastward in the direction of Yanina, to cut off the Greeks' route of withdrawal to the south and complete their encirclement. Realising the hopelessness of the situation, the Greek commander offered to surrender his 14 divisions. After brief negotiations, the surrender was accepted with honourable terms for the defeated. In recognition of the valour with which the Greek troops had fought, their officers were permitted to retain their side arms. The soldiers were not treated as prisoners of war and were allowed to go home after the demobilisation of their units.

Mount Olympus

As the advance continued apace, Boehme, XVIII Mountain Corps commander, had been forced to wait until the rear elements of his divisions that were lagging behind in the Rhodope Mountains were able to close up. The advance in the direction of the Vardar River was resumed as soon as the bulk of the corps had been reassembled. Once the Vardar crossing had been accomplished on 11 April, 6th Gebirgs Division drove in the direction of Edhessa and then turned southward toward Verroia. After capturing that town the division established a bridgehead across the Aliakmon and pushed on to the high ground at the foothills of Mount Olympus. The 2nd Panzer Division, with the 5th Gebirgs and 72nd Infantry Divisions closing up along the route of advance, continued on the left flank down the Aegean coast. The force crossed the Aliakmon near the river bend and entered Katerini on 14 April. That same day, the lead units reached a point where the slopes of Mount Olympus drop sharply to the sea.

Meanwhile the remainder of Stumme's force continued the advance in the direction of Athens and the Allied line. On 13 April, the 9th Panzer Division clashed with a British tank brigade at Ptolemais, devastating Wilson's armoured reserves. That same evening the division established a bridgehead across the Aliakmon River, and on the next day captured Kozani on the west side of the Vermion Mountains. For the next three days, however, the advance was stalled in front of the strongly fortified mountain positions held by the British.

Now without armoured support, Wilson reached the conclusion that his position was no longer tenable. The rapid progress of XL Panzer Corps was alarming enough, but in recent days General Boehme's XVIII Mountain Corps had regrouped in Salonika and was advancing down the Aegean coast.

With the threat of encirclement by these two pincers looming, and reinforcement from elsewhere in the Mediterranean out of the question, Wilson reluctantly ordered a withdrawal from the Vermion Mountains and lower Aliakmon River to Thermopylae, leaving rearguard units to hold up the advance.

Simultaneously with the main thrust into central Greece, the Twelfth Army completed the pacification of eastern Macedonia, western Thrace and the Aegean Islands. Following its capitulation, the Greek Second Army was demobilising in orderly fashion, leaving only isolated hostile forces active in these areas. Airborne units, together with elements of the 6th Gebirgs Division, were employed in the seizure of some of the larger Cyclades and Sporadhes Islands.

On the coast 2nd Panzer worked through an attack on rearguard positions held by New Zealand XXI Battalion on the Platomon Ridge. At first the tanks tried a frontal assault but made no headway. Then an infantry battalion managed to climb the western side of the ridge and encircle the defenders, who were forced to retreat to the Pinios Gorge, the last potential stronghold before Thermopylae.

Here the New Zealanders were reinforced by two Australian battalions and some artillery, which thwarted initial attempts by the panzers to push through the gorge at dawn on 18 April. However, hoping to outflank the New Zealand battalion, Boehme had dispatched the 6th Gebirgs Division on an arduous trek across the mountains to seal the western exit of the gorge. In the afternoon, infantry began to cross the Pinios River on floats, secured the road on the far side, and effectively cut off the defenders' line of retreat. Lacking proper radio equipment and fighting in isolated units, the defenders did not realise their plight and were all but annihilated in the ensuing struggle. With the fighting for the Pinios Gorge at an end, XVIII Mountain Corps entered the Plain of Thessaly hard on the heels of the Allied forces. The two days that it had taken for Boehme's corps to break through had been just sufficient for Wilson to pull back his right wing and avoid encirclement.

Larisa

During the night of 17 April, the rapid advance of XVIII Mountain Corps onto the Plain of Thessaly, threatening the British route of withdrawal through Larisa, forced an evacuation of the Aliakmon position. The British succeeded in breaking contact with the German outposts and left their positions, which had remained intact throughout the relentless attacks. On 19 April, the first XVIII Mountain Corps troops entered the town, where they found extensive stocks that the British had not had time to destroy. The capture of Larisa also brought the prize of the airfield, where the British had left their supply dumps intact.

During the fighting in the Mount Olympus area, the corps had encountered severe logistical problems because of the bad roads and traffic congestion. These difficulties had been only partially alleviated by airdrops and by shipping ammunition, rations and gasoline by lighter along the Aegean coast. The capture of rations and fuel stocks at

Below: Mountain infantry company on the march.

Larisa, ensured that Boehme's spearhead units were able to leave the Lamia area with adequate supplies. At Volos too, the Germans captured large quantities of diesel and crude oil, although Volos, the only port in central Greece that had a satisfactory capacity, could not be cleared of mines before 27 April.

For the German forces it was now primarily a question of maintaining contact with the retreating British forces and countering their evacuation plans. The infantry divisions were withdrawn from action because they lacked mobility. The 2nd and 5th Panzer Divisions, the 1st SS Motorised Infantry Regiment, and the 5th and 6th Gebirgs Divisions were ordered to continued the pursuit. As early as 16 April, the German command had realised that the British were evacuating their troops aboard ships at Volos and Piraeus. Numerous units were re-embarked during the last few days before the ports fell on 21 April.

XL Panzer Corps drive

Simultaneously with Boehme's advance down the Aegean coast, the 9th Panzer Division was attacking the western Aliakmon positions. In the face of stout defence by New Zealand troops, Stumme sent the bulk of his force on a wide flanking movement beyond the fringe of the British line, but this could only move at a crawl on appalling roads and took until 17 April to arrive. As soon as General Stumme realised that the enemy rearguard had withdrawn beyond the immediate reach of his spearheads, he issued orders giving Luftwaffe ground personnel traffic priority along the Kozani–Larisa road, as large-scale demolitions were delaying the German pursuit on the ground. However,

Below: Mountain troops on the Balkans Front make use of an 'acquired' Italian Semovente L40 da 47/32 SP gun. Armoured vehicles were not part of the Gebirgsjäger establishment, officially at least.

tactical air support units were able to operate from fields close to the fast-moving mobile forces, and harried the retreating British columns incessantly.

Thermopylae Pass

It appeared to all eyes that the not so distant calamity at Dunkirk was about to be repeated in the Balkans. Mindful of this General Wilson ordered a rearguard to make a last stand at Thermopylae Pass, the gateway to Athens, to permit the evacuation of the main body of British forces. On the evening of 21 April German air reconnaissance information indicated that the British defence line consisted of light field fortifications, the construction of which did not seem to have progressed beyond the initial stage. Other air reconnaissance reports showed that British troops were still being evacuated from the ports of Piraeus and Khalkis.

By 22 April a flying column of the 5th Panzer Division was attacking the Thermopylae positions defended by ANZAC infantry, artillery and armour. Although the initial German probing attacks were unsuccessful, a wide enveloping movement was undertaken the next day by 6th Gebirgs Division troops who crossed the difficult terrain west of the ANZAC positions. This operation took place in concert with another outflanking manoeuvre performed by a tank-supported motorcycle battalion advancing via Molos. After offering strong resistance along the Molos road, the ANZAC troops abandoned the Thermopylae Pass during the night of 24–25 April.

Drive on Athens

After abandoning the Thermopylae area the British rearguards withdrew to an improvised position south of Thebes, where they erected a last obstacle in front of Athens. The motorcycle battalion of the 2nd Panzer Division, which had crossed to the island of Euboea to seize the port of Khalkis and had subsequently returned to the mainland, was given the mission of outflanking the British rearguard. The motorcycle troops encountered only slight resistance, and on the morning of 27 April the first Germans entered the Greek capital. They captured intact large quantities of fuel, several thousand tons of ammunition, 10 trucks loaded with sugar and 10 truckloads of other rations in addition to various other equipment, weapons and medical supplies.

By 30 April the last British troops had either escaped or been taken prisoner and hostilities ceased. During the spectacular campaign in Greece, List captured 90,000 Yugoslavs, an estimated 270,000 Greeks, and more than 12,000 British, Australian and New Zealand troops. However, although the BEF lost much of its vital heavy equipment during the Greek campaign, some 50,000 men were able to make good their escape to the island of Crete.

List's own losses were 1,100 killed and 4,000 wounded or missing. After the fall of Athens the Twelfth Army and 5th Gebirgs Division stayed in Athens, where they enjoyed a brief rest before the next phase of the Balkans conquest got underway.

Below: The ability to move quickly over rough terrain without heavy equipment made demands on the skill and ingenuity of the Gebirgs engineers.

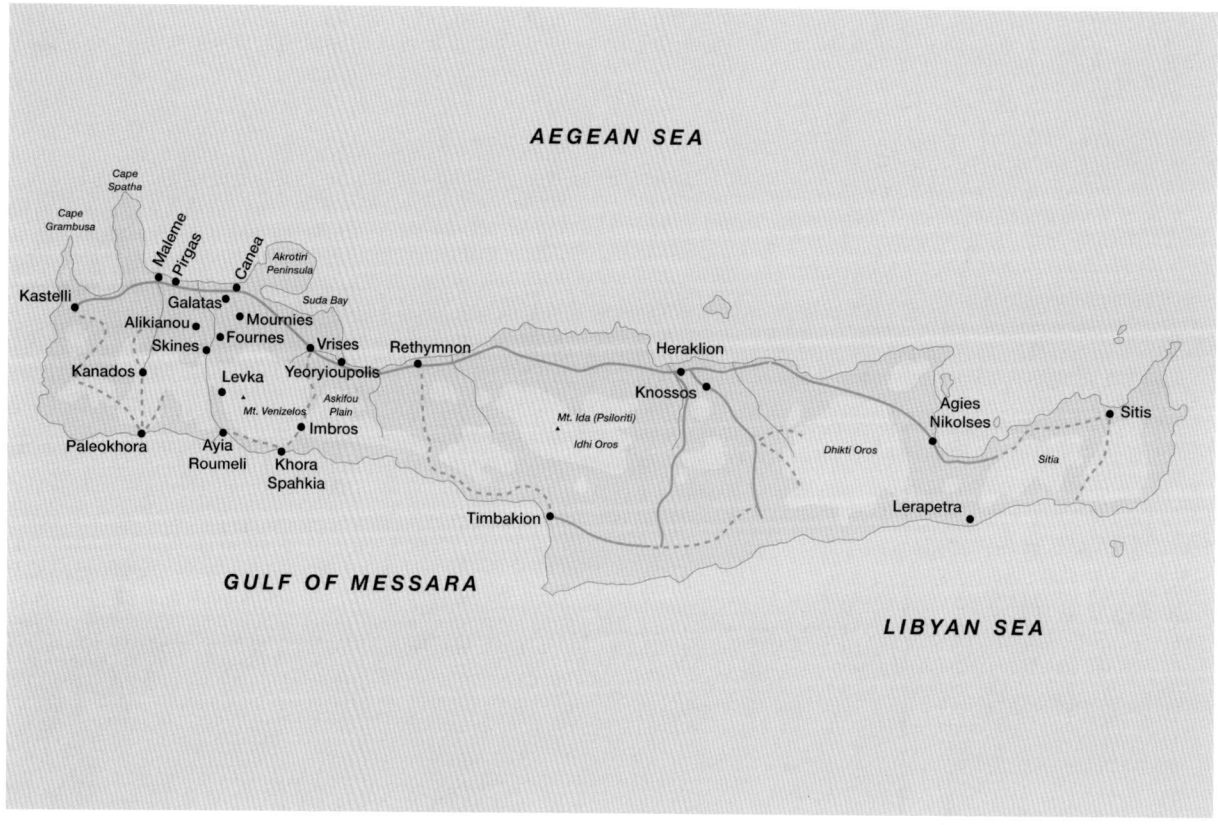

Above: Map of Crete.

CRETE

Recognising the supremacy of the Royal Navy in the Eastern Mediterranean, Hitler intended to break off the Balkans campaign in southern Greece. But the rout of Allied forces in Greece left them badly weakened, and Luftwaffe commanders were quick to recognise the opportunity to seize another prize – the island of Crete – by airborne assault.

The strategic importance of Crete lies in its position guarding access to the Eastern entrances to the Mediterranean, and during the Second World War it also offered an important staging point for flights to North Africa. British forces had occupied the island in October 1940 with a view to using it for future operations in the Balkans, the source of much of Germany's oil and minerals. Furthermore, the occupation offered an opportunity to maintain naval supremacy in the eastern Mediterranean, as the Cretan port of Suda provided the Mediterranean Fleet with a forward base 420 miles north of Alexandria.

The staff of Luftflotte 4 – which had been committed to the Balkans under command of Alexander Löhr – conceived the idea of capturing the island with airborne forces and forwarded the plan to Göring at the time of the invasion of Greece. He thought highly of it but the OKW (Oberkommando der Wehrmacht) preferred action against Malta, a crucial link in the Allied chain of supply to North Africa.

However, on 20 April, after a conference with Generalleutnant Kurt Student (commander of XI Fliegerkorps), Hitler decided in favour of Crete. His decision was influenced by two key factors. First, any opportunity to remove the threat to the Ploesti oilfields in Romania warranted attention. As an added incentive, capture of the island would offer an ideal forward base from which to conduct offensive air and naval operations and

Above: 5th Gebirgsjäger Division was the follow-up force during Operation *'Merkur'* on Crete. A significant number of men was to be air-landed. Here, members of the division wait next to the Junkers Ju52 transports.

to support the ground offensive in Egypt. Hitler was adamant that there was to be no further delay to the start of the Russian campaign, and five days later Directive No. 28 (Operation *'Merkur'* – Mercury) was issued. This was to be a Luftwaffe operation under the executive responsibility of General Löhr, and was scheduled for 16 May.

Although both Luftflotte 4 and XI Fliegerkorps submitted detail plans, it was the latter's scheme that was adopted. Since the troops were to be entirely resupplied by air in the initial stages, success depended on the capture of one of Crete's airfields. Recognising this fact, the XI Fliegerkorps plan envisaged the simultaneous landing of gliders and air drop of parachute troops at seven points. The first wave of airborne troops was to strike at H-Hour against Maleme and Canea. The second wave was to descend at H plus 8 hours on Rethymnon (modern Retimo) and at Heraklion. These 15,000 combat troops were to link up from distances of about 10 to 80 miles apart as soon as possible.

On the second day, elements of the 5th Gebirgs with heavier weapons were to be airlifted to the three airfields captured by the first assault, followed by a third wave carried across the sea to Heraklion, Suda Bay and any minor ports open to shipping in Konteradmiral Karlgeorg Schüster's convoy. This would land 6,000 further troops and heavy equipment that could not be airlifted, including the field guns, anti-tank guns and panzers of the 31st Panzer Regiment, ammunition, rations and other supplies. The Royal Navy maintained a strong naval presence around Crete, and there were no Kriegsmarine units available. The convoys were made up largely of small caiques and coastal freighters that had been captured during the Greek campaign and were assembled in the port of Piraeus. Clearly, the convoys would be frighteningly vulnerable if still at sea at night, when the Luftwaffe could not provide air cover and the Royal Navy ruled the sea.

Throughout the operation, the 716 fighters, bombers and recce aircraft of VIII Fliegerkorps would be providing powerful tactical support. This was the formation which

Above: Many mountain troops were transported by sea during the battles for Greece and Crete. Loaded at Piraeus and Chalkis in flotillas of Greek caiques, two battalions of the 85th Gebirgsjäger Regiment were en route to Crete with an escort of Italian warships when the Royal Navy intercepted the convoy. Over 500 Gebirgsjäger died in the battle.

had swept the Royal Air Force out of Greece in April and achieved almost total domination of the skies over Crete in the first weeks of May.

Considered in hindsight, this plan had the advantage of putting the Germans in possession of all strategic points on the island in one lightning strike, after which a follow-up operation would clear any remaining pockets of opposition. But dispersing the troops over great areas, inevitably without tactical air support at certain junctures, was a boldly calculated risk. Furthermore, from the outset of the operation, the absence of the airborne troops of the VIII Fliegerkorps Infantry Division was to be a major problem. It could not be transferred in time for the operation from Romania, where it guarded the Ploesti oil fields, and the 5th Gebirgs Division, which was brought in to replace it, had no practical experience in airborne operations.

All units for Operation 'Merkur' were hurriedly assembled within two weeks, although logistical problems caused the start date to be put back to 20 May. Student's XI Fliegerkorps was to be responsible for the actual assault on the island. It had 10 air transport wings with a total of approximately 500 Ju52 transports and 80 DFS 230 gliders available to airlift the attacking forces from recently captured airfields in Greece. The assault troops consisted of the *Luftlande Sturmregiment* (Airlanded Assault Regiment – Generalmajor Eugen Meindl), the 7th Flieger Division (Generalleutnant Wilhelm Süssmann) and the 5th Gebirgs Division under Ringel.

The topography of Crete in many ways favoured the invader, because at that time there were virtually no communication lines running north–south down the 160-mile-long, narrow, barren island. The only usable port on the south coast was the small harbour of Sphakia, which was inaccessible to motor traffic. In the north the only efficient port was in Suda Bay, connected by a single road that ran close to the north coast with the towns of Maleme, Canea, Rethymnon and Heraklion. The British defenders, who could only resupply Crete from Egypt, were handicapped by the shortage of adequate ports, and by the fact that their airfields were situated close to the exposed north coast at Maleme, Rethymnon and Heraklion.

At the beginning of the German invasion of Crete, the swollen island garrison consisted of about 27,500 British and Imperial troops and 14,000 Greeks under the command of Major-General Bernard C. Freyberg, commander of the New Zealand division. The original garrison, numbering approximately 5,000 men, was fully equipped, but the troops evacuated from Greece were battle weary, disorganised, and equipped only with the small arms they had saved during the withdrawal. Furthermore, the Greek and Cretan soldiers were mostly inadequately armed recruits. There was a general shortage of heavy equipment, transportation and supplies. The armour available to the defenders consisted of eight medium, and 16 light tanks, and a few personnel carriers; these were divided equally among the four groups formed in the vicinity of the airfields and near Canea. The artillery was composed of some captured Italian guns with a limited supply of ammunition, ten 3.7-inch howitzers and a few anti-aircraft batteries. The construction of fortifications was far behind schedule.

During May 1941 the British air strength on Crete never exceeded 36 planes, and only half of these were operational at any time. With the German preparatory attacks from the air growing in intensity and the British unable to operate from their airfields, the latter decided to withdraw their last few planes the day before the invasion began. Thus, all told, Crete was ill equipped to face an attack from the air. Freyberg, however, regarded such an operation as impractical and dispersed his ground forces with a view to preventing seaborne landings in Suda Bay and the adjacent beaches, and airborne landings on the three airfields at Maleme, Rethymnon and Heraklion. He divided his forces into four self-supporting groups, the strongest of which was assigned to the defence of the vital Maleme airfield. The lack of transportation made it impossible to organise a mobile reserve force.

Above: 'O group' on Crete.

The British naval forces defending Crete were based on Suda Bay, where the port installations were under constant attack during the period immediately preceding the invasion, restricting the unloading of supplies to the early hours of the morning. The only aircraft carrier in the eastern Mediterranean was unable to provide fighter cover because of aircraft losses during the evacuation of Greece.

The British were well appraised from their Ultra intelligence intercepts of the German intentions against Crete, and their counter-measures were based on the assumption that an airborne invasion could not succeed without the landing of heavy weapons, reinforcements and supplies by sea. By intercepting these at sea, Freyberg believed, 'Crete will be held'.

At 07:15 on the morning of 20 May, after a short, vicious pounding from the air had driven the defenders into their bunkers, I Battalion of the Luftlande Sturmregiment began landing their DFS 230 gliders at Maleme Airfield, where they immediately ran into heavy opposition from the XXII New Zealand Battalion on Hill 107, and the 5th New Zealand Brigade.

Meanwhile, a gliderborne assault by Kampfgruppe Altmann (1 and 2 Companies of the Luftlande Sturmregiment) was heading to secure vital objectives near Canea, to split the main force of defenders. But as Hauptmann Altmann's men tried to land on the Akrotiri Peninsula near the AA emplacements, a storm of flak was roused that destroyed four gliders and scattered the rest. Once on the ground, Altmann discovered that the emplacement was a dummy, and within hours his No 2 Company had ceased to exist. No 1 Company under Oberleutnant Genz landed in nine gliders southeast of Canea and captured the AA batteries, but had to then withdraw southwards to join the other paratroops who had dropped there, as they were unable to link up with Altmann.

Above: The Kübelwagen was the largest vehicle that could fit inside a Ju52 troop carrier and was much used by motorised units of mountain regiments, such as the anti-tank companies.

Chaos still ruled on the ground as the first wave of paratroops roared over the coast, heading for Maleme. Groundfire brought down several Ju52s, but the drop of II and IV Battalions onto positions west of the airfield, and of III Battalion to the east, began as planned. II and IV Battalions landed virtually unopposed but III Battalion came down over strong Allied positions. Of the 600 men who jumped, 400 were killed – many before they reached the ground.

Meanwhile, a German force consisting of I, II and III Battalions of the 3rd Fallschirmjäger Regiment and an engineer battalion was dropped near Canea. III Battalion parachuted directly onto positions held by the 10th New Zealand Brigade and sustained heavy casualties. So too did the engineer battalion, which dropped to the southwest onto the fury of a Greek regiment. When the fighting abated, the commander of the regiment gathered together the survivors: scarcely 1,000 of his original 3,000 men. The combined efforts of I and II Battalions succeeded in securing Agia, but during the day the regiment was unable to progress in the direction of Canea and the situation appeared critical.

By midday on 20 May, none of the prime objectives assigned to the first wave had been secured. The Luftlande Sturmregiment had failed to take Hill 107 and Maleme airfield, and the 3rd Fallschirmjäger Regiment was hemmed in around Agia in what was termed 'Prison Valley'. Communications with headquarters on the Greek mainland had been practically non-existent. Furthermore, problems with refuelling the Ju52s and the dust on the Greek airfields were disrupting the timetable for the second wave.

Because of these logistical problems the second wave could only be dropped piecemeal, instead of en masse as planned. At 15:00 I and III Battalions of the 2nd Fallschirmjäger Regiment began landing at Rethymnon, in a sector held by elements of the 19th Australian Brigade. Many were scattered and some troops were dropped in the wrong place, with many injured when landing on rocky ground. However, the few hundred survivors managed to drive the Australians from a hill and set up a roadblock to prevent Allied reinforcements from moving in.

The final drop, three battalions of paratroops totalling 2,000 men, was to capture Heraklion, the ancient capital of the island. This drop descended into carnage when Australian AA gunners unleashed a torrent of fire on the transports as they lumbered overhead. Fifteen were lost, and troops from the surviving aircraft were widely dispersed in a chaotic drop that lasted for nearly three hours. In the face of such a determined defence there appeared little chance of taking the airfield at Heraklion that day.

The operation was now perilously close to crisis. On the first day Student had lost thousands of his elite troops, nearly a third of the 7th Division. Gruppe West had managed to gain a foothold at Maleme but had not taken the hill or the airfield, Gruppe Mitte was in a critical situation at Canea and Rethymnon, and Gruppe Ost had failed to gain Heraklion or the airfield there. News was then received that the flotilla of boats carrying the 5th Gebirgs Division reinforcements to Heraklion had been delayed and would not be ready to depart until the next day.

At this critical juncture, Student decided that the foothold on the western edge of the airfield and northwest shoulder of Hill 107 at Maleme was the one position that could be exploited. He decided to concentrate on Maleme and employ the 5th Gebirgs Division there instead of in the Heraklion sector. The new plan was to roll up the British and Dominion positions from the west, despite the risk of a counterattack by Freyberg.

Maleme

Early on 21 May, a stroke of fortune befell the Germans. Convinced that he was about to be overrun, the commander of XXII New Zealand Infantry Battalion made the crucial mistake of ordering back A and B Companies from Hill 107, overlooking Maleme airfield. In the confusion, small parties of German paratroops moved cautiously up the hill and found it abandoned. Student seized the moment to take his gamble. At 05.00, with the airfield still under artillery fire, the first Ju52s came in at wave-top level for a straight-in landing run at Maleme, carrying a full battalion and the headquarters staff of the 100th Gebirgsjäger Regiment. With shells exploding around the landing aircraft the scene rapidly became chaotic, with burning machines wrecked in collisions or by artillery fire littering the field.

By evening the bulk of the battalion was on the ground and had reinforced the Maleme sector. A further air drop of the reserves of the 1st and 2nd Fallschirmjäger Regiments in the early afternoon finally overran the airfield defences, and it seemed that Student now held the key to victory.

The situation remained serious, however. There were still fewer than 1,800 Germans fit for action; the Allies had 7,000 troops, and another 6,000 within 10 miles. Gruppe Mitte near Rethymnon and Gruppe Ost near Heraklion faced heavy concentrations of Allied troops. To the west of the airfield Hauptmann Wiedemann's III Battalion had to dig in near Perivolia just east of the town. The Germans managed to hold out for several days against determined counterattacks by heavy artillery and armour.

Convoy disaster

Since there were not enough aircraft to carry out both the initial landing and the rapid build up of forces on the island, a flotilla of 63 requisitioned Greek vessels had been put together in advance of the attack to carry part of the 5th Gebirgs Division to the island. Most of these commandeered vessels were caiques – a type of fishing boat dependent on a sail and a small auxiliary engine – and the rest of them a motley mix of coastal freighters. There were to be two flotillas; one was to carry some 2,300 Gebirgsjäger to Maleme; the other to carry 4,000 to Heraklion. On the night of 19 May, the first flotilla arrived at the island of Milos and anchored there. But with the situation on Crete grown critical, a change of plan occurred and both convoys were ordered to sail to Maleme. The first convoy departed on 20 May escorted by one small Italian corvette. At around 22:00, making only 7 knots, and still some 18 miles from the landing beaches at Maleme, they

Below: Piraeus harbour – Gebirgsjäger talk with the Italian sailors who would form their escort.

Above: A Cretan donkey pressed into service.

were picked out by the probing searchlights of a British naval task force led by Admiral Rawlings. Unknown to the ships crews, they had been spotted that afternoon by a British reconnaissance aircraft. For two and a half hours the British hunted the caiques and freighters down, sinking 12 of them. The survivors straggled back north towards Greece, leaving many of the Gebirgsjäger floating in their lifejackets in the warm waters. The III Battalion of the 100th Gebirgsjäger Regiment was decimated by the naval action and virtually disappeared as a fighting force. In the morning, Italian boats and planes mounted a rescue effort, and as the Ju52s resumed the airlift of the 100th Gebirgsjäger Regiment into Maleme, the troops in the planes dropped life-rafts to their comrades below. Some 178 survivors were rescued by seaplanes and another 64 by launches. By 16:00 in the afternoon on 22 May, the rescue effort had been completed, and miraculously only 300 of the 2,331 on board the ill-fated flotilla were dead. A few managed to reach land, suffering from exposure but still carrying their weapons!

The second flotilla set sail southwards from Milos on 22 May. At about 09:30 they came within range of another naval task force under Admiral King, but were saved by the timely arrival of Luftwaffe aircraft that forced King to break off the attack. This second flotilla was recalled to spare it the same fate as the first, and no further seaborne landings were attempted until the island was in German control.

22 May saw renewed action by the Luftwaffe against the British naval task forces in which two cruisers and a destroyer were sunk, and two battleships and two cruisers damaged. After these attacks, Admiral Cunningham, commander of the Mediterranean fleet, decided that he could not risk further losses by operating during the day near Crete or in the Aegean Sea, and withdrew.

Reinforcements and supplies were now arriving on Crete in a steady stream. By midnight on 22 May, the whole of I Battalion of the 100th Gebirgsjäger Regiment had been brought in, followed by II Battalion, I Battalion of the 85th Gebirgsjäger Regiment and then the 95th Gebirgs Engineer Battalion under Major Schatte. That evening the 5th Gebirgs Division's commander, Generalmajor Julius Ringel, flew in with orders to clear the British out of Crete. He assumed command of all forces in the Maleme area, and set about organising the forces there into three *Kampfgruppen* (battle groups). Kampfgruppe Schatte was to protect the Maleme area from any western threat and push westwards to capture Kastelli. A second group, made up of paratroops under command of Oberst Ramcke, was to strike northwards to the sea to protect the airfield and then extend eastwards along the coast. The third, under the command of Oberst Utz, was to move eastwards into the mainland, in a flanking movement across the mountains. The New

Above: General Ringel with staff officers questions captured British troops on Crete.

Zealand commanders had already opted to withdraw to strengthened positions in readiness for the German advance, but in effect, as Freyberg's chief of staff later remarked, 'this amounted to accepting the loss of Crete'.

On 23 May, the three battle groups moved cautiously forward. I Battalion of the 85th Gebirgsjäger Regiment headed eastwards of Kampfgruppe Utz and reached the village of Modi in the afternoon, where it was engaged by New Zealand troops. To outflank the enemy position, I Battalion of the 100th Gebirgsjäger Regiment marched across the mountains to the south, and after a brisk fire fight the village fell. Next, advancing up the bare slope of a tactically important position known as Hill 259, the Gebirgsjäger fought hand-to-hand with the New Zealand defenders. During the night they pulled back to avoid being cut off, and moved their artillery back southeast of Platanias. As a result of these actions, Maleme airfield was left virtually undefended.

On each line of advance, the German troops were harried incessantly by Greek and Cretan irregulars. Numerous reports were already circulating that these bands had carried out atrocities on the German dead and wounded – some of whom were apparently tortured before dying. Then, on the west of the island, the 95th Engineer Battalion came under attack from armed civilians (including women and children), and as a result the 5th Gebirgs Division announced that henceforth, for every German soldier killed in this fashion, 10 Cretans would be shot in reprisal. The Luftwaffe also dropped leaflets warning the population of the measures that would be taken against partisan activity.

With the pressure on Maleme eased, the volume of traffic into the airfield increased dramatically, to about 20 aircraft every hour. II Battalion of the 100th Gebirgsjäger Regiment, newly landed in the morning, was sent eastwards to support Kampfgruppe

Utz. As more and more reinforcements landed on the island Ringel was able to regroup. During the night of 24–25 May, the 100th Gebirgsjäger Regiment gained contact with the paratroops under Oberst Heidrich, who had been surrounded in 'Prison Valley' since the 20th.

During the day, the 95th Gebirgs Engineer Battalion entered Kastelli to the west after air support from Stukas. Meanwhile, southwest of Canea, Oberst Ramcke's paratroops continued the advance from Pirgos along the coastline on the left flank. In the centre Kampfgruppe Utz, with two battalions of the 100th Gebirgsjäger Regiment, ran into the 10th New Zealand Brigade at Galatas. Fierce hand-to-hand combat raged between the mountain troops and the New Zealanders in the afternoon heat, but by nightfall two Gebirgs battalions had succeeded in forcing their way into the village. As they edged along the narrow streets in the dark, a counterattack by two companies of XXIII Battalion and the 5th New Zealand Brigade, supported by two tanks, forced Utz to retreat back into the surrounding hills, but the defenders were withdrawn to Canea on Freyberg's orders during the night and the next morning the mountain troops were able to re-enter the village.

Early in the morning of 27 May, Ringel began to attack Canea in earnest, as he deployed a battle group of two battalions of the 141st Gebirgsjäger Regiment (which had arrived on the 25th and 26th) under command of Oberst Jais on the right of the 100th Gebirgsjäger Regiment.

In front of Canea the British had deployed a rearguard dubbed 'Force Reserve'. It resisted fiercely, but of its 1,200 soldiers only 400 were able to escape the encircling Germans. By 15:00 on the 27th, the 100th Gebirgsjäger Regiment had penetrated the town defences.

Late in the evening before Canea fell, and despite suggestions that he retreat to Rethymnon, Freyberg ordered a general withdrawal through the mountains to the fishing village of Sphakia, where the ships of the Royal Navy were waiting to evacuate his forces. To the southwest of Suda, the 141st Gebirgsjäger Regiment beat back counterattacks by New Zealand and Australian troops. Unbeknown to Ringel, this was actually a rearguard action aimed at slowing his advance. When the Germans finally entered Canea and Suda bay, they found the area deserted.

Relief at Rethymnon

Oberstleutnant Wittmann's 95th Gebirgs Artillery Regiment was now ordered by Ringel to advance east as quickly as possible toward Rethymnon, and then Heraklion, to relieve the paratroopers cut off there. Under pressure from Student, who was agonising over the fate of his men, Ringel seconded virtually every mobile unit to Wittmann's command. Early on 28 May, Kampfgruppe Wittmann began the advance along the coast via Suda, where the road was found to be blocked by craters blown by a British commando unit that had landed during the night. A flanking attack was mounted, while mortars, anti-tank and mountain guns opened against New Zealand Maori troops and commandos behind the obstacle. At midday, resistance was overcome and contact with elements of Kampfgruppe Krakau was gained. From here the pursuit continued without interference as far as Kaina, where Kampfgruppe Wittmann met up with the main force. Lacking good observation points for artillery, Wittmann had to wait for support from Kampfgruppe Krakau, but by last light the odds were turned.

The pursuit continued on the 29th; Rethymnon was entered at 13:00 and contact with III Battalion of the 2nd Fallschirmjäger Regiment established. After a further artillery bombardment, the 700 Allied defenders, short of almost all supplies and unaware of the evacuation order of 27 May, laid down their arms. They had inflicted terrible losses on the 2nd Fallschirmjägers: 700 dead and wounded, 500 captured. Fewer than 200 men from

Top and Above: Two members of a Gebirgsjäger mortar team. The man at top carries a rangefinder, the one below the mortar.

the once proud regiment were still fit to fight when relief arrived.

Although the evacuation order had not reached Allied troops in Rethymnon, it had been received at Heraklion. Leaving the wounded behind, 4,000 men were embarked during the night of 28–29 May aboard ships under the command of Admiral Rawlings.

Leaving a detachment to guard the prisoners at Rethymnon, Kampfgruppe Wittmann resumed the march east toward Heraklion at 07:30 on the 30th. An hour later contact was made with the eastern group of the 2nd Fallschirmjäger Regiment. At 11:45 contact was gained with a reconnaissance patrol from the 1st Fallschirmjäger Regiment, which had been holding out in the Heraklion area since the afternoon of the first day. The advance continued with a couple of tanks (which had been landed by sea) leading the way for safety. The airfield and town were taken without a shot being fired.

Sphakia

Wittmann's drive to rescue the paratroops at Rethymnon had resulted in the deliverance of Freyberg's fleeing troops, as the German command had failed to realise that the main body of the Allied force was evacuating from the south in the fishing village at Sphakia. When the Allies had pulled back, Ringel had assumed they were retiring along the coast road towards Rethymnon, and although the bulk of the Luftwaffe had been withdrawn to prepare for the invasion of the Soviet Union, enough aerial reconnaissance remained for pilots to report there was no sign of the British to the east. In fact, significant forces were not sent south towards the port until 31 May.

In the meantime, scattered patrols of the 85th Gebirgs Regiment under Kampfgruppe Krakau, trying to follow the retreat south, had toiled through the mountains to outflank enemy positions guarding the Suda–Sphakia road, vital for the push eastwards and equally vital to the Allied withdrawal plan. On the night of 26–27 May the battle group occupied the heights above Stilos. As the Gebirgsjäger approached the town at about 06:30 the following morning, fire from a blocking position of artillery and tanks suddenly pinned it down. With a barrage of anti-tank weapons, artillery and mortar fire, the defence was breached. At 08:50 on 29 May, I Battalion of the 100th Gebirgsjäger Regiment (Kampfgruppe Utz) was sent southwards, and that afternoon II Battalion followed. The advance continued until 18:00, when a determined rearguard action was encountered just north of Kares. The attack was resumed in the morning and further progress was made to a point about two and a half miles from the coast. By the evening of 30 May the whole of Crete, except the Loutro–Sphakia area, was in German hands.

Above: Battalion command post in the mountains.

General Freyberg left the island that evening by flying boat. The Royal Navy evacuated almost 15,000 men to Egypt, with several ships damaged and sunk in the course of their operations. However, the Germans were unable to push down to the coast until 09:00 on 1 June, when the tenacious Allied rearguard forces finally surrendered. The war diary of the 5th Gebirgs Division recorded that the final resistance was overcome at 16:00 in the mountains north of Sphakia.

For Britain and its Allies, Crete was yet another stunning defeat. Hitler had secured his southern flank and gained a valuable staging ground for operations in the eastern Mediterranean. The British and Dominion casualties were more than 4,000 killed or wounded and 11,835 taken prisoner. Furthermore, the British naval presence in the theatre had been reduced to a skeleton by the loss of three cruisers and six destroyers sunk, and of one aircraft carrier, three battleships, six cruisers and nine destroyers damaged.

Yet it was in many ways a Pyrrhic victory for the Germans. Of the 22,000 men committed to the operation, approximately 6,000 were casualties. The 5th Gebirgs Division alone lost 20 officers and 305 other ranks killed in action. Of the 18 officers and 488 other ranks listed as missing, most were presumed drowned in the convoy attack. Nearly 271 of the 500 transport aircraft involved were lost, which was to have major ramifications in the forthcoming Russian campaign. Despite this enormous sacrifice, Hitler never pursued the opportunity to dominate the Eastern Mediterranean from Crete. Ringel offered a fitting epitaph: 'This sacrifice would have not been too great if the Crete campaign had meant a beginning, not an end.' In mid-July Student and Ringel flew to East Prussia to receive decorations for valour. Student was bluntly informed by the Führer that 'the days of the paratroop are over', and after Crete the German parachute arm was never used again in large-scale airborne operations.

Below: The Ju52 landings at Maleme were extremely dangerous – 80 of the aircraft were damaged as they landed as a result of heavy shelling.

LIECHTENSTEIN

With the formal cessation of hostilities on Crete, the 5th Gebirgs Division remained on the island as part of the occupying force. The role the division was scheduled to play in Operation 'Tyr', the planned invasion of the tiny mountain city-state of Liechtenstein, part of Hitler's plans for total European conquest, is not well known. (Contingency plans also existed for the takeover of Spain, Portugal, and Sweden.)

During the late 1930s Nazi agents provocateur failed in their attempts to subvert the plebiscite process in Liechtenstein and arouse calls for a union with Germany, as they had successfully done in Austria. As the tiny state posed no threat to the Nazi regime, it was left untouched.

Nonetheless, Hitler ordered plans be drawn up for the invasion of that country in May 1941. His astrologer had advised him that 'pebbles in the shoe can become boulders that roll and crush', and that Liechtenstein was key to that prophecy. Immediately, Hitler demanded a 'Liechtenstein Solution' from Field Marshal Keitel. Keitel acceded to the Führer's request, as usual, and delegated the planning to his chief of staff, General Jodl.

Above: Gebirgsjäger in summer uniform moving up a hillside on Crete.

Jodl felt insulted at having to plan an operation against a country as insignificant as Liechtenstein while being left out of most of the planning for 'Barbarossa'. He submitted Operation 'Tyr' calling for four divisions, justifying his numbers on the grounds the Swiss might renounce their neutrality and intervene on behalf of the mountain duchy. He requested the 1st and 4th Gebirgs Divisions from Army Group South, together with the 5th and 6th Gebirgs Divisions, which were both garrisoning Crete after the fierce campaigns there. The 188th Reserve Gebirgs Division, a training outfit based in northern Austria, would provide a garrison for the area.

Jodl submitted his plans, and Keitel delivered them to Hitler. The Führer swallowed whole Jodl's fantasies of Swiss intervention and approved the plan without modification. He ordered the divisions be brought up to crush Liechtenstein. As soon as they found out, Field Marshal Gerd von Rundstedt, commander of Army Group South, and General Ringel of the 5th Gebirgs Division who commanded the garrison in Crete, protested strongly about the commitment of their forces to such a pointless venture. Hitler would hear none of it and considered having them relieved of command. Only the vociferous objections of Halder and Field Marshals Leeb and Bock saved von Rundstedt from being dismissed. Ringel was currently riding on a crest of popularity after the Cretan campaign, and Hitler's staff recommended that he too be retained.

Nevertheless, the divisions prepared to move out to conquer Liechtenstein. The Cretan garrison was to be withdrawn first, as it would be the most difficult to extricate and other divisions would have to be sent in as replacements. Just before the transports loaded up the replacement units, an emergency cable arrived from Berlin: Operation 'Tyr' had been called off.

The reasons for its cancellation are still not entirely clear, but documents so far point to a change in the stars and a modification of the prophecy made by Hitler's astrologer. That the plan was suddenly abandoned is very clear. The 5th and 6th Gebirgs Divisions remained in Crete, and the 1st and 4th Gebirgs Divisions remained attached to Army Group South. Although Hitler expected to be able to execute Operation 'Tyr' in mid-1942, it was rapidly shelved. It was briefly dusted off in June 1943, in the overconfidence preceding the Kursk campaign, but in the wake of Germany's resounding defeat at Kursk it was consigned to the dustbin. Documents relating to this operation were only recently uncovered in a mass of German Army horsefeed requisitioning forms.

After moving to Germany between September and October, the 5th Gebirgs Division spent the winter of 1941–2 preparing for a move to the Eastern Front. On 16 October the *Armelband Kreta* or Crete cuff-title was instituted for those who had taken part in operations on Crete between 20 and 27 May 1941. Then, on 1 November, Aufklärungs Abteilung 95 and Panzerjäger Abteilung 95 were exchanged with the 3rd Gebirgs Division for Aufklärungs Abteilung 68 and Panzerjäger Abteilung 48, but these two battalions remained in Finland and were assigned as army troops on 5 January 1942.

EASTERN FRONT

The Battle of Leningrad

'When Operation "Barbarossa" is launched, the world will hold its breath!' said Adolf Hitler before German forces began their invasion of Russia on 22 June 1941. And so it did as he unleashed the mightiest army ever assembled on the ill-prepared Red forces. Initially the gains were stunning, but with the onset of the autumn rains, the assault faltered and halted along the whole 1,800 mile front, and his enemies breathed a collective sigh of relief.

Below: After the battle – a Gebirgsjäger relaxes with a trio of *Deutsches Rotes Kreuz* (DRK German Red Cross) nurses.

At the end of July, Hitler had given Leningrad (now St Petersburg) priority over Moscow as the most important objective of 'Barbarossa', and wanted to divert a panzer group from Army Group Centre to hasten the advance northward, but the OKW persuaded him to transfer only a corps. After considering the problem and arguing with his generals several weeks longer, Hitler announced his final decision on 21 August. He intended to give priority to the flanks, in the south taking the Crimea and the Donets Basin industrial region and cutting the Russians off from the Caucasus oil, and in the north taking Leningrad and joining forces with the Finns. Only after Leningrad had been secured and Army Group South was well on its way would the advance toward Moscow resume. In the meantime, Army Group Centre would divert strong forces to assist Army Group South to push southward into the Ukraine.

On the northern flank, fighting had been continuous through to 8 August when the Germans attacked Krasnogvardeisk. In the second half of August, the Finnish Army and Army Group North closed in rapidly on Leningrad. On 30 August Germans forces cut the rail-link to Moscow, isolating Leningrad off from the rest of Russia. On 31 August, the Finns reached their pre-1940 border on the Karelian Isthmus 30 miles north of Leningrad, and on the same day an Army Group North division arrived at the Neva River 10 miles southeast of the city. Four days later, the Finnish Army opened an offensive east of Lake Ladoga toward the Svir River, where it expected to make contact with German forces coming from the southwest.

On 8 September, Army Group North took Shlisselburg (or Schlüsselburg, in German) and with it the communication system, isolating Leningrad from the outside world. Already the only means of resupplying the city was by air drop or by crossing Lake Ladoga. By 9 September the Germans were within cannon range of the city, and when tanks broke through the last fortified line, which stood less than 10 miles from the outskirts, it appeared to all that Leningrad was doomed.

Below: Time out of combat wasn't all DRK nurses – here Gebirgsjäger are instructed on the intricacies of the Czech 7.92mm 26(t) light machine gun which was issued to some units instead of the MG34 or MG42.

Above: MG34 in the air defence role. (See pages 72–3.)

The city probably could have been taken in a few weeks despite exceptionally stiff Soviet resistance had it not been for several unusual circumstances. In the first place, Hitler decided that Leningrad was to be surrounded and not entered, and the army group therefore had to try to manoeuvre into the narrow isthmus to the east. Secondly, the Finnish commander in chief, Field Marshal (later Marshal of Finland) Baron Carl G. E. Mannerheim, refused to cross the border and close in from the north. Apparently he did not want to do what he conceived to be the Germans' work for them, and he also did not want to lend substance to the old Soviet argument that the Finnish border on the Karelian Isthmus was a threat to Leningrad. Finally, in the second week of September, Hitler removed Army Group North's armour. He left the army group one motorised corps, and demanded that it be withheld for a thrust toward the east to meet the Finns on the Svir when the time was ripe.

Hitler had decided on 6 September to concentrate German strength on Moscow after all. Army Group Centre was to be reinforced at the expense of its two neighbours, and Army Groups North and South were to complete their missions with the forces remaining to them. With the panzer units badly needed elsewhere, the OKW appealed to Hitler to institute a siege at Leningrad so that these units could be redeployed. On 29 September 1941, Hitler gave his approval to the plan. Furthermore, he ordered that the city be reduced so that the Germans would not have to feed its population. Thus began the epic siege of Leningrad, established on a line that began on the shore of the Gulf of Finland at Novoikerzon and curved eastward to Petergof and Uritsk, both within view of the city. Relentless shelling and air raids continued for the next 872 days, until Red Army troops finally drove away the German besiegers in mid-January 1944.

On 16 October 1942, Army Group North launched a limited attack across the Volkhov River toward Tikhvin and the Svir River, which the Finnish Army had reached at the end of September. After the first two or three days the autumn rains overtook the operation, and before the end of the first week the troops were leaving their tanks and trucks behind, bogged down on muddy roads. On 8 November German troops broke into Tikhvin, but there they stayed only until mid-December, when Russian units closing in on all sides forced them back to the Volkhov.

The Soviet winter offensive

During the summer and fall of 1941 the Soviet armies retreated because they had to and not (as was claimed as long as Stalin lived) because of a masterful strategic plan. The nation suffered staggering losses, including two-thirds of its pre-war coal-producing areas, three-quarters of its iron and manganese ore production, and 35 million people. Nevertheless, the sacrifices bought time, which the Soviet regime exploited with ruthless energy. Even while they were in full retreat, losing, destroying, or tearing down and shipping to the east entire industrial complexes, the Russians managed to recruit and equip fresh armies. As of 1 December, Soviet casualties probably totalled between 4 and 5 million men, but at the same time the Germans identified at or near the front 280 rifle and cavalry divisions and 44 tank or mechanised brigades.

The Soviet High Command did not share Hitler's doubts about the strategic importance of Moscow. In the summer and autumn it sacrificed entire armies and groups of armies in attempts to hold the western approaches to the capital. It would have sacrificed more in the battle for the city itself had not the earliest and coldest winter in half a century almost literally frozen the German armies in their tracks.

The long delays in August, September and October and the German loss of momentum on the northern and southern flanks in November had given the Russians time to assemble strong reserves around Moscow. Possibly, had the cold not set in, the German armies would have battled their way through that mass of men as they had

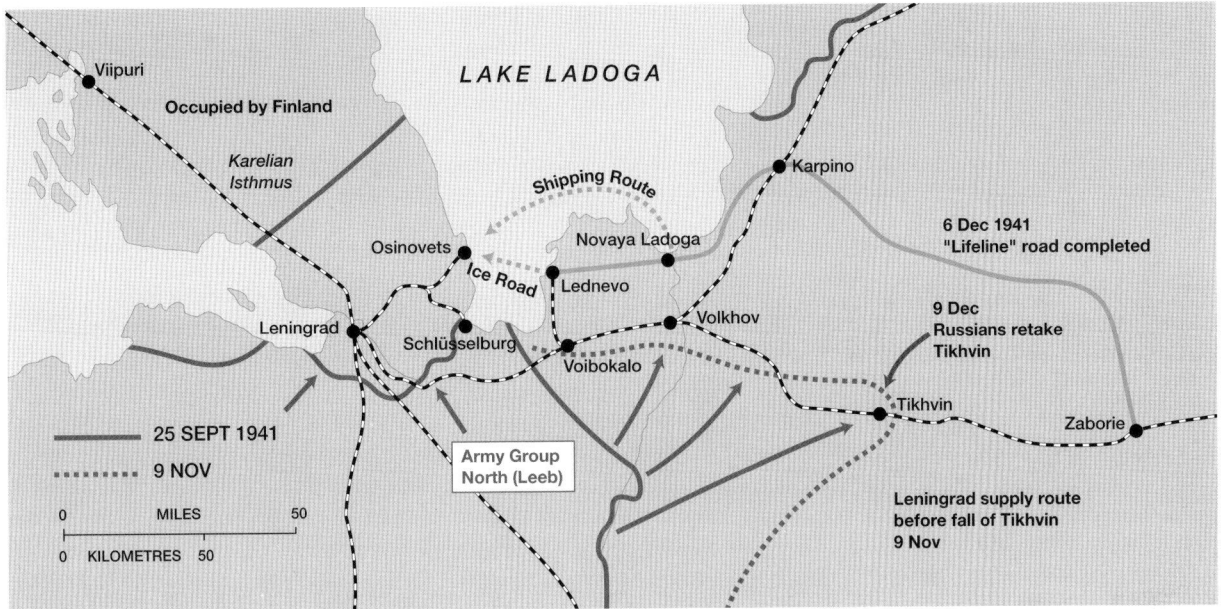

Above: The siege of Leningrad.

through others, but victory, as Bock predicted late in November, would have been achieved by the narrowest of margins. As it was, the German offensive ground to a halt on 5 December.

But as winter descended on the front the Soviets launched a mighty counteroffensive. The first stage, beginning on 6 December and lasting approximately a month, consisted of furious Russian attacks against Army Group Centre. These blows were to drive the Germans back from the gates of Moscow and, in so doing, destroy the advanced German panzer groups if possible. The attacks breached the thin German lines at several points and sent Hitler's armies reeling westward until a stand-fast order braked their retreat. By the end of December, the front had temporarily stabilised, with most German units on the central sector driven to a form of strongpoint defence.

Encouraged by the success of these first attacks, Stalin ordered an even greater counteroffensive effort on 5 January 1942. This second stage mounted major Soviet efforts against all three German army groups and aimed at nothing less than the total annihilation of the Wehrmacht's armies in Russia. Tearing open large gaps in the German front, Soviet armies advanced deep into the German rear and, in mid-January, created the most serious crisis yet. Grim reality finally succeeded where professional military advice had earlier failed, and Hitler at last authorised a large-scale withdrawal of the central German front on 15 January. Even with this concession, the German position in Russia remained in peril until Soviet attacks died out in late February.

The first stage of the Soviet winter counteroffensive drove the Germans back from Moscow but failed to destroy the advanced German panzer forces. The divisions of Army Group Centre adopted a strongpoint style of defence as they retreated.

When Hitler ordered the German armies to stand fast on 16 December, the opening Soviet drives had already spent much of their offensive energy and were unable to sustain their far-ranging attacks with supplies, replacements and fresh units.

During the latter part of December, both sides struggled to reinforce their battered forces. Hitler ordered the immediate dispatch of 13 fresh divisions to the Eastern Front from other parts of German-occupied Europe, including the 5th Gebirgs Division, although there was a considerable delay in the arrival of these reinforcements. In a curious parallel to Hitler's command actions, Soviet leader Joseph Stalin assumed

Above: Gebirgsjäger relax in their farmhouse billet; Russia 1942.

Right: This Gebirgsjäger Leutnant talking to the crew of a Panzer IV has a Bergführer (mountain leader) badge on his breast and a tank destruction badge on his right arm.

personal control over the strategic direction of Russian operations in late December. In Moscow, Stalin saw in the Red Army's surprising early success the makings of an even grander counteroffensive to crush the invaders and win the war at one stroke. Pushing Russian reinforcements forward as fast as they could be assembled, Stalin sketched out his new vision for this second stage of the Soviet counteroffensive. The Leningrad, Volkhov and Northwestern Fronts would smash in the front of Army Group North and lift the siege of Leningrad. The Kalinin, Western and Bryansk Fronts would annihilate Army Group Centre by a colossal double envelopment. In the south, the Soviet Southwestern and Southern Fronts would crush Army Group South, while the Caucasus Front undertook amphibious landings to regain the Crimea.

This Red Army avalanche fell on the Germans during the first two weeks of January, thus beginning the second stage of the winter campaign. The objectives were far too ambitious and greatly exceeded what could be done with Red Army resources. The attacking Soviet armies managed to penetrate the German strongpoint belt in several areas, but once into the German rear, they had not sufficient strength or impetus to achieve a decisive victory.

As part of this ambitious offensive, during the winter Marshal Meretskov's Volkhov Front repeatedly tried to break through the blockade of Leningrad. His orders of 17 December 1941 were to smash German armies on the west bank of the Volkhov River and gave the 2nd Soviet Shock Army, commanded by General A. A. Vlasov, the main task of breaching through defence line on the west bank.

Vlasov made the area south of Kirishi on the River Volkhov the focus of his attack. Here, the terrain was predominantly swamp and primeval forest, making military operations difficult in winter (and well nigh impossible in the summer months). On 13 January, while there was still frozen ground enough to manoeuvre, the Second Shock Army ripped through the German lines to the south of the 254th Infantry

Above: Refreshment break – note the ankle boots and canvas gaiters rather than the usual German Army jackboots.

Division. By 20 January the breach had been expanded to a width of nearly 20 miles. Vlasov's forces advanced through the breach and began to move in a northeasterly direction. By mid-February, after advancing over 60 miles, they had reached the Lyuban area and had thus covered half the distance to Leningrad. However, the advance was hampered by the lack of reserves and materiel resources (tanks, ammunition, self-propelled artillery and the rest), and a general lack of coordination between the Leningrad and Volkhov Fronts. By the end of February, Stalin's great offensive had run its course.

The German forces too were restricted by the terrain, a lack of reserves and Soviet attacks on other parts of the front, forcing them to take individual battalions from their parent divisions and commit them in ad-hoc battle groups in an attempt to build up a defensive front. But having vehicles and a good network of roads, they could manoeuvre these groups and concentrate them on the spearheads of the Soviet drive. By early March, a stable defensive line had been formed. For the next three months fierce combat ensued all around the salient, with the Soviets striving to expand their gains and the Germans attempting to halt them, and also to cut Second Shock Army off from its supply.

In early March, the 5th Gebirgs Division was transferred to I Corps in the Eighteenth Army of Army Group North and moved into positions southwest of Leningrad, in the area east of Lyuban, where it would stay to fight a series of defensive battles until November of the following year. The flat, swampy terrain was wholly different from anything that it had trained or fought in up to this time.

Destruction of the Volkhov 'Kessel'

The arrival of the spring thaw turned the area into a vast, mosquito-infested swamp, to the total misery of both German and Soviet troops. The front line stood as stark evidence of the confused winter fighting: instead of spanning the front in a smooth arc marred by a few minor indentations, it snaked tortuously back and forth, its great swoops and bends marking the limits of Russian offensive and German defensive endurance.

The most conspicuous point was the narrow but long salient that had been created by the advance of General Vlasov's Second Shock Army: the Volkhov Front. As a result of German counterattacks, by 26 March Vlasov's forces – which included the 372nd Rifle Division, 24th and 58th Rifle Brigades, 4th and 24th Guards Rifle Divisions and 7th Tank Brigade – were in danger of encirclement. Another advance on 9 April by the SS Polizei Division to the southwest of Spasskaya Polist finally cut off the Soviet salient. In the 'Kessel' (cauldron or encircled area) were troops of seven rifle divisions, each of them numbering between 18,000 and 20,000 troops.

Then, on 22 May the Germans launched a final operation designed to eliminate the Second Shock Army, and by the morning of 6 June had driven between 59th and 52nd Soviet armies attempting to relieve the pocket. The 5th Gebirgs Division, to the northeast of the trapped forces, countered efforts by the 54th Army to drive southwest into the pocket via Lyuban. Fierce fighting in the primeval swamps and forests continued for the next month, but on 24 June communication with the staff of Second Shock Army was interrupted. Finally, on 12 July, General Vlasov surrendered 30,000 of his men into captivity.

Above: The ski stretcher for casualty recovery was standard mountain troops' equipment and was handled by a four-man team as seen here. (See also page 75.)

Lake Ladoga

On 7 April, Red Army troops managed to force a very narrow corridor to Leningrad, opening a tenuous rail link to the city. Trains ran into the city with desperately needed supplies and came out with civilians and the wounded, all under heavy artillery fire from the Germans. Soon, however, this link was cut and Leningrad was once again isolated.

In the late spring and early summer of 1942, the 5th Gebirgs Division was tasked with clearing out the various pockets of resistance that remained at large after the crushing defeat of the Second Shock Army. The terrain, covered with mile after mile of heavy, dank, pine forests, provided ample places to hide and favoured the prey. Hitler's Directive No 44 (Operations in Northern Finland) of 21 July 1942 makes it clear that the division was intended for the 20th Mountain Army in Finland 'by the end of September', but this was based on the assumption that 'Leningrad will be captured in September at the latest'. But the Soviet forces showed no signs of relinquishing the city. On 24 August they launched another major offensive to relieve it. On 27 August the offensive expanded to an attack by the Leningrad Front in the city and the Volkhov Front outside the siege lines. Both fronts were aimed against the German positions at Schlüsselburg on Lake Ladoga. The 5th Gebirgs Division was rushed into positions to counter the mighty blows, and successfully withstood a series of human wave assaults. On 10 September, after taking heavy losses in attack, the Red Army forces halted their operations for the winter as rains once again made movement nearly impossible.

1943

Beginning on 1 January 1943, there were renewed attacks on the German positions in the Pogoste Kessel and south of Kolpino, as a result of which the 5th Gebirgs Division moved to shore up the defences on the Neva at Kolpino. Then, on the 12th, Operation '*Iskra*' (Spark) hit the narrow sector of the southern coast of Ladoga Lake. Strengthened by reserves, the armies of the Volkhov and Leningrad Fronts, supported by the 13th and 14th Air Armies and artillery of the Baltic fleet and Ladozhskaya flotilla, struck from two directions at the German defences. Although the German troops offered strong resistance, the defence was pierced at the Mga–Sinyavsk projection, and after seven days of bitter fighting the Germans were driven back some six miles from the southern coast of Lake Ladoga. The blockade of Leningrad was finally broken by Soviet troops on 18 January 1943, when Schlüsselburg was liberated. By the end of the month a railway was built on the corridor that now connected Leningrad with the mainland. Supplies were rushed into the city while wounded and non-combatants were shipped out. All of this was done under constant artillery fire against the cordon. A week later the Soviet leadership announced that the siege of Leningrad was raised. For the first time in many days, the populace could walk openly in the streets without fear of air attack.

Despite this, rations in the city were still very limited, and German artillery was still in range of any part of the city. Because of the shortages in food and supplies, an offensive to break the blockade was impossible. Attempts to widen the corridor (only six miles wide) failed at a heavy cost in men and matériel.

Between November 1941 and October 1942 alone, 641,803 people died of starvation in Leningrad.

Operation 'Polar Star'

Between 15 and 28 February the Soviets tried to consolidate their newly won positions by a series of limited thrusts. The main attack was on the Demyansk salient (Operation 'Polar Star'), where six German divisions of II and X Army Corps were entrenched. By 23 February the Soviet formations had penetrated only 6–10 miles, by which time the bulk of the German forces had been withdrawn through the tightening noose.

Left: MG42 on its AA mount (see also pages 72–3). Its crew wear the 1943 pattern anorak suit with its tan brown side outwards. The other side was white.

In the second half of March, further attempts were made to continue the offensive in the direction of Sinyavsk–Mga. As part of LIV Corps in the Eighteenth Army, the 5th Gebirgs Division was committed to a series of defensive actions near Novgorod, during which time a light reconnaissance detachment (95th Schnelle Abteilung) was attached to the division. In the middle of April the German forces southeast of Leningrad launched a series of counterattacks, but these were swiftly put down by the Soviet Fourteenth Army. Then, on 14 May, a fresh attempt was made to cut the land bridge to Leningrad, but this operation too quickly fell apart.

Throughout the summer German operations around Leningrad continued to vacillate between defence and attack. In late July another Soviet attack fell on the German positions on the Mga, the purpose of which was to disrupt German plans to organise a new offensive on Leningrad and tie down their forces in the area. In the face of this new onslaught all reserves of Lindemann's Eighteenth Army and significant forces from other front areas were committed, including the 5th Gebirgs Division Although their defences held fast, after a month of fighting the Germans had incurred heavy losses, most of them from artillery fire and aircraft attacks. Some of the most serious losses were incurred by the fire-brigade units such as the 5th Gebirgs, which was all but destroyed in these battles.

Mga offensive

When in September the Soviet armies took possession of the powerful defences near Sinyavsk, the staff of Army Group North recognised that their positions on the Volkhov had become precarious. In October German troops were removed from their positions on the river through the Kirishi bridgehead and rearranged in newly constructed defences.

On 7 October another setback occurred when the Red Army launched a fresh offensive at Nevel. By the end of December the army group comprised only 40 incomplete divisions, defending a front extending 500 miles. Permission was urgently sought to withdraw from Leningrad and move west to the 'Panther Line'. Although such movement offered the chance to shorten the defence line by 120 miles, Hitler rejected the request.

Already, the 5th Gebirgs Division had received the welcome news that it was to leave the Eastern Front for Italy, where the Allied campaign was slowly gathering momentum, First however, it was transferred to the reserve of Generaloberst von Vietinghoff's Tenth Army of Army Group C (Kesselring) in northern Italy to rest and refit.

It was a much-needed furlough for the Gebirgsjäger, as the battles in which they had fought in the past months were some of the bloodiest and most wasteful of the war, with neither side able to make appreciable gain despite monumental sacrifice. Indeed, the Leningrad

Below: Winter transport for a 10.5cm leichte Feldhaubitze 16 being horse-drawn in the snow on a wood skid in northern Russia. The men are wearing the two-piece winter suit and the horses have white camouflage sheeting.

Front has since come to symbolise the horrors of the Eastern Front. During the siege, starvation claimed hundreds of thousands of lives but, incredibly, war production continued in Leningrad's bombed-out factories, even through the frozen winter. In many ways the failure of the German offensive can be attributed to actions elsewhere, particularly at Stalingrad, which consumed resources needed to carry the offensive.

Though the Germans would never take Leningrad the defence of the city would be one of the costliest for Russia in the war.

MONTE CASSINO AND THE GUSTAV LINE

After the Axis retreat and Allied victory on the island of Sicily, in the autumn of 1943 the Allies had landed uncontested on the mainland of Italy, the so-called 'soft underbelly of Europe', at Reggio and Taranto. After further landings at Salerno timed to coincide with the Italian armistice, Kesselring sent the 16th Panzer Division to the Salerno area to meet the invasion, and mobilised the Tenth Army behind it to help drive the Allied force back into the sea. By 16 September, Vietinghoff was forced to concede that the Allies were not to be dislodged from the Salerno beachhead. He began a phased withdrawal, satisfied in the knowledge that he had disrupted the timetable for the capture of Naples. As they withdrew the Germans demolished everything that could not be shipped north, while engineers began to construct a series of defensive lines across the Italian peninsula. The first of these, Viktor, began 18 miles north of Naples, next came the Barbara and Bernhardt Lines and finally the Gustav. Kesselring believed that this could be made almost impregnable and prevent the Allies from reaching Rome for many months.

Above: Mountain troops' observation post, with winter camouflaged binocular sight.

The terrain certainly favoured the defenders, as running down the spine of Italy is the long Apennine range, at its highest point rising to 6,000 ft. From it a series of ridges and valleys radiate out onto narrow coastal strips – only 25 miles wide on the west side and 10 miles on the east. Even in good weather the roads were barely adequate for motorised columns and supply convoys. In winter they would become quagmires, dictating that the war would have to be waged by foot soldiers, fighting mile by mile.

Through the late autumn and into the winter months Vietinghoff slowly withdrew through the prepared positions. On 15 November the worsening weather forced General Alexander, commander of the Allied Fifth Army Group, to call a halt to the advance. By the time he was ready to resume the advance, the Germans were firmly entrenched on the Gustav defensive line in expectation of the allied offensive.

The Gustav Line
The Gustav Line ran across the width of central Italy, from the mouth of the Sangro River in the east, through the Abruzzi mountain region to the mouths of the Rapido/Garigliano Rivers on the west coast. The dominating feature on the defensive line was a defile on which stood the town of Cassino. Less than a thousand yards west of Cassino town is Monte Cassino, towering 1,700 ft above the town. On top of Monte Cassino stood the centuries-old Benedictine monastery, the scene of many battles over the years. It dominated the surrounding countryside, including the Liri valley that ran through the mountains to the north and Route 6, the main highway linking the south to Rome, which snaked around Monastery Hill.

To defend Cassino and the Gustav Line Vietinghoff, newly promoted to Generaloberst, had 15 divisions including the 44th Infantry Division (Generalleutnant Ortner) and the 5th Gebirgs Division (Generalleutnant Schrank), which in January was attached to XIV Corps and moved into positions on the Gustav Line south of Rome. Added to this was the 1st Fallschirmjäger Division (Generalleutnant Heidrich) of LI Mountain Corps

Above: Wearing 1939-pattern anoraks in both camouflage and plain pattern, this infantry ski company moves up to positions in the Gothic Line.

(General der Gebirgstruppen Feuerstein); this brought together the paratroops and the Gebirgsjäger who had fought together in Crete two years previously. Under XIV Panzer Corps (Generalleutnant von Senger und Etterlin) were the 71st Infantry Division (Generalmajor Raapke), 94th Infantry Division (Generalmajor Steinmetz) and the 15th Panzergrenadier Division (Generalmajor Rodt).

Facing the Cassino front the allies now had seven Commonwealth divisions, containing men from India, New Zealand, South Africa (who had an armoured division in reserve) and Brazil, as well as five American, five British, four French and three Polish divisions. On the eastern flank, LI Mountain Corps faced forces of the British Eighth Army. In the west, XIV Panzer Corps, by this point desperately short of tanks and heavily reliant its infantry units, faced the US Fifth Army.

The Allies faced an ominous task, as along the whole front German engineers had made very skilful use of terrain to fortify their positions. Mines were planted on the roads and trails, at the heads of gullies and in the natural cross-country approaches. All bridges and culverts were destroyed, and sites for bypasses were mined. Machine-gun and mortar emplacements, many of them dug four or five feet into solid rock, covered nearly every path. Not even intense artillery concentrations could smash these positions. On the slopes of mountains, behind stream beds, and across narrow valleys, dozens of mutually supporting machine guns were sited to weave a deadly pattern of cross fire. As a result of these defences, small forces of the enemy could hold the gullies, draws and difficult trails that led into the mountains, even in the face of strong attacks. To further impede the Allied advance, the countryside in front of the Rapido east of Cassino town had been flooded.

Allied attacks on the Gustav Line commenced on 15 December, with coordinated attacks by II Corps in the San Pietro area and by VI Corps in the mountains to the north.

The main objectives were the heights north of Cassino at the head of the Rapido River Valley, but between lay 10 miles of rugged mountain country.

VI Corps' offensive opened with an attack toward the village of Lagone, which fell on 16 December. Just to the north of Lagone, fighting on 15 and 16 December brought the first contact with the 5th Gebirgs Division. Before daybreak on the 15th, the 1st Platoon of the 45th Reconnaissance Troop ventured out on a volunteer mission to capture Hill 895, held by elements of the 100th Gebirgs Regiment. Although the Gebirgsjäger broke up the platoon's assault, their hold along this sector was weakened. After dark a platoon of Company C, 179th Infantry, was able to take La Bandita without opposition, and the next day the 100th Gebirgs Regiment was forced to yielded Hill 895 to French troops of the 5th Rifle Regiment.

On 17 December all the German front-line units on VI Corps' front began a general withdrawal. Though the penetrations were nowhere deep enough to cause great alarm, the positions had become increasingly difficult to hold. It was therefore decided to make a limited withdrawal, regroup on a new line, and thus gain a breathing spell. A withdrawal would also lengthen the enemy supply lines through the mountains and bring him into new and unfamiliar terrain.

The first battle

The next concerted assault on the Gustav Line was launched on 17 January 1944, in coordination with the landings at Anzio planned for the 22nd. The British X Corps was to cross the Garigliano River west of Cassino and try to outflank German positions around the Liri Valley. The French Expeditionary Force was to move through the mountains in the east and complete a flanking manoeuvre. In the centre, the US II Corps would cross the Rapido River a few miles south of Cassino and enter the Liri Valley.

In support of the Allied assault, troops from the French 3rd Algerian Division struck the 5th Gebirgs Division and 8th Panzergrenadier Regiment positions on Mt Belvedere, flanking Cassino. Meeting heavy resistance, they were quickly checked, while to the west the British were halted and failed to execute the western flanking manoeuvre. With neither objective met, the Allied troops dug in around the hills and mountains around Monte Cassino.

Two days into the operation, the US 36th Division assaulted across the Rapido. The going was unexpectedly tough in the fast-flowing, steep-sided river, and many boats and their occupants were lost in the crossing. Those men who reached the other side of the river established a small bridgehead, but as the sun rose artillery fire was brought down on them from positions on Monte Cassino. Through the next night, more bridges were built across the Rapido to reinforce the bridgehead, but still they were held at bay. On 22 January, as the division's casualties escalated, the order was given to pull back. Two days later, the US 34th Division crossed the Rapido east of Cassino to try and outflank German positions. Over the next few days they advanced to within a few hundred yards of Monastery Hill, but again at a heavy cost, and were unable to approach any closer to Monte Cassino.

With this first assault on the Cassino front of the Gustav Line repulsed, it seemed that Kesselring's maxim, that the British and Americans would 'break their teeth' on the Gustav Line would ring true. But already the Axis commander faced another problem, for on 22 January, British and Americans under command of the US VI Corps had carried out an almost unopposed landing on beaches at Anzio, 60 miles to the north. This landing behind the German lines was designed to draw German forces away from the Cassino front, and thus weaken the Gustav Line defences. The Allied forces on the Cassino front could then head north and link up with the US VI Corps before advancing on their goal, Rome. However, contrary to expectations, parts of the newly reconstituted German

Below: The 8cm Granatwerfer 34 was the standard mortar for mountain troops, as with other German fighting units.

Above: Gebirgsjäger regimental HQ with commander and senior staff housed in a *mittlerer Kraftomnibus* command vehicle built by Magirus.

Fourteenth Army, which had been taking part in the occupation of northern Italy, were rushed to Anzio. Although only two German battalions stood between Anzio and Rome, VI Corps chose to consolidate their beachhead before attempting a breakout. This was quickly contained, and stalemate set in. There would be no easy road to Rome.

During this lull, command of the 5th Gebirgs Division passed on 10 February to Generalleutnant Max Schrank, who was to hold the position until January 1945. The highly popular and respected Generalleutnant Ringel, who had led the division through Greece, Crete and Russia, was promoted to the command of LXIX Mountain Corps.

The second and third battles

Focus returned to the Cassino Front where, on 14 February, leaflets were dropped onto the monastery informing the occupants and refugees that the allies had decided to bomb it and the surrounding German positions from the air. Up to this point both sides had tacitly agreed to avoid the destruction of Italy's historical assets unless it was a military necessity. However, many Allied troops, chief among them the commander of the New Zealand II Corps, General Freyberg, insisted that the destruction of the monastery was indeed necessary, and Alexander felt forced to assent. On the next day wave after wave of heavy bombers, acting in a tactical role, pulverised the monastery with heavy bombs. This highly controversial attack drew condemnation from all sides, and succeeded only in turning the monastery into a fortress; the ruined walls, which had been up to 15 ft thick, made excellent defensive positions which the Germans quickly occupied.

Following the aerial barrage, the second battle of Cassino began in earnest as US and Commonwealth troops attacked key points on the approaches to the battered monastery. After four days of fierce fighting the assault was called off. The survivors dug in, some of them only yards from the enemy dugouts and as heavy snow and freezing rain forced another break in the fighting, they watched nervously for the next attack.

On the morning of 15 March, as spring weather broke out over the bloodied slopes, another Allied bombardment fell on the German positions. When this ceased, the Fallschirmjäger holding the hill beat off an attack by 2nd New Zealand Division. Although tanks were sent in, they got bogged down in shell craters and mud and could only be used as static artillery.

The next morning, the monastery was again bombed, but the defenders remained largely untouched in their underground bunkers. Now being supplied solely by air drops, they continued to put up a determined resistance. On 19 March the Allied high command ordered yet another push to take German strong points in the town, and a frontal assault on Monte Cassino from Hangmans Hill by Gurkhas. It was hoped that tanks, which were being brought in on a newly carved track north of Cassino, would back up this assault. However, the advance on the town was kept at bay by tenacious German defenders, using tanks which had been half buried in the house ruins. By the afternoon the frontal assault was called off, and the Allied troops once again prepared to dig in around Monte Cassino. Only a week after the operation had started, the Allies had already lost 3,000 men.

Cassino was by now a pressing issue, for it had already been decided that the Gustav Line had to be broken before the Normandy invasion, planned for June, could take place. The Allies had to try and smash as many German divisions as they could, and rob Hitler of men that could be used in France.

And so another assault was planned for May. Parts of the British Eighth Army on the Adriatic front of the Gustav Line were secretly moved westward to the Cassino front. Fortunately for the Allies, the code-breakers at Bletchley Park were intercepting coded messages, which they read with the Enigma machine, and which contained details of the under-strength German formations facing them.

A four-pronged attack was planned, with the US II Corps attempting a breakthrough along the west coast following Route 7 and heading north in an attempt to link up with the US V Corps, who were attempting to break out of the Anzio beachhead.

The French Expeditionary Force of four divisions was to advance north through the Liri Valley, attacking German positions in the areas behind Monte Cassino. The British VIII Corps was to cross the Rapido River, clear the town and advance across the Gustav Line, cutting off the road west of Cassino. The Polish II Corps, comprising two infantry divisions and one armoured, had Monte Cassino as its objective. It was to encircle the mountain and attack from the north, first taking the German positions on Calvary Hill behind it.

At Cassino, the 1st Fallschirmjäger Division regrouped in preparation for the assault. The 5th Gebirgs Division was positioned some 10 miles north of Cassino and tasked with holding the line against the opposing Italian Motor Group (X Corps, Eighth Army). On Schrank's left flank, the 114th Jäger Division faced the 24th Guards Brigade and 4th Indian Division.

The final battle

Late in the evening of 11 May, 2,000 artillery pieces began to bombard the German positions on Cassino. Within an hour Polish forces were on Calvary Hill, just over 1,000 yards northwest of Cassino. The next day, pontoon bridges were constructed across the Rapido. The British VIII Corps crossed and advanced four miles, while the French Expeditionary Force moved up the Liri Valley. As the US II Corps thrust northwards up the coast towards Anzio, the German position began to deteriorate rapidly.

Another armoured assault on 16 May by Polish forces secured Calvary

Below: Gebirgsjäger moving into positions near Monte Cassino.

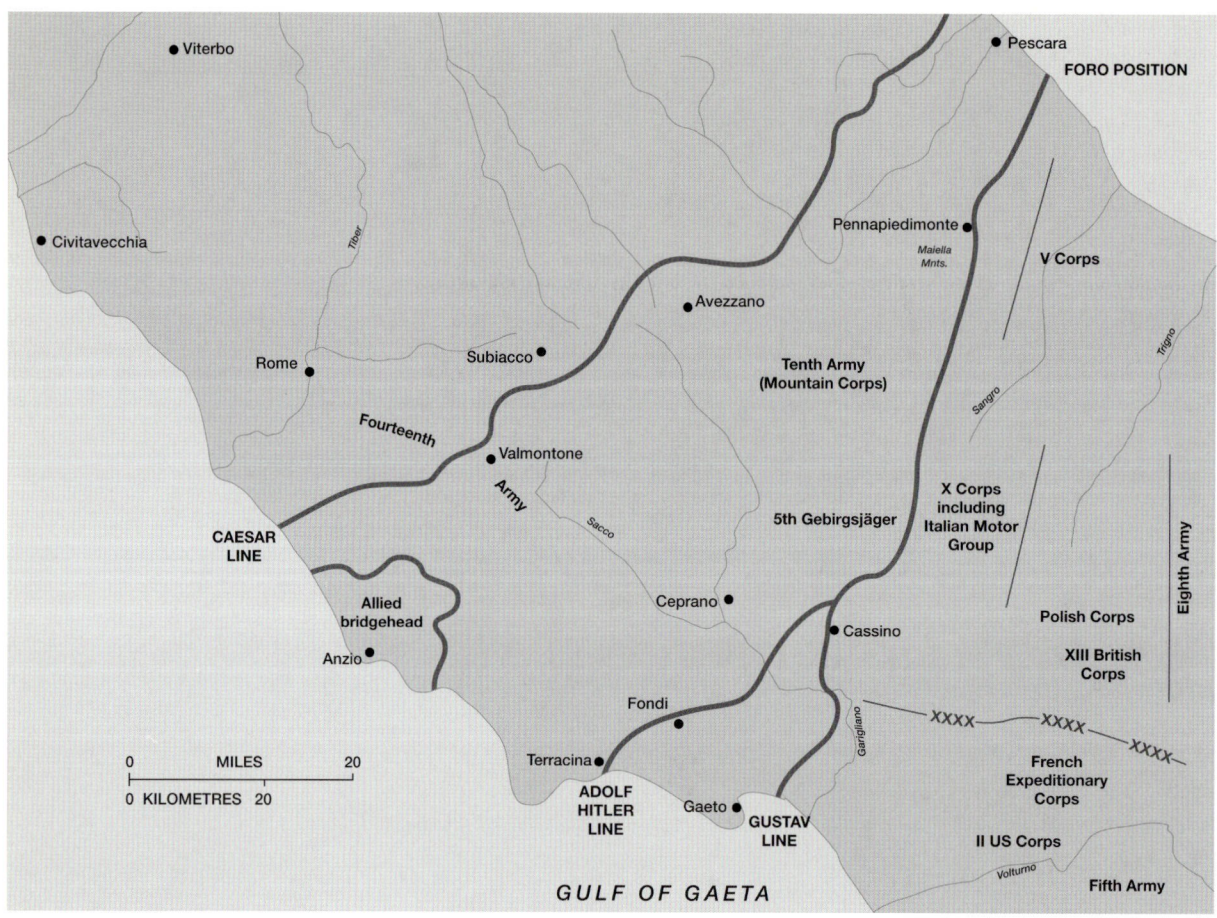

Above: The fourth and final battle for Monte Cassino – the Italian Front as at 11 May 1944.

Hill behind Monte Cassino, threatening the German line of retreat. With Allied forces now pouring through gaps in the line and bypassing German positions, Kesselring decided he could delay no longer and ordered the withdrawal from positions in the town, monastery, and surrounding hills and mountains. Thousands of German troops began an orderly retreat northwards on Route 6, the main highway linking the south to Rome. In failing to cut the highway, the Allies missed a sterling opportunity to score a major victory.

The town of Cassino finally fell on 17 May to Polish troops. The next day the Polish flag flew over the ruins where so many men had sacrificed their lives. Altogether the Germans had suffered 20,000 casualties in the defence of the Gustav Line, but their sacrifice had seriously delayed the Allied advance in Italy.

ROME

Between Rome and the Gustav Line, the Germans had constructed two delaying positions. The first, the Hitler/Dora Line, was sited six miles behind the Gustav Line and had been built to contain any forces that managed to break through the main position. It was half a mile deep, and laid with minefields, anti-tank traps, barbed wire and pillboxes. Behind this line a third defensive position, situated in the Alban Hills 20 miles south of Rome and named the Caesar Line, was under construction, but this was never finished.

Neither position could stem the Allied advance and both were quickly breached, forcing the German Tenth Army to make further withdrawals north and the Fourteenth

Army to retreat eastwards to avoid the Allied forces advancing from Anzio. During the retreat they destroyed bridges, laid mines on roads and prepared ambushes, all designed to delay the advancing Allied forces.

On 23 May, the US VI Corps finally broke out of the beachhead at Anzio, and two days later linked up with the US II Corps, advancing up the Liri Valley. The German Fourteenth Army at Anzio and the Tenth Army, withdrawing from their defensive positions, were partially encircled by this joint US force as they moved north, but avoided encirclement when it was decided that the Americans would head for Rome, which they then entered in triumph on 4 June 1944. Even as they paraded victoriously through the streets, German forces were slipping past the outskirts of Rome, heading north.

By the end of the first week of August 1944, members of the British Eighth Army stood on the Ponte Vecchio, bridging the Arno River in recently liberated Florence. The Eighth Army had just completed a campaign, in conjunction with the US Fifth Army, that had kept Axis forces in Italy in full retreat. For the first time since the Italian campaign had begun, Allied leaders were optimistic that they were on the verge of pushing the Germans out of the northern Apennines and sweeping through the Po Valley beyond. After that, many hoped for a rapid advance into the Alps, the Balkans, and perhaps into Austria, before winter and the enemy could stem their advance.

THE GOTHIC LINE

Axis forces, however, were preparing to frustrate any continuation of the Allied drive by building another belt of fortifications, the Gothic Line.

The new line generally consisted of a series of fortified passes and mountaintops, some 15 to 30 miles in depth north of the Arno River. It stretched for 200 miles from La Spezia on the Ligurian Sea through the Apennines, Pisa and Florence, to Pesaro on the east coast.

Along the Adriatic coast where the northern Apennines sloped down onto a broad coastal plain, the Gothic Line defences were generally anchored on the numerous rivers, streams and other waterways that flow from the mountains to the sea. One key to the line appeared to be the central Italian city of Bologna, a major rail and road communications hub located only a few miles north of the defensive belt.

The intense combat operations of the summer were not destined to continue into the fall. With the liberation of Rome on 4 June, and the invasion of Normandy two days later (Operation 'Overlord'), Allied resources earmarked for Italian operations, already considered of secondary importance, steadily diminished. The Allied invasion of southern France (Operation 'Anvil-Dragoon') on 15 August further reduced the limited resources available for the Italian theatre. More important, 'Anvil-Dragoon' stripped the Allied armies in Italy of seven first-class divisions, three American and four French.

Despite this scaling down the Allies planned to continue offensive operations in the northern Apennines in the hope of breaking through the Gothic Line and advancing into northern Italy. A continuation of the offensive, they hoped, would at least prevent the Germans from transferring their forces in Italy elsewhere.

Operations

In August 1944, Kesselring's Army Group C faced a still formidable Allied force. Field Marshal Alexander's command included troops from 16 Allied nations; Lieutenant General Mark W. Clark's Fifth Army (IV Corps and II Corps) held the western portion of the Allied line, from the Ligurian Sea at the mouth of the Arno River to a point just west of Florence. To the east Lieutenant General Sir Oliver Leese's larger Eighth Army, consisting of the Polish II Corps (two divisions), the Canadian I Corps (two divisions), the

British V Corps (six divisions), the British X Corps (two divisions), and the British XIII Corps (three divisions), held the line from the Florence area to just south of Fano on the Adriatic coast.

Opposing Clark's Fifth Army was Generalleutnant Joachim Lemelsen's Fourteenth Army, which contained 10 divisions belonging to I Parachute and XIV Panzer Corps. To the east, opposing the British Eighth Army, was the Tenth Army commanded by General Heinrich von Vietinghoff. This army consisted of 12 divisions belonging to LXXVI Panzer and LI Mountain Corps, which included the 5th Gebirgs Division. The two other Axis forces in northern Italy, the Ligurian Army and the Adriatic Command, controlled four more divisions and generally performed anti-partisan and reserve missions.

Operation 'Olive'

Soon after British forces reached the Arno River on 4 August 1944, planning for the next phase of the Allied attack had begun. Under this operation, code-named Olive, General Leese's army was to attack up the Adriatic coast to Rimini. Once this attack had drawn Axis units away from the Fifth Army's front, General Clark could hit the Gothic Line in a secondary assault from Florence directly north toward Bologna with his more limited force. The Fifth and Eighth Armies could then converge on and capture Bologna and move to encircle and destroy Axis forces in the Po Valley, putting Eighth Army forces in a favourable position to move into the Balkans and the Danube Valley.

Below: When radio silence demanded – or when atmospheric necessities dictated – mountain troops used signal flags.

The shift of British forces over battle-damaged and circuitous mountain routes to their start positions began on 15 August, while Fifth Army units maintained pressure on their front to convince the German commanders that the main thrust was coming in the Florence area. The movement, made easier by the almost total lack of German air reconnaissance, took all the following week; by 22 August, however, 11 divisions and nine separate brigades faced the German forces that were holding a 25-mile-wide stretch of the Gothic Line anchored on the Adriatic.

German radio communications and order-of-battle reports, intercepted and decrypted by ULTRA code-breakers in July and August, revealed to Alexander, Clark and Leese that neither Kesselring nor any of his subordinates had detected the eastward shift of Fifth Army and Eighth Army units. Similarly, the Axis command did not realise that a change in Allied operational strategy had occurred or that an attack along the coast was imminent.

Operation 'Olive' commenced on 25 August 1944, as the British V Corps and Canadian I Corps attacked through two Polish divisions on a 17-mile front along the Adriatic. The 5th Gebirgs Division was holding positions on the right against the 9th British Armoured Brigade, with 71st Infantry Division to their left and 278th Infantry Division holding the coast. The offensive, supported by the British Desert Air Force, rapidly gained ground, with the Canadian 5th Armoured Division in the centre moving far forward against light resistance. Polish and Canadian troops penetrated the Gothic Line near the coastal town of Pesaro on 30 August, threatening to turn the entire Axis front.

Originally believing that the Eighth Army assault was a diversion to draw troops from central Italy, Kesselring delayed steps to reinforce units on the coast for four days. However, the heroic resistance displayed by units such the 100th Gebirgsjäger Regiment (see below), maximising the defensive advantages provided by inclement weather and numerous rivers and ridges, inflicted a total of 8,000 casualties on the attackers and stalled Eighth Army forces short of their Rimini and Romagna Plain objectives by 3 September. The same cautiousness that had characterised previous Eighth Army engagements began to play to Kesselring's advantage, and he managed to plug the breach with rapidly mobilised reinforcements.

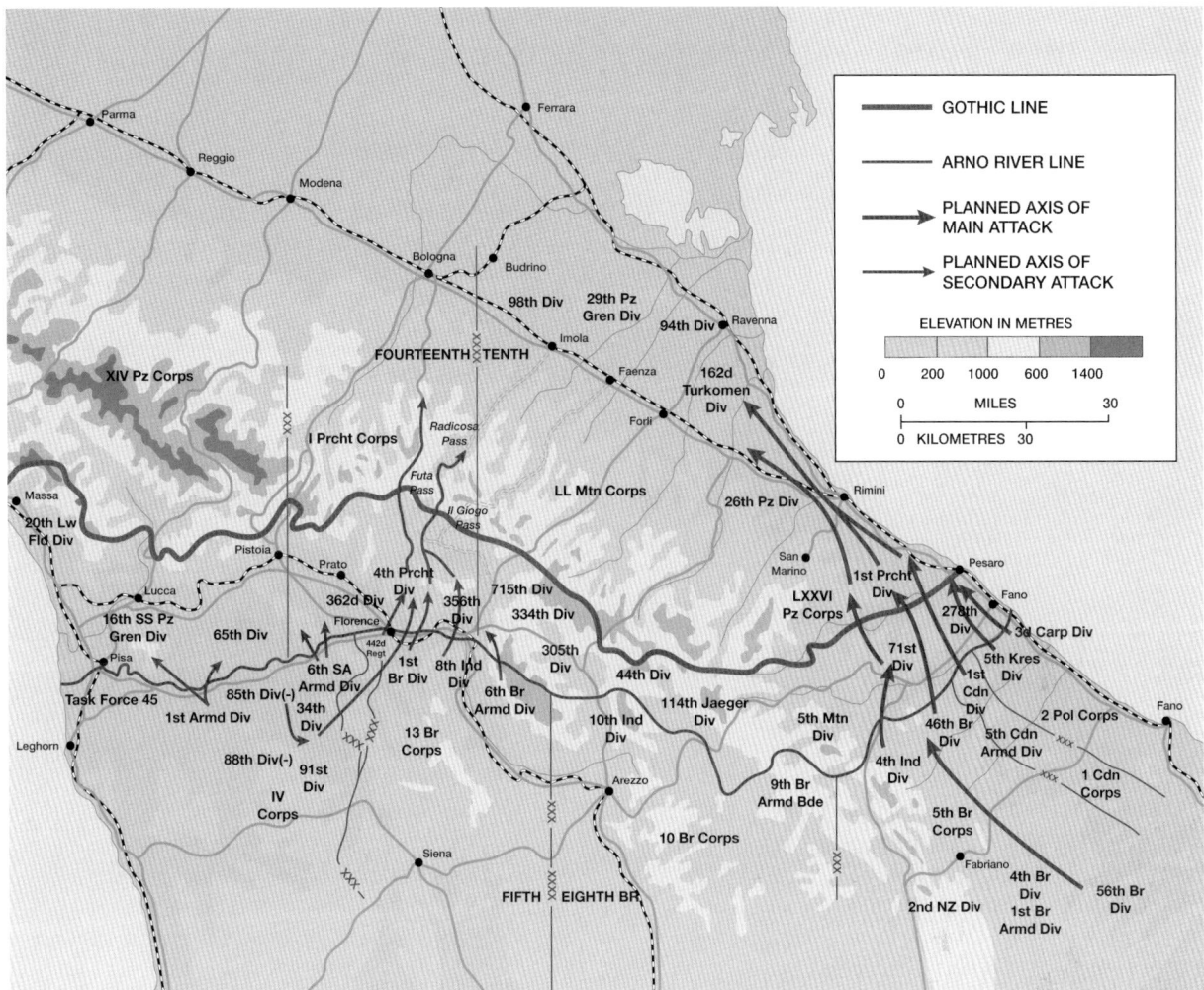

Above: The Allies attack the Gothic Line – Operation 'Olive', 25 August 1944.

Gemmano

When news of the breakthrough at Pesaro came through, 100th Regiment was deployed in Emilia-Romagna, holding a sector of the Galla Placidia anti-landing line between Rimini and Cesena. At that time the regiment, under the command of Oberstleutnant Richard Ernst, consisted of three Gebirgsjäger Battalions under Hauptmanns Hermann and Bachmaier and Major Zwickenpflug, and four fighting companies (reconnaissance, artillery, engineers and anti-tank), with a total of about 4,500 men.

On 1 September the regiment received orders to move to the River Conca valley and was put under the orders of the 71st Infantry Division, whose commander, General Raapke, ordered it to garrison a salient in the line at Gemmano. From 4 to 14 September, 100th Regiment fought tooth and nail against British Empire forces for the key points of the battlefront: Gemmano, Borgo, San Francesco height, Monte Gardo (Point 449), and Zollara were taken, lost and retaken at least 10 times by the combatants. The Gebirgsjägers' stubborn defence in the face of almost continuous attacks, often in close combat, became an epic in the German military history. A week into the battle German news radio broadcast the following dramatic announcement:

In the hard defensive fighting on the Adriatic, in the sector of Gemmano, the 100th Mountain Regiment, under the orders of Oberstleutnant Ernst, together with an artillery group under his orders, with its indestructible firmness and gallant counterattacks has behaved particularly well.

Three days later, following an order to withdraw to Montescudo, the last two German soldiers (one of whom was Ernst himself) left the Gemmano battlefront. The valour demonstrated during the battle of Gemmano earned the regiment no fewer than six *Ritterkreuz des Eisernes Kreuz* (Knight's Cross of the Iron Cross) awards as well as hundreds of Iron Crosses. The action for which August Rappel was awarded the Ritterkreuz, highly unusual for a common soldier, is described here by Ernst:

Rappel defended his blockhouse, then ejected the British from another blockhouse, then recaptured his own blockhouse, which had fallen to the enemy. Later he gave to his own artillery the order to fire against the positions, his own and those of the enemies, who were obliged to retire. And when a shell set fire to his blockhouse he saved his comrades from the flaming house. At last, when the flames were burnt out, he returned to the blockhouse.

When the battle was over, Ernst penned this epitaph for Gemmano:

How much blood this unhappy heap of ruins has drunk! Even if this waste of men had not the proportions of Cassino, the fighting here had the same obstinacy; with the same rage we fought for every house, for every ruin. And as Cassino was the tomb of the 1st Fallschirmjäger Division, so Gemmano was the tomb of my Regiment.

Exhausted by the tough battles on the Arno River and Gothic Line, at the end of August the 5th Gebirgs Division was placed on the reserve of the Ligurian Army and moved to the Western Alps (Alps Maritime). In September, the division was transferred to General der Gebirgstruppen Hans Schlemmer's LXXV Army Corps which, together with the Lombardy Corps of General der Artillerie Kurt Jahn, formed the Ligurian Army. Commanded from the end of October by Marshal Rodolfo Graziani, the Ligurian Army was charged with defending a line through the Western Alps from the Gulf of Genoa to the Franco-Italian frontier against Allied forces that had landed in southern France under Operation 'Dragoon'. It was also engaged in operations against partisans targeting German supply lines. The 5th Gebirgs Division fought under this formation until the end of the war, although various of its sub-units, notably the 100th Gebirgsjäger Regiment, were used to reinforce sectors of the line when breakthroughs threatened. Throughout the autumn the division held positions surrounding the plateau of Mount Cenis in Haut-Maurienne, preventing any attempt to break through the frontier and into Piedmont, behind the German armies from the Gothic Line. It was used variously to reinforce the 4th Alpine Division 'Littorio' in the Tarentaise sector, the Varese battalion on the Col du Petit-saint-Bernard, the Bergamo battalion on the Col du Tauchy and Col du Mont, and the Edolo battalion, which was being held in reserve. Facing them were three brigades of French Chasseurs Alpins, plus numerous irregular units such as the Francs Tireurs Partisans, Section des Eclaireurs Skieurs and Armee Secrete.

Through September and into October the US Fifth and British Eighth Armies continued to slog up the peninsula on roughly parallel lines of advance, using to full advantage the overwhelming air, armour and infantry firepower they now enjoyed in battles of attrition.

Rimini, gateway to the Romagna Plain, was finally taken by the Eighth Army on 21 September. Following this, British Empire forces pressed their attack northward, beginning a three-month operation known as the 'battle of the rivers'. On the Fifth Army front, the capture of the Il Giogo and Futa Passes ended the American phase of Operation 'Olive'. Advancing up Highway 65, by the end of September General Clark was in sight of the Po Valley and the snow-covered Alps beyond. Clark believed that both were now within his grasp, although winter weather now began to slow the advance to a crawl. Furthermore, German forces had inflicted heavy casualties on his troops and were still proving stubborn foes.

On 10 October, the US II Corps launched an assault against the ten-mile-long Livergnano Escarpment, a steep east–west line of solitary mountain peaks constituting Army Group C's strongest natural position in the northern Apennines. Here, as elsewhere, however, sustained Axis resistance, the exhaustion of the American troops, rugged terrain and poor weather halted the advance 10 miles south of Bologna.

Field Marshal Alexander now paused to consider another attempt at capturing Ravenna and Bologna, using the Fifth and Eighth Armies in concert. Meanwhile, across the lines, Kesselring's staff pressed their commander to fall back to the more easily defended Alps. Hitler however, facing Red Army gains on the Eastern Front and mounting pressures in northwest Europe, was loath to cede any territory voluntarily and ordered Kesselring to hold his current line. The field marshal, fearing to oppose the Führer, complied, placing two units from his reserve in front of II Corps.

Above: Gebirgsjäger in 1943-pattern reversible anorak armed with a StG44.

In the last two weeks of October, the Allies rained hammer blows onto the German line, but all attempts to smash the defence and achieve a decisive breakthrough were fruitless. Instead the Fifth Army had to battle their way from mountain to mountain, while Polish, Canadian, Indian and British units of the Eighth Army fought north of Rimini in a continuation of the 'battle of the rivers'. On 27 October, General Sir Henry Maitland Wilson, the Supreme Allied Commander in the Mediterranean, ordered a halt to these offensives, citing Allied munitions and shipping shortages, troop exhaustion, the lack of replacements (largely due to the continued Allied emphasis on combat operations in northwest Europe and southern France and the priority given those areas in terms of manpower, munitions and supplies) and the ever more rapidly deteriorating weather conditions.

Field Marshal Alexander, still striving for an eleventh-hour breakthrough before winter, decided that another attempt on the German defences should be made by both armies with whatever strength they could muster. Eighth Army planners outlined another 'one–two punch', ordering its units to attack to the northwest toward Imola and Budrio, and north toward Ravenna and beyond. After 7 December or after the Eighth Army had taken Imola, whichever came first, Clark would launch the Fifth Army's assault with two divisions of II Corps.

> **BATTLE GROUP 7**
>
> Battle Group 7
> Staff 4th Alpini Division
> Staff, 7th Mountain Regiment
> III/7th Infantry Regiment
> I/8th Infantry Regiment
> II/5th Marine Infantry Regiment (from the 3rd 'San Marco' Marine Infantry Division)
> II/4th Mountain Artillery Regiment
> IV/4th Mountain Artillery Regiment
> 4th Engineer Battalion
> 4th 'Cadelo' Reconnaissance Group

The offensive began on schedule on 2 December, ending the two-month stalemate, but immediately ran into stiff enemy resistance from the 90th Panzergrenadier and 98th Infantry Divisions. Although the Canadian 5th Armoured Division entered Ravenna, a city liberated in large part by a massive uprising of Italian partisans on 4 December, Vietinghoff succeeded in stabilising his front along the Senio River, 10 miles farther north, and repulsed all subsequent attacks launched by Canadian, Polish, Indian and New Zealand units. When it was reported that the Germans had not reduced their strength in II Corps' area as anticipated, Alexander decided on 7 December to postpone further Allied offensive operations, and the front temporarily quieted.

In December there were major reorganisations in both the Axis and Allied high commands. On 23 October Field Marshal Kesselring had been severely injured when his staff car collided with a towed artillery piece on a crowded mountain road; the lengthy recuperation required effectively ended his tenure as Axis commander in Italy. Although he returned to duty in late January 1945, in early March Hitler gave him command of Army Group B in Western Europe, replacing Field Marshal von Rundstedt. General Vietinghoff commanded Army Group C until transferred to the Eastern Front in late January, and then returned to permanently replace Kesselring in March 1945. General Lemelsen stood in for Vietinghoff in the Tenth Army until 17 February 1945, when he was replaced by Generalleutnant Traugott Herr. At Fourteenth Army, Generalmajor Fridolin von Senger und Etterlin replaced Lemelsen before relinquishing command to Generalleutnant Kurt von Tippelskirsch, who in turn gave Lemelsen his old command back in February.

In the Allied camp, Wilson went to Washington as chief of the British Military Mission. Alexander succeeded him as Supreme Allied Commander in the Mediterranean and General Clark took command of the Fifteenth Army Group in place of Alexander. Major-General Lucian K. Truscott, Jr., returned from France to head the Fifth Army. General Sir Richard L. McCreery, who had replaced General Leese as Eighth Army commander on 1 October, remained in command of that force.

5TH GEBIRGSJÄGER WAR SERVICE

Dates	Corps	Army	Army Group	Area
10.40	Forming	Wehrkreis XVIII	–	Home
11.40–2.41	XVIII Corps	Second Army	Army Group C	Home
3.41–10.41	XVIII Corps	Twelfth Army	–	Greece, Crete
11.41	Recuperating BdE	Wehrkreis V	–	Home
12.41–3.42	BdE	Wehrkreis VII and XVIII	–	Home
4.42	I Corps	Eighteenth Army	Army Group North	Leningrad, Volkhov
5.42–7.42	L Corps	Eighteenth Army	Army Group North	Leningrad, Volkhov
8.42	XXVIII Corps	Eighteenth Army	Army Group North	Leningrad, Volkhov
9.42	XXVI Corps	Eighteenth Army	Army Group North	Leningrad, Volkhov
10.42	XXVI Corps	Eleventh Army	Army Group North	Leningrad, Volkhov
11.42	XXX Corps	Eighteenth Army	Army Group North	Leningrad, Volkhov
12.42–3.43	LIV Corps	Eighteenth Army	Army Group North	Leningrad, Volkhov
4.43–11.43	XXVI Corps	Eighteenth Army	Army Group North	Leningrad, Volkhov
12.43	Reserve	Tenth Army	Army Group C	Upper Italy
1.44–5.44	XIV Corps	Tenth Army	Army Group C	Italy (south of Rome)
6.44–7.44	LI Corps	Tenth Army	Army Group C	Italy
8.44	Reserve	Ligurian Army	Army Group C	Western Alps
9.44–4.45	LXXV Corps	Ligurian Army	Army Group C	Western Alps

Left: Wearing the 1943-pattern reversible anorak snow-side outwards, a reconnaissance team watches for the enemy.

OPERATION '*WINTERGEWITTER*'

On 26 December 1944, Axis forces launched Operation '*Wintergewitter*' (winter storm), a limited attack against the inexperienced 92nd Division of the US IV Corps, some 20 miles north of Lucca. Their forces, however, advanced only a few miles beyond Barga, before beginning a withdrawal on 27 December, and in four days of intense fighting in bitter weather they were pushed back to their original positions.

In early January 1945, the Allied commanders in Italy ceased large-scale military operations, to prepare for a new offensive scheduled for 1 April 1945. Despite two months of planning, limited offensives, and much manoeuvring, the Allied units came to rest on a winter line that had changed very little since late October 1944. Early in the year Clark decided to launch three small attacks to obtain the best possible starting points for the planned spring offensive, and achieved some small incremental gains. Except for these limited advances, the Allies contented themselves with resting, receiving reinforcements and stockpiling munitions, especially artillery shells and other supplies. As spring approached, the fully rested and resupplied Fifteenth Army Group prepared to renew the offensive in a campaign that most anticipated would take it into the Po Valley and mark the final Allied push of the war in Italy.

Axis forces, having successfully held the Gothic Line through the autumn and early winter, also used the lull to rest and refit, and attempted to strengthen their fallback positions. Although Vietinghoff's front still stretched from sea to sea, his military situation was deteriorating rapidly. Behind his lines, bands of Italian guerrillas harassed what remained of his bomb-shattered transportation system, setting roadblocks and blowing up railway tracks. From January 1945, the 50,000 tons of supplies that normally arrived each month from Germany ceased altogether, and his troops were forced to live off the land.

On 18 January, Generalmajor Hans Steets assumed command of the 5th Gebirgs Division, becoming its penultimate commander. Attempts were made to reinforce the badly depleted division with elements of the Italian 4th Alpini 'Monte Rosa' Division. This was divided into two elements, Battle Groups 7 and 8, and in February–March 1945, Battle Group 7 was parcelled out between the 5th Gebirgs Division and the 2nd Grenadier Division 'Littorio'.

ADVANCE TO THE ALPS

In April 1945, the months of inching progress through mud and mountains came to an abrupt end, when the US Fifth and British Eighth armies erupted into the Po Valley. Within three weeks the campaign in Italy was brought to a decisive end, as the now numerically vastly superior Allied forces raced to the Alps. But even as these last actions were played out, in the Western Alps there were further heroics from the men of the 5th Gebirgs Division.

The Battle of Mount Froid

In April 1945, the III Battalion of the 100th Gebirgsjäger Regiment and a company of the Italian Fascist Folgore Regiment occupied a key sector in the northwest of the Plateau du Mount Cenis in the Haut-Maurienne. In all they numbered about 1,500 soldiers with 20 howitzers and several heavy mortars. In the valley below them were three chasseurs alpins battalions of the 27th French Mountain Division, mostly composed of former maquisards. These 3,000 volunteers, although inexperienced and poorly equipped, were supported by 45 field guns.

On 5 April 1945, cloaked by a bitter wind and icy snow, the three French battalions facing the 5th Gebirgs Division on the frontier launched an offensive against the plateau of Mount Cenis, which controls access to the Suse Valley and Piedmont. The first target was Mount Froid, a peak 8,500 ft tall that commanded the valley and formed the cornerstone of the German stronghold. Its summit, a narrow ridge 2,100–2,400 ft long, was shielded by three strong points: the east and west blocks with two tumbledown casemates and a centre block with a network of trenches. Although the Gebirgsjäger fought back stoutly under a withering barrage of French artillery fire, the 4th Company of the XI Chasseurs Alpins battalion succeeded in conquering the middle and the western strong points. The next day, after a fourth attack, the same unit seized the eastern block, and Mount Froid fell into French hands.

In the course of 6 April, the French brought fresh troops and ammunition through the deep snow to the fog-shrouded mountaintop positions. Shortly before midnight, after a violent bombardment, a detachment of one German company and two Italian platoons, in five assault groups, approached the eastern casemate in a howling wind. While three groups made a frontal attack, the two others moved to outflank the position. The French garrison was quickly overwhelmed and, facing annihilation, took refuge in the centre block. The assault groups came on again, charging the casemate with submachine guns and hand grenades. The French chasseurs alpins defended themselves energetically, driving back first one then another assault. As dawn began to break on the exposed slope, the attackers were forced to retire.

After three failed counterattacks, German commanders resolved to evacuate the sector but Vietinghoff, fearing an Allied breakthrough to Turin in his rear, overruled them and ordered the 5th Gebirgs Division to recapture Mount Froid at any price. Reinforced by other elements of the division, the troops retook the position on 12 April. It was, however, to prove a hollow victory gained at a heavy cost. Two weeks later, Steets received orders to evacuate his men from the region.

On 20 April, Vietinghoff ordered the retreat, previously denied him by Hitler, to prepared positions on the Ticino and Po Rivers. That night, with defeat in Italy growing imminent, Gebirgsjäger of the 5th Gebirgs Division mounted one last defiant attack against the French VII Battalion Chasseurs Alpins' positions on Roc Belleface. Seven men made a night climb up the precipitous northeast wall of the mountain, and overcame the garrison's defences. It was a gallant act but, with the final battles in Berlin now being played out, ultimately futile.

Above: MG34 team wearing the winter reversible suit field grey side outwards.

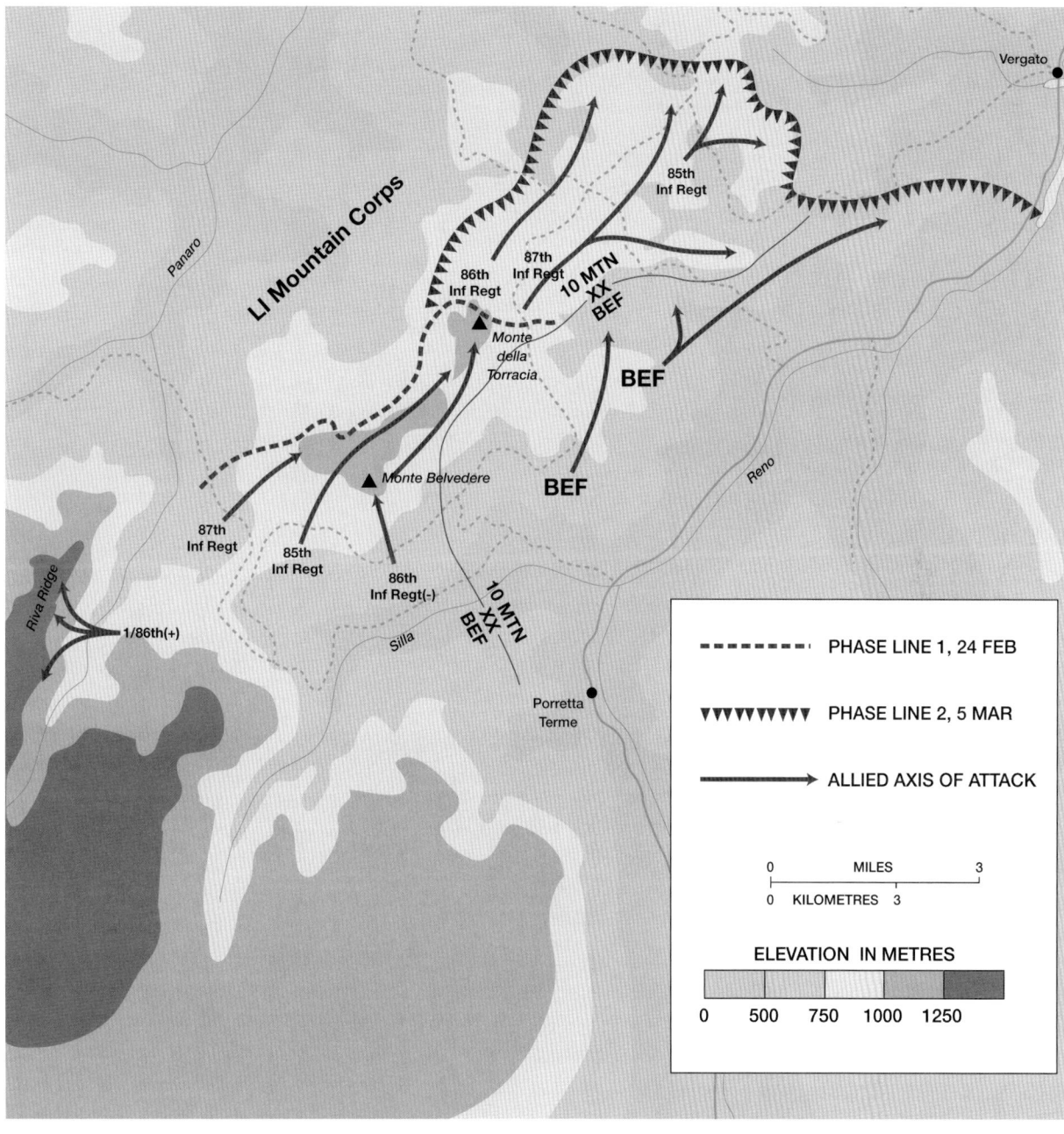

Above: The Allied Operation 'Encore' – 19 February to 5 March 1945.

In the final days of April, the 5th Gebirgs Division continued to fight tenaciously, ignoring the inevitability of defeat. By now they were the last mountain division still fighting in high Alpine terrain. At the beginning of May, the division was regrouped for the last time and marched in full order eastwards toward Milan. During the journey there were skirmishes with Italian partisans, before the troops laid down their arms en masse to the US Fifth Army just north of Turin.

EQUIPMENT, MARKINGS AND CAMOUFLAGE

Some basic details of the insignia, uniforms and equipment (including weapons) used by the 5th Gebirgs Division is provided below. For information on German army rank insignia, award badges and so on, refer to one of the many reference works on this subject listed in the bibliography.

INSIGNIA

The distinctive edelweiss insignia of both army and SS mountain units was based on a small white flower that grows exclusively in the high Alpine regions of continental Europe. It was first adopted under the Habsburgs in 1907 by the Austrian Landesschützen as their official unit insignia. In 1915 it was donated to the German Alpenkorps as a gesture of camaraderie, and from that time on it was worn on the troops' *Bergmütze* (mountain cap). After the First World War the edelweiss was used by a few Freikorps units, although in the Reichswehr only the soldiers of III Gebirgsjäger Battalion of the 19th Jägerregiment were allowed to wear it. On 2 May 1939, it was reintroduced as the insignia of all Gebirgstruppe in response to a request by General der Gebirgstruppe Ludwig Kübler to the OKH (Army High Command).

The 5th Gebirgs Division took as its divisional emblem the Gamsbock, a type of mountain goat noted for its agility on precipitous rock faces. The figurative representation of one of these animals was also used as a marking to distinguish divisional vehicles, and was one of the nicknames given to the division.

Above: Gebirgsjäger Edelweiss badge.

Right: Oberleutnant showing Edelweiss badge on right sleeve and left side of Bergmütze.

Below: The *Gamsbock* emblem of 5th Gebirgsjäger.

HEADGEAR

All ranks were issued with the standard German *Stahlhelm* (steel helmet) in either the 1935 or 1942 pattern, depending on their date of entry into service. Painted flat grey with no decals, this could be covered with a white 'winter' helmet cover. Gebirgsjäger were also issued with the standard German Army peaked cap (*Schirmmütze*) piped with the grass green Waffenfarben and with a small metal edelweiss worn between the national emblem and the wreathed cockade.

Away from the barracks and the parade ground, the mountain cap or *Bergmütze* was far more commonly seen was, and was highly prized by those who had won the right to wear it. Closely modelled on the cap worn by Austrian mountain units in the First World

ELITE ATTACK FORCES: 5TH GEBIRGSJÄGER DIVISION

War, this was produced in field-grey wool or tricot, and had a short peak and side flaps that could be folded down and fastened under the chin to protect the wearers ears and nape from the cold. The flaps were usually fastened at the front with flat green buttons. A cast-metal edelweiss insignia was worn on the left side, and on the front the national cockade and emblem. From 1943 this was replaced a new general issue field cap, based on the Bergmütze but with the longer peak of the tropical field cap. Also produced was a white camouflage cover.

Troops serving in the Mediterranean were issued with an olive-brown tropical field cap, with the same insignia as the Bergmütze. Until 1943 the national emblem and cockade were backed with an underlay of Waffenfarben, and even after this was discontinued many Gebirgsjäger continued the practice.

UNIFORMS

The general service dress of the Gebirgsjäger units followed the German Army standard. A four-pocket, grey, wool *Feldbluse* (field tunic) in either the 1941 or the simpler 1943 pattern was worn, with appropriate rank insignia and the embroidered edelweiss badge on the upper right sleeve. Collar and cuff patches, edelweiss insignia and officers' shoulder straps had an underlay of w*iesengrun* (grass green), the branch-of-service colour (*Waffenfarbe*) of the mountain troops. The same grass-green piping was applied to NCOs' and other ranks' shoulder straps, and to the front, collar, cuffs and trouser seams

Above: Cover of *Signal* magazine showing a mountain leader descending a rock face.

Right: 1941 view of Gebirgsjäger mountain artillery hauling their weapon by mule.

Left: Colour views from *Signal* magazine of rock-climbing training.

Below: Early war mountain troops rifle section ski patrol.

Left: This excellent portrait shows well the Edelweiss cap badge and 1939-pattern reversible anorak which was white one side, sage green the other.

Right: NCO wearing standard-issue greatcoat and Bergmütze.

Far Right: Windproof anorak suit issued 1943–4 to replace earlier types. It was white on one side, sage green the other.

Below: Gebirgsjäger in the two-piece winter suit pass PzKpfw IVs.

of walking-out dress. Finally, there was a grass-green strip in the centre of each officer's *Litzen* (collar patch), and on the earlier issues of NCOs' and other ranks' Litzen.

In addition, to the Waffenfarben, the following system of identification was used by Gebirgsjäger units on the shoulder straps and collar patches:

- Rifle and mountaineering units: unit number.
- Alpine and mountain troops school: gothic 'S'.
- Mountain troop divisional staff: embroidered 'D' with divisional number below.

Instead of the standard issue, field-grey, straight-legged trouser of the *Landser* (general infantryman), Gebirgsjäger were issued distinctive wide-cut mountain trousers (*Keilhose*), with reinforced seats and inside legs, tapered to allow them to be tucked into the boots.

For service in the Balkans and the Mediterranean theatres, Gebirgstruppen were issued with a regulation olive-coloured, cotton, four-pocket tunic, which could be worn with matching shorts, trousers or wider breeches. Puttees were usually discarded; instead socks were simply rolled down over boot-tops.

Winter clothing

Other standard items of clothing designed for use in cold climates, which were not exclusive to but used by the Gebirgsjäger, were the padded, reversible,

Below: Sighting for an MG42 gunner, this man wears a sage-green windproof jacket and has an ice pick and Bergen-style rucksack.

white/camouflage, hooded winter suit with matching mittens, a woollen balaclava to be worn under the helmet, standard army greatcoat, and felt overboots.

Unique to the Gebirgsjäger are the weighty (5 lb or 2.36 kg) ankle-length mountain boots and windproof jacket. The former had thick, studded and cleated leather soles, were fastened by eyelets and hooks, and could be worn with skis, crampons or snowshoes. In warmer climates a lighter boot was sometimes worn. The boots were topped with grey-green, woollen puttees (*Bergstiefel*) some 76cm long, fastened by a buckle and worn either to ankle or knee height. On occasion, canvas gaiters were preferred.

Also peculiar to the Gebirgsjäger was the sage-green *Windjacke* (windproof jacket) made from heavy-duty, close-woven calico, and designed to be worn over the field service blouse, primarily to cut wind-chill. It was double breasted with adjustable cuffs, a rear half-belt, skirt and 'muff' pockets, and provided some protection from the icy winds often experienced in mountains. The jacket could be worn over the belt with ammo-pouches. It had the same buttons and shoulder straps as the field service blouse, but some of the insignias were not worn on the *Windjacke*.

Above: First aid for an injured Gebirgsjäger – his rifle has been slung in the tree above. The men are wearing the 1939-pattern reversible anorak, white side outwards.

Below: The cuff-title 'Kreta' was instituted in 1942. (See next page.)

Right: MG34 with drum magazine.

Below right: MG42 gunner wearing sage green windproof jacket.

Below: Detail photograph of the MG42.

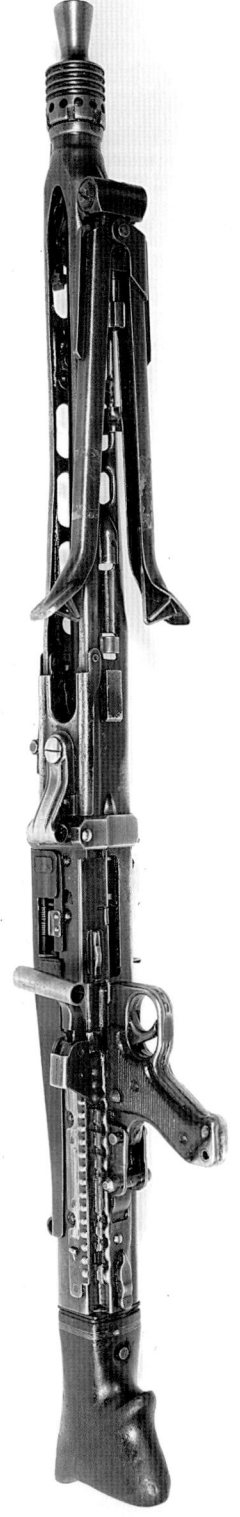

From 1942 a reversible, field-grey/white, hooded anorak with matching overtrousers was issued to the Gebirgsjäger. The cagoule-style, hooded anorak had a large flap to cover the neck opening, three breast pockets, a waist drawstring and a crotch strap that fastened to the front. The overtrousers had a drawstring waist. Neither item was particularly warm, and the anorak was generally less popular than the *Windjacke*.

Officers often wore privately purchased mountain caps, made of finer wool. Before 1942 there was no silver cord around the top on the mountain caps for officers, and only with the introduction of the field-cap Model 42 were officers allowed this distinction to their uniform. Generals wore a golden cord.

SPECIAL AWARDS

Along with the numerous awards for close combat, marksmanship, anti-partisan operations and the like issued to every branch of the services, men who had fought in the Narvik campaign in Norway were awarded a white metal shield bearing the legend 'Narvik 1940' (with an edelweiss for Alpine troops, or a propeller or anchor for Luftwaffe or Navy personnel). Of further interest is the Armelband Kreta, instituted in October 1942 for those men who had taken part in operations on Crete between 20–27 May 1941. Worn on the lower left sleeve, it was a white cloth band edged with golden-yellow Russia braid; in the centre was the embroidered legend 'Kreta', flanked with acanthus leaves. Far more rarely seen was the enamelled *Heeresbergführer* (army mountain leader) badge, worn on the left breast pocket and awarded only to those men, regardless of rank or age, who had achieved the highest level of mountaineering skill. This high-quality piece, keenly sought by collectors today, consists of an enamelled metal oval with a white outer border and green central field, surrounding an embossed silvered edelweiss with gilt stamens. At the base in gothic script is the title Heeresbergführer.

PERSONAL EQUIPMENT

This included all of the standard combat equipment of the German infantry along with other, more specialised kit. Standard equipment included a black leather belt with buckle, ammunition pouches, Y-shaped yoke straps of leather, a canteen, bread bag, bayonet, shelter (*Zeltbahn*), mess tin and cutlery, gas mask canister and entrenching tool. As bayonets, gas masks and helmets were too heavy for Alpine warfare, and of little worth, these were often left behind with the baggage train.

For operations in the high mountains the Jäger was issued with a 'Grosse' rucksack, the contents of which had to sustain him for days, weeks and often months. Inside the rucksack he carried his

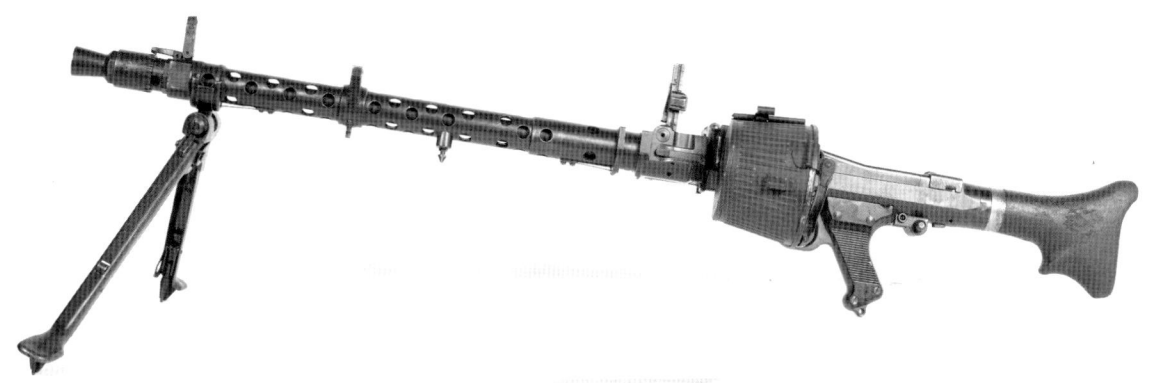

windcheater, spare shirt, spare trousers, spare socks, a groundsheet and woollen blanket. This last item proved less popular than the lighter, warmer and more compact Russian sleeping bag issued to Siberian troops, and examples of this were highly sought after. In addition, there was a Balaclava helmet, waist belt, gloves and the basic fighting ration: a kilo of bread (2.2 lb), one large tin of meat, and one small tin of lard. This had to satisfy dietary needs for two days, after which it was expected (but by no means guaranteed) that pack animals would bring supplies up to the front line.

To supplement this 'fighting ration', the troops were given a selection of high-calorie, low-bulk foodstuffs. Many calories were required to provide for the physical demands of marching and climbing in mountainous regions. These foodstuffs had to be edible either raw or very quickly cooked, since at high altitude the process of heating food requires more time and thus expends precious fuel. Air-dried meats, canned food, dehydrated vegetables and biscuits proved the best for these conditions, although on shorter operations chocolate, grape sugar or dried fruit were also practical. (Dried fodder for the pack animals was often provided in the form of cattle cake to avoid the problems of transporting bulky hay and grain.)

In his musette bag, the trooper carried an iron ration with chocolate and similar foodstuffs, washing gear, patching gear and candles or flashlight. In his blouse pockets he typically had two first-aid field dressings, a clasp knife, cigarettes, matches, pen and ink, and service pay book.

Platoon and section commanders (and runners) had to carry binoculars, message bags or signal pistols. The compass and binoculars were vital in the mountains and were issued right down to squad level.

MOUNTAIN EQUIPMENT

The Gebirgstruppe also had various specialised mountain equipment to hand, including skis, snow goggles, ice axe, a length of rope (three-eighths of an inch thick), the Grosse rucksack mentioned earlier, and ice hammer, crampons, snowshoes and pitons.

For traversing snow-covered terrain at speed, skis or snowshoes were essential, although both the army and the Waffen SS had their own Skijäger units. In icy conditions, crampons were used.

Snow goggles were standard issue as they provided protection for the eyes against harsh winds and were slightly tinted to protect against snowblindness. In the event that a snow storm, fog or darkness reduced visibility on the line of march, coloured ropes and flags were used to mark out a given route. Rope railings were employed for crossing crevasses in glaciers and were fitted with noise-making devices such as empty cartridge cases to aid orientation.

Rock-climbing equipment was issued to all Jäger units to suit their own personal requirements. Medical teams, for example, were issued with special stretchers that allowed the wounded to be lowered vertically down the side of a rockface. The medical teams had to deal with various types of injury, including snowblindness, frostbite and rope burns, which in some cases could be severe. Evacuation was almost always necessary in the case of severe injury, and ski stretchers were often employed for this task. These stretchers could be broken down and had folding legs, and in an emergency could be used as an operating table. Specially designed tents, some 16 ft in length, were employed to treat the wounded. They were made of light, windproof material and could be broken down into loads and transported by pack animals.

All told the average trooper was expected to be able to shoulder about 70 lb total weight, and be able to carry that over a vertical distance of rather more than 6,000 feet. However, as already mentioned it was impossible to fight with such a load, and the

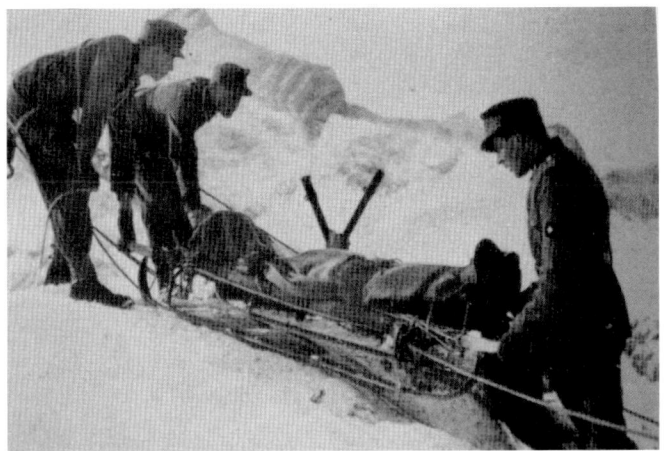

Above: Casualty evacuation on ski stretcher.

Below: A tree trunk has been called into use with a block and tackle to haul a K15 gun to its firing position.

Right: Mountain stretcher of proofed canvas.

Below right: Specially designed MG34 snowshoe for front bipod legs.

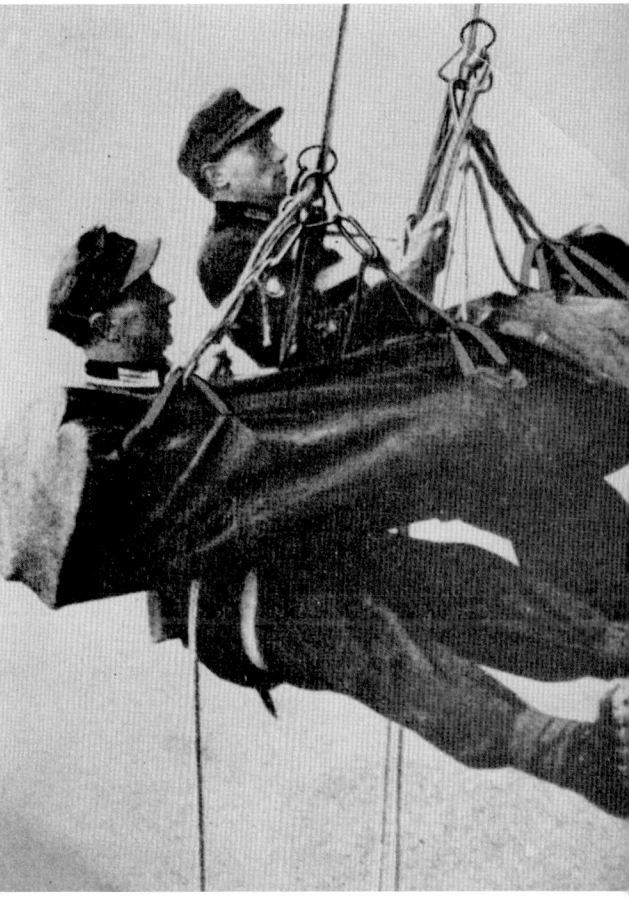

Left: The 7.5cm Geb G36 – note wicker mats under wheels to give grip in snow. This weapon is emplaced at 18,400ft on Mount Elbrus, the furthest point of the German advance into the Caucasus.

Right: Kübelwagen towing a 37mm Pak 36 anti-tank gun. There were 12 of these weapons in each motorised anti-tank company.

Below: A 10.5cm leichte Feldhaubitze 16 – not specifically a mountain troops' weapon – being emplaced by Gebirgsjäger gunners in north Russia. Note the skid chassis for ease of handling in snow.

Grosse rucksacks were often laid down and brought up later from behind in the baggage train.

MOUNTAIN ARTILLERY

The light mountain artillery used by heavy companies and platoons in the direct fire support role was designed so that it could be fully dismantled and transported by pack animals to the fighting front. Trials with standard issue equipment had proved unsuccessful as the guns could not be broken down easily, so special equipment was introduced. As a rule, mountain artillery pieces had to be both light and very robust. Thus, different manufacturing techniques were devised. Extensive use was made of pressed parts rather than the more conventional machined parts.

To suit the specific needs of the mountain artillery, designs dating from the First World War were revised and updated, including the 75 mm (3 inch) Gebirgskanone (1915) and the 1918-vintage 75 mm leichte Gebirgskanone. A weapon based on the latter design was introduced in 1935. It weighed a little under 900 lb (400 kg) and had a range of rather over two miles (just over 3.5 km). Both remained in service until the end of the war. They were supplemented by the 75 mm Gebirgskanone 28 and, from 1938, by the 75 mm Gebirgsschütze 36 model, weighing in at 1,650 lb (750 kg) and capable of firing a 13 lb (6 kg) projectile to a maximum range of just over 5 miles (9.25 km).

Heavier fire support was provided by the *Gebirgshaubitze* (mountain howitzer) batteries. These used the 100 mm Gebirgshaubitze 16 or Gerät 77, and one of two 105 mm pieces. The Gebirgshaubitze 42, produced by the Austrian firm of Boehler did not reach the mountain artillery battalions until 1943–4. It weighed 1.66 tons, had a range of nearly eight miles (12.6 km), and could be broken down easily into four large parts to be towed by NSU Opel *Kattenkrad* (tracked motorcycle) in single axle carts.

Both German-made and captured guns were used. French guns included the 6.5 cm Gebirgskanone 221, the 7.5 cm Gebirgskanone 238 and the 10.5 cm Gebirghaubitze 322. Czech guns such as the 10 cm Gebirghaubitze, and the Russian 7.62 cm Gebirgskanone 307 were also adopted for use.

The mountain artillery regiments of the mountain divisions (in the case of the 5th Gebirgs Division, the 95th Gebirgs Artillery Regiment) also had the standard *schwere Infanterie Geschütze* (heavy infantry guns) and *schwere Feldehaubitze* (heavy field howitzer) of the German forces, for use in long-range fire support missions. Generally there was one battalion each of 105 mm and 150 mm howitzers. The 150 mm (6-inch) howitzer had a range of rather over eight miles (13.3 km), but due to its size and weight the heavy batteries had to operate on the lower slopes and valley floors, from where their support could be called on as required.

Below: 7.5cm light mountain gun IG 18 on the Russian Front in 1944.

INFANTRY WEAPONS

Kar 98k rifle
K/G43 semi-automatic rifle
MP40 submachine gun

Above: Artillerymen and mule team carry a K15 mountain gun to its position.

Left: Another view of the K15 mountain gun. The gunners are wearing calico wind jackets.

MP38/42 Beretta machine pistol
MP44
MG34 light machine gun
MG42 light machine gun
stick or egg grenades
P38 pistol
P08 pistol
G33/40 mountain carbine

In common with other branches of the infantry the standard issue rifle was the excellent Mauser Kar 98k, although large numbers of the so-called Gebirgskaribiner (Gewehr 33/40), a Czech-made variant of the Mauser with a shortened (46cm) barrel were also issued. As the distances at which combat took place could be considerable, these weapons were often equipped with either the zF41 (x 2.5 magnification) or zF4 (x 4 magnification) telescopic sights.

For close combat both the MP38 machine pistol and the MP40 submachine gun were used, primarily by squad leaders, and later in the war the semi-automatic Gewehr 43 and Sturmgewehr StG44 assault rifle were introduced in significant quantities. Captured examples of the simple yet tough and reliable Soviet PPSh-41 submachine gun were

Below right: Telefunken pedal power generator with signaller transmitting by morse key in the background.

Below: Funkgerät d2 radio set with three-man carrying team. The second man carries the battery pack.

highly prized. Officers carried either the Luger, P08 or, less frequently, Walther PPK automatic pistols.

In the squad support role the Gebirgsjäger used the ubiquitous MG 34 and later MG 42 light machine guns, both of which proved reliable in the harsh conditions of the mountains. With the aid of a mount that could be attached to either breech or barrel, it could be used as a fully automatic heavy machine gun or a light anti-aircraft weapon. Ammunition for the personal weapon was carried in belt pouches, and each man was usually also required to carry ammunition for the light machine guns.

Extensive use was also made of hand grenades for close quarter fighting, both the familiar stick pattern and smaller, egg-shaped *Eierhandgranate*. Light fire support was provided by easily disassembled and transportable mortars, flak and light artillery. Particularly effective in the mountains, because of their high trajectory, were the mortars. The Gebirgs divisions used three main types: the 5 cm (2 inch) leichte Granatwerfer 36, 8 cm kurzer Granatwerfer 42, and 12 cm kurzer Granatwerfer 42. The 5 cm GrWf 36 was a sturdy little weapon weighing only weighing just over 30 lb (14 kg) and comprising just two basic components, a barrel and a base plate. It could fire a projectile weighing rather over 7.7 lb (3.5 kg) over 500 yards. From 1941 this was phased out in favour of the 8 cm (3 inch) kurzer Granatwerfer 42, which had more than double the range and nearly double the weight. This failed to live up to expectations and so from 1943 a 12 cm (4.75 inch) heavy mortar based on a Russian design was introduced.

Above: Signaller laying field telephone cable from skis.

The Gebirgs divisions also had dedicated anti-aircraft battalions equipped with a light 20 mm AA gun that could be broken down into eight major sub-components and be transported by pack animals. Towards the end of the war, this weapon proved particularly useful in defending the high passes of the Western Alps.

As in other units, the 5th Gebirgs Division's Panzerjäger (anti-tank) battalion was equipped with 37 mm L45 PAK 35/36, a weapon that proved wholly unsatisfactory against heavily armoured British and Russian tanks. Not until the introduction of the 50 mm gun did the situation improve.

COMMUNICATIONS

Given the lack of a transport infrastructure, communications in the mountains presented unique challenges. Radio transmitters were the principal means of communication over distance. Early sets included the Tornister Funkgerät, which weighed in at nearly 80 lb (35 kg) and required a three-man team to operate and transport it. Two of them carried the set – one the transmitter, one the batteries – and the other was the operator. This bulky set had a range of 2.5 miles (4 km) for voice, or 10 miles (16 km) sending a Morse signal. Later on in the war, much lighter radio equipment was developed, including the Feldfunk Sprecher B and C that could be carried and operated by one man.

Radio sets were issued right down to company level but could sometimes be rendered useless by high mountain peaks or atmospheric conditions that blocked their signals. Larger aerials were required than those used on conventional radio sets, and in an attempt to the combat the loss of signals experienced under certain atmospheric or topographical conditions, these were often attached to the tops of trees. Another tactic was to relay signals between stations. All of this equipment could be broken down into mule loads for transportation. A simpler and widely used method of signalling, and one less susceptible to interference, was semaphore. Provided visibility was good, a trained signaller could send messages to another man up to five miles away. Trained dogs were also used to send messages. (Large St Bernard dogs were also often employed to carry ammunition, food and medical packs, and were used by rescue teams.)

MOUNTAIN ENGINEERS

Within each Gebirgsjäger division there was a dedicated engineer battalion. As well as performing the normal combat engineer duties – mine-clearing, bridge laying, demolition and so forth – the *Gebirgspioniere* had numerous other tasks, among them improving mountain passes and roads by rock blasting, avalanche blasting and the draining of water from mountain roads. For these tasks they were equipped with the same tools and equipment as a regular infantry division and other more specialised kit. The Gebirgs engineer battalion could construct cable lines that could support loads of either 330 lb (150 kg) or 1,100 lb (500 kg) for moving men and equipment down from high areas. A difference in height of about 400 yards was required for them to be usable, and they could span an distance of 1,000 yards.

Below: Gebirgsjäger engineers repair a road to allow supporting StuG IIIs to advance.

Where roads were in poor condition or non-existent, new ones often had to be built. In the swampy areas around Leningrad, the engineers of the 5th Gebirgs Division were often called upon to build corduroy roads of logs so that vehicles could move through the cloying mud. Where a bridge had been blown, or simply did not exist, the engineers would be called on to construct anything from a simple rope walkway to a heavy pontoon bridge able to bear the weight of vehicles and heavy weapons. For this purpose, three types of bridging equipment were supplied to the Gebirgs engineer battalions. The Military (Mountain) Bridge Equipment G-Gerät kit provided the components to build a simple footbridge 120 yards in length, a 4-ton suspension bridge capable of supporting motor vehicles and horse-drawn carts, or a 2-ton inflatable-boat bridge that could span 60 yards. The B-Gerät kit enabled the construction of an 8–16-ton bridge supported by pontoon ferries; the K-Gerät was particularly useful in that it enabled the construction of a 20-yard-long, 16-ton bridge without assistance in only 20 minutes.

In addition, endless amounts of mines and mine-clearing equipment, snow probes, demolition explosives, detonators, electric and cordite fuses, power-saws, flame-throwers, rope and construction tools were required.

TRANSPORT

As mentioned earlier, when fighting in the mountains the Gebirgsjäger divisions were heavily reliant on the physical strength of their troops for logistics. At other times, when other assets could be employed, flexibility was important. In many cases, whatever was at hand would be pressed into service. The Gebirgstruppe in Lapland followed the example of the Finnish troops and used reindeer, while in the Caucasus Bactrian camels

Left: As has been shown aplenty in this book, the Gebirgsjäger used mules and horses to carry mountain guns and other equipment. Here the wheels of a K15 mountain gun are transported – note the handler (leading) has slung his rifle across his chest as per regulations.

Overleaf: A variety of means of transport for Gebirgsjäger – bicycles, skis, sledges, horses and Kettenkrads.

and small donkeys were pressed into service. The loads that these animals could carry were quite considerable, but without doubt the most widely used pack animals were mules and small sturdy ponies. Although in general mountain units were not fully motorised, two vehicles proved both suitable and popular in such terrain. These were the Kettenkrad tracked motorcycle, which could negotiate tight mountain passes and rocky terrain, and the light mountain car known as the *Erlkönig*, specially developed for the mountain units. It was light and fairly manoeuvrable while at the same time being quite robust. Artillery units had prime movers for their bigger weapons, but of course these were restricted to the roads, as were the plethora of other trucks and cars available to the units. Where there were no roads, lighter calibre artillery pieces had to be dismantled and drawn by animal teams on sleds, or else manhandled into position.

SHELTER

In the high peaks, access to some form of shelter from wind, rain and snow is vital given the constantly changing weather. On most occasions this had to be constructed by hand, and often very quickly. Men were taught how to dig caves in the ice or snow, and to make use of natural caves that were sometimes found on mountains. Finnish plywood shelters that could be broken down and transported, were often used, and proved effective as well as windproof. If a more permanent installation was required, the engineer units could throw up log cabins. The construction of mountain strongpoints and safety installations, with snow-fences and avalanche deflectors to guard against rock falls and avalanches, and fortified with barbed wire, was also the responsibility of the mountain engineer units. High winds often prevented conventional shelters from being constructed, however. In this case, simple stone walls were thrown up to act as windbreaks, behind which men could sleep.

PEOPLE

COMMANDERS OF 5TH GEBIRGSJÄGER

Generalleutnant Julius 'Papa' Ringel	to April 1944
Generalleutnant Major Max-Günther Schrank	to February 1945
General Hans Steets	to 3 May 1945
General Karl Kurz	to the end of war

Right: 'Papa' Ringel.

JULIUS 'PAPA' RINGEL

Julius Ringel, or 'Papa' as he was known by his devoted men, was commander of 5th Gebirgs Division from its inception and during its most celebrated actions. Both charismatic and highly able, easily distinguished from most army officers by his goatee beard, Ringel was one of the best of the Gebirgstruppe commanders.

He was born on 16 November 1889 at Volkermarkt in Austria and in August 1909 joined the army. A year later he was a Leutnant with 4th Infantry Regiment and at the outbreak of was on the general staff (Ia) of the 3rd Gebirgs Division.

In August 1938, when the Austrian Army units were absorbed by the Wehrmacht, Ringel was promoted to Oberstleutnant. Now an officer in the German Army, three years later he was Oberst and a general staff officer (Ia) with 268th Infantry Division. At the end of October came his first command, 266th Infantry Regiment. Prior to the invasion of France Ringel was given his first divisional command, the still organising 5th Gebirgs Division. In early June, with the campaign mostly concluded, preparations began for the invasion of England ('Sealion') and for this Ringel was chosen to lead 3rd Gebirgs Division. He was returned to 5th Gebirgs Division when Operation 'Sealion', was cancelled and led it into the Balkans. His leadership on Crete won him the Knight's Cross, to which Oakleaves were added in 1943 after service on the Leningrad Front. After the division was transferred to Italy, in April 1944 he moved up to command LXIX Mountain Corps for a brief period. In June came promotion to General der Gebirgstruppe and commander of XVIII Mountain Corps. Finally, in February 1945, Corps Ringel was created. After the war he wrote an account of the 5th Gebirgs Division titled *Hurra! die Gamsbocks*, which remains its finest history. He died on 10 February 1967.

MAX-GÜNTHER SCHRANK

In February 1944 command of the 5th Gebirgs Division passed to Generalleutnant Max-Günther Schrank. Schrank was born in 1898 and died in 1960. He won the Knight's Cross in July 1941.

Above: Ringel decorates men of the division after the invasion of Crete.

HANS STEETS

Steets took comnand of 5th Gebirgs Division in Febuary 1945 and led it until succeeded by Karl Kurz.

KARL KURZ

Last of the commanders of the 5th Gebirgs Division, and the most short-lived, was Karl Kurz. He took command on 3 May 1945 and led it until the general surrender.

KNIGHT'S CROSS HOLDERS

Below is a complete list of Knight's Cross winners, and the date of the award, from 5th Gebirgsjäger Division.

Friedrich Bachmaier	9 January 1945
Max Burghartswieser	9 July 1941
Josef Ehinger	22 August 1943
Richard Ernst	20 October 1944
Albin Esch	13 June 1941
Albert Gaum	13 June 1941
Anton Glasl	11 October 1943
Franz Gnaden	8 August 1941
Josef Hampl	10 September 1943
Helmut Hermann	18 December 1944
Adolf Hofmann	15 November 1941
Franz Holzinger	13 April 1944
August Krakau	21 June 1941
Matthias Langmaier	29 February 1944
Franz Pfeiffer	13 June 1941
Franz Poeschl	23 February 1944
Heribert Raithel	13 June 1941
August Rappel	29 November 1944
Karl Riesle	29 February 1944
Julius Ringel	13 June 1941
Siegfried Rupprecht	10 September 1943
Johann Sandner	13 June 1941
Lorenz Schmied	29 November 1944
Max-Günther Schrank	17 July 1941
Leopold Schrems	27 July 1944
Otto Schury	17 July 1941
Egon Teeck	8 August 1941
Willibald Utz	21 June 1941
August Wittmann	21 June 1941
Hans Zwickenpflug	5 April 1945

Note: It worth noting that the first soldier of the Wehrmacht to be awarded the coveted Oakleaves to the Knight's Cross of the Iron Cross was a Gebirgsjäger, Generaloberst Eduard Dietl. His name was adopted by the Gebirgsjäger training school of the post-war Bundeswehr, the 'Dietl Kaserne'.

AUGUST WILHELM KRAKAU

One of the most celebrated 5th Gebirgs Division officers, Krakau was born on 12 September 1894, at Pirmasens in the Rhein-Pfalz, Bavaria.

He volunteered for service at the outbreak of the First World War in August 1914, and a year later was promoted to Gefreiter. By the end of 1917 he was a Leutnant and deputy commander of the 1st Company of the Bavarian 2nd Jäger Battalion, and ended the war as commander of the 3rd Company of the Bavarian 2nd Jäger Battalion upon the demobilization in Germany.

After a spell as a militia leader, he joined the post-war Reichswehr and took part in the suppression of internal unrest in central Germany. During the 1920s and early 1930s he slowly climbed the promotion ladder until appointed commander of the II. Battalion/Infantry Regiment 41 of the 10th Infantry Division on 12 October 1937. In September 1939, the 10th Infantry Division took part in the invasion of Poland where it participated in the capture of Warsaw. In February 1940 he was commander of Infantry Regiment 85 of the 10th Infantry Division and took part in the invasion of France as a component of Generaloberst Wilhelm List's Twelfth Army.

On 5 October 1940 the 85th Infantry Regiment was redesignated the 85th Gebirgsjäger Regiment and assigned to the 5th Gebirgs Division, and under Krakau fought in the spring of 1941 first in Greece and then Crete. In May 1942, Krakau was delegated with the leadership of the 7th Gebirgs Division in Finland, which he led until captured in Norway on 9 May 1945. He died in January 1975 at Oberpfalz.

ASSESSMENT

Right: A warning notice to mule or horse teams to beware of falls.

Although far less publicised than the elite Panzertruppe, Fallschirmjäger and Waffen-SS, the Gebirgstruppen of the German Army deserve equal recognition.

By a considerable margin, 5th Gebirgsjäger Division was the best trained, led and motivated of the 10 mountain divisions within the German Army during World War II, and by some measure the best of any nation. It was certainly the only one used consistently in its intended role and environment. Although mountain troops are already reckoned something of an elite, within that small group 5th Gebirgsjäger Division has few peers.

In their very first combat, at the Metaxas line in Greece, 5th Gebirgsjäger Division men showed considerable mettle in breaching this fiercely defended, seemingly impregnable fortification. Following on from that, the speed with which they maintained the pursuit of the retreating British forces through the Greek mountains to the south coast is testimony to their hardiness.

In Crete, the division flew into a cauldron and put out the fire. Gambling all on a highly risky assault into Maleme while this was still under fire, the Gebirgsjäger can be credited for averting the disaster that otherwise would have befallen Student's Parachute Corps. And this despite suffering one of their own at the hands of the Royal Navy in the waters off the island, when the motley collection of boats that had been hastily collected together to transport them to the island was intercepted. Then, in driving the defenders across Crete into the sea, the division was able to demonstrate the abundant skills of mountain craft and physical endurance in rapid advances across difficult terrain.

In Russia, fighting a very different kind of war in the miserable swamps around Leningrad, these skills were largely wasted. Nevertheless, the division gave a good account of itself in the stagnant defensive battles on this front, acting in the role of a 'fire brigade' on the porous sectors.

Transferred to Italy, the division was again relegated to a defensive role. In the brutal battles on the Gustav Line at Cassino, and on the Gothic Line to the north, it mounted a tenacious defence despite merciless pounding by Allied aircraft and artillery, which helped frustrate Allied ambitions time and again and prevented them from redeploying units that could have shortened the war on other fronts. In the final months of the war, fighting once again in the mountains, this time on the Franco-Italian border, 5th Gebirgs Division successfully fended off attempts to break through to the rear of the retreating German Army.

It should be emphasised that for an infantry division, 5th Gebirgsjäger Division was comparatively lightly armed, and furthermore depended for mobility on its men and pack animals. Morale seems to have been consistently high, even under the most trying of circumstances. What is more, the problems with discipline that afflicted other lesser parts of the German army do not seem to have touched the 5th Gebirgsjäger Division, and it ended the war with honour intact. In final judgement, this truly was an elite.

REFERENCE

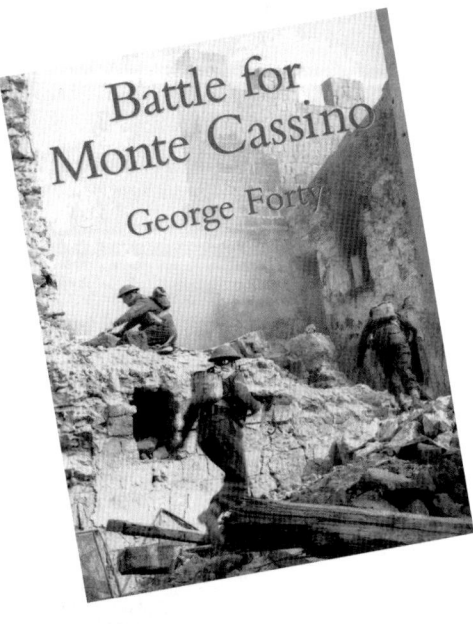

BIBLIOGRAPHY

Clark, Allan: *The Fall of Crete*; Cassell, 1962.
Excellent general description of the battle.

Clark, Mark: *Calculated Risk*; Harper, 1950.
Commander of Fifth Army gives the best war memoir on Italy.

D'Este, Carlo: *World War II in the Mediterranean, 1942–1945*; Algonquin Books/Chapel Hill, 1990.

Dunnigan, James F. (ed.): *The Russian Front: Germany's War in the East, 1941–45*; Arms and Armour, 1978.
Excellent general survey of the Eastern Front battles.

Fisher, Jr., Ernest F.: *Cassino to the Alps*; Washington Center Of Military History, 1977.
The most comprehensive work on the Italian campaign.

Forty, George: *Battle for Crete* and *Battle for Monte Cassino*; Ian Allan Publishing, 2001, 2004.
Two heavily pictorial surveys of these important battles.

Gordon-Douglas, S. R.: *German Combat Uniforms 1939–45*; Almark, 1970.
The focus of this book is on combat equipment and field uniform.

Hogg, Ian: *The Encyclopedia of Infantry Weapons of WW II*; Regent Books, 1984.
A fully comprehensive, illustrated work, including every type of weapon used by every army in the Second World War.

Keegan, John (ed.): *Encyclopedia of World War II*; Bison Books, 1977.
A short, many-sided history of the war as a whole. It includes biographies, details of major weapons, weapon systems, and details of all major battles.

Kaltenegger, Roland: *Weapons and Equipment of the German Mountain Troops in World War II*; Schiffer, 1995.
Largely pictorial record of the German mountain troops with brief details of their organisation.

Lucas, James: *Alpine Elite*; Jane's Publishing Company, 1980.
Lucas, James: *Hitler's Mountain Troops: Fighting at the Extremes*; Cassell, 1999.
Merriam, Ray: *Gebirgsjäger: Germany's Mountain Troops*; World War II Journal, No. 9.
Three good surveys of the Gebirgsjäger.

Mitcham, Samuel W.: *Hitler's Legions*; Cooper, 1985.
The organisation and technical aspects of the German divisions are described. Every part of the army is covered.

Mitcham, Samuel W.: *Hitler's Field Marshals*; Guild Publishing, 1988.
Biographies of the German field marshals and accounts of their major battles.

Orgill, Douglas: *The Gothic Line, Autumn 1944*; Heinemann, 1967.
Good detailed battle history.

Purnell-Hart/Pitt (eds): *History of the Second World War*; Purnell, 96 parts, published weekly during the 1960s.
Written in the main by the soldiers themselves, this is a real trove of information.

Williamson, Gordon: *German Mountain and Ski Troops 1939–45*; Osprey, 1996 and *Gebirgsjäger – German Mountain Trooper 1939–45*; Osprey, 2003.
Two classic Osprey equipment titles.

WEBSITES

http://www.Gebirgsjäger.4mg.com/
Currently the most detailed source of information on the German mountain troops currently available on the web.

http://www.geocities.com/Gebirgstruppe/index-e.html
'The mountain troops of the Wehrmacht.' Good colour pictures of uniforms, and details of divisional markings.

http://www.kameradenkreis-Gebirgstruppe.de/
Kameradenkreis der Gebirgstruppe E.V. In der Internationalen Föderation der Gebirgssoldaten (IFMS). German language site of the German Gebirgsjägers past and present. Also honours the mountain soldiers of other nations.

http://www.thirdreichruins.com
Has a picture of the Gebirgs memorial at the Gebirgsjäger barracks.

http://www.feldgrau.com
Excellent site providing detailed information and statistics on the German armed forces during from 1919–45.

http://www.axishistory.com/
Axis History Factbook. Another excellent site, still under construction, providing detailed information and statistics on the German armed forces from 1919–45. Currently one of the most detailed online sources of information on the Third Reich.

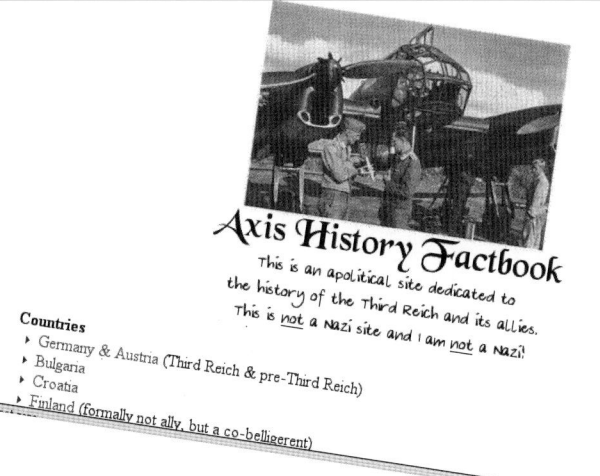

http://www.onwar.com/maps
Campaign maps from the Second and other wars.

http://www.tankclub.agava.ru/sign/sign.shtml
Russian-language site with excellent illustrations of the tactical signs of the German Army.

RE-ENACTMENTS

5th Gebirgsjäger 100th Regiment 1st Battalion 2nd Company
Virginia-based living history unit with members from VA, MA, NY.
Email: scvoli@aol.com

1./Gebirgsjäger.Regiment 98.
US-based living history unit who can be contacted via:
http://www.reenactor.net/units/gjr98/1-gjr98-home.html

FURTHER RESEARCH

Bundesarchiv – Militärarchiv
Federal Records Office – Military Archive
Postfach, 79024 Freiburg
Wiesenthalstrasse 10
D-79115 Freiburg
Deutschland

Bundesarchiv – Zentralnachweisstelle
Federal Central Record Office
Historical records office of the German Federal Republic. Available upon application for use by researchers and authors.
Bundesarchiv-Zentralnachweisstelle
Abteigarten 6

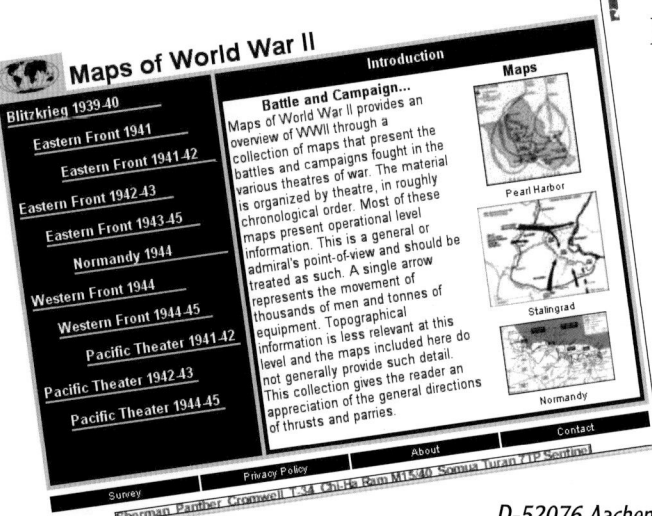

D-52076 Aachen
Deutschland
http://www.bundesarchiv.de

Bundesarchiv-Personalarchiv
Federal Records Office – Personnel Archives
Information on personnel questions relating to Second World War survivors.
Bundesarchiv-Personalarchiv
Abteigarten 6
D-52076 Aachen
Deutschland

Bundesministerium der Verteidigung
Ministry of Defence
Bundesministerium der Verteidigung
Postfach 13 28
D-53003 Bonn

Deutschland

Verband des Krieges
German War Veterans Organisation
*Verband des Krieges
Wurzerstrasse 2-4
D-53175 Bonn
Deutschland*

Volksbund Deutsche Kriegsgräberfürsorge
German War Graves Commission
Maintains German war graves all across the world. Has a database of fallen or missing German soldiers, with the location of their graves (if known).
*Volksbund Deutsche Kriegsgräberfürsorge
Werner-Hilpert-Strasse 2
D-34112 Kassel
Deutschland*
http://www.volksbund.de/homepage.htm

Arbeisgemeinschaft für Kameradenwerke und Traditionsverbaende e.V
Kameraden Veterans Magazine
The official newsletter for German Second World War veterans.
*Arbeisgemeinschaft für Kameradenwerke und Traditionsverbüde e.V
Tuebinger Strasse 12-16
D-70178 Stuttgart
Deutschland*

MEMORIALS

At the Gebirgsjäger barracks in Berchtesgaden-Strub, Bavaria, in Germany is a memorial to German mountain troops of the Second World War. It takes the form of a lion mounting a peak, which itself stands on a stone plinth.

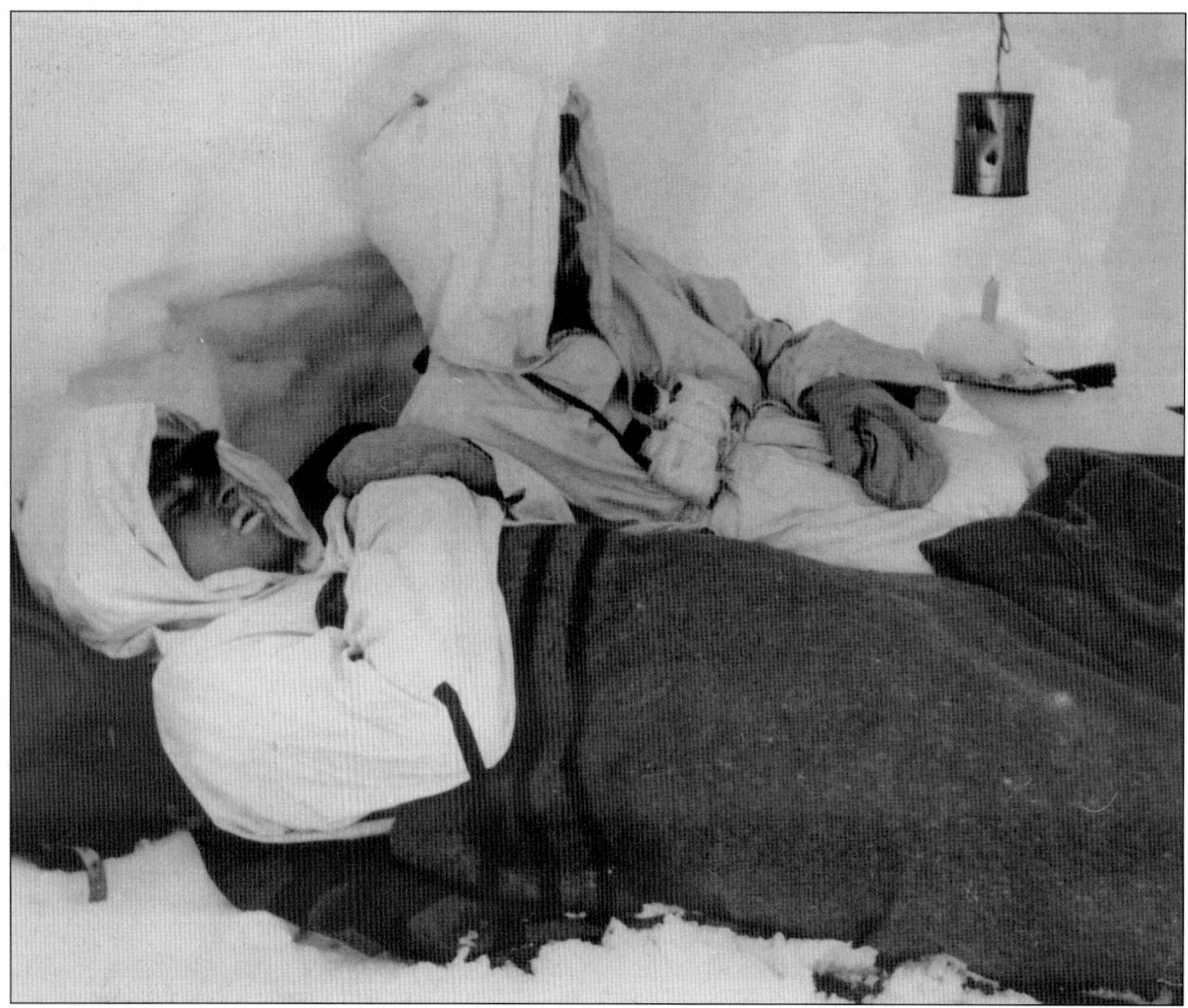

Above: Mountain troops from 5th Gebirgsjäger Division in white two-piece winter suits bed down in the snow on the Eastern Front. Note white cloth covering the binoculars.

Right: This reconstruction of a late 1944 Ardennes campaign scenario shows two Waffen-SS soldiers in front of an American M48 armoured car. The man on the left is wearing a black muffler pulled up round his face. Among the weaponry on view is a Panzerfaust hand-held anti-tank launcher leaning against the armoured car. *Daniel Peterson*

BRANDENBURGERS
The Third Reich's Special Forces
Ian Westwell

ORIGINS & HISTORY

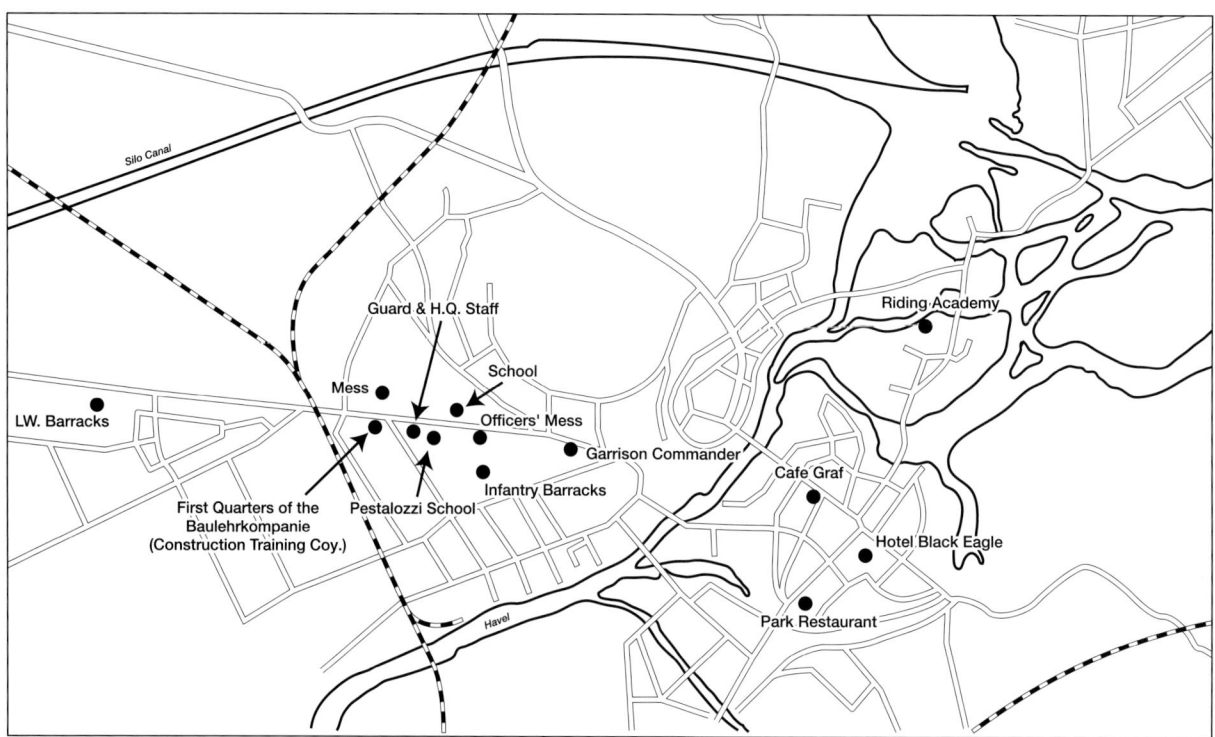

Above: Brandenburg an der Havel and the Brandenburgers' barracks.

For the most part, Nazi Germany went to war in 1939 expecting to win its battle and campaigns through the use of large conventional forces employing Blitzkrieg tactics. Little thought had been given to, or interest shown in, developing small units capable of conducting what are now commonly referred to as special operations. Although the major branches of the armed forces virtually ignored such units — and, indeed, doubted their worth, the *Abwehr* (German intelligence service) was more responsive to such ideas and successfully raised just such a formation on the eve of war. Members of this multinational clandestine force were commonly known as the 'Brandenburgers' after their chief base at Brandenburg-an-der-Havel in western Berlin, and performed roles similar to those conducted by Britain's Special Air Service or Commandos. They scored several noteworthy coups in the early campaigns of World War II, yet the ultimate fate of the Brandenburgers did not revolve around events on the battlefield but lay with the much murkier world of the internal power-politics of the Third Reich.

The *Abwehr* was formally established as a section of the Ministry of War on 21 January 1921, just over three years after the Armistice that had ended World War I and little more than two since the Treaty of Versailles, which among its provisions had outlawed the creation of a German military intelligence organisation and emasculated the country's regular armed forces. Post-1918 Europe was unstable and impoverished; Germany itself was riven by political unrest and menaced by newly independent and expansionist Poland on its eastern border. The Poles had launched several attempts to annex parts of the German provinces of Prussia, Silesia and Saxony but had been thwarted thanks only to the intervention of Freikorps units — bands of right-wing former World War I servicemen. The head of the new *Abwehr*, naval Captain Konrad Patzig, was constrained by an acute lack of funds for much of the interwar period and the meagre resources that were available were split between just two departments — Eastern and Western. *Abwehr* personnel from these departments, particularly the former, were attached to the seven military districts into which postwar Germany was divided and their main objective was to assess the military capabilities and intentions of neighbouring countries.

The activities of the *Abwehr* remained modest throughout the late 1920s and early 1930s as Germany was crippled by economic hardship and political upheaval, but its fortunes were transformed by Adolf Hitler's assumption of power on 30 January 1933. Under a new commander, 47-year-old Captain Wilhelm Canaris, from 1 January 1935, the *Abwehr*, which had developed plans for expansion during the lean years of the interwar period, received much greater funding and was transformed in size between 1936 and 1938. On top of this, its areas of responsibility expanded well beyond the original defensive remit. In February 1938 the Ministry of War was subsumed within the *Oberkommando der Wehrmacht* (OKW/High Command of the Armed Forces), the supreme planning body of the military, and a year later Canaris was made head of a transformed organisation known as the *Amt Ausland/Abwehr* (Foreign Intelligence Office), which was seen as a key department within the OKW. *Abwehr* liaison officers were also attached to the armed forces at virtually every level. In the case of the army this stretched from the *Oberkommando des Heeres* (OKH/ High Command of the Army) all the way down to divisional level in the field, and a similar pattern was followed in the air force and navy. Canaris, who had a background in clandestine operations during World War I, was well-travelled and spoke several languages, had successfully overhauled the somewhat moribund service from his offices on the Tirpitzufer in Berlin and, having gained Hitler's confidence, was rewarded with a series of rapid promotions, reaching the rank of admiral in 1940.

The much-expanded *Abwehr* consisted of several sections, whose efforts were co-ordinated and administered by *Abteilung* (Department) Z under Maj-Gen Hans Oster, Canaris's deputy and an officer later revealed to be deeply involved in the anti-Nazi resistance movement. *Amtsgruppe Ausland* was established to oversee overt intelligence gathering by military attaches and diplomats overseas, but three other *Abteilungen* conducted more clandestine operations that went far beyond the remit of the *Abwehr* in the 1920s and early 1930s. Department I was responsible for foreign espionage, the classic world of spies and spying, and Department III was given a counter-espionage role, combating foreign subversion and spying networks in both Germany and, during World War II, German-occupied lands. Unlike other intelligence services of the time, however, the *Abwehr* was not involved in one highly fruitful area of intelligence gathering — that of intercepting and decoding the enemy's radio transmissions. These operations were generally left to separate bodies within the air force, army and navy.

Partly because of this rather awkward division of responsibilities regarding radio interception, both *Abteilungen* I and III performed with mixed results immediately before and during World War II. *Abteilung* I was, perhaps, the least successful, not least because it had little experience of, or indeed time to develop, foreign spy networks before 1939.

BRANDENBURGER LOCATIONS
Initially based at Brandenburg/Havel's Generalfeldzeugmeister-Kaserne, the unit expanded to battalion size with companies based at Brandenburg; Innermanzing, Wienerwald; and Münstereifel. Later there were several smaller barracks scattered over Germany and Austria, including Rathenow/Havel (airborne), Admont/Steiermark in Austria (mountain) and Swinemünde on the Baltic Sea (coastal raiders), later at Langenargen (Lake Constance). Subunits were headquartered at various times at Baden-Unterwaltersdorf (near Vienna), Freiburg im Breisgau (Black Forest), Allenstein (East Prussia), Ploesti (Romania) and Gatron (Libya).

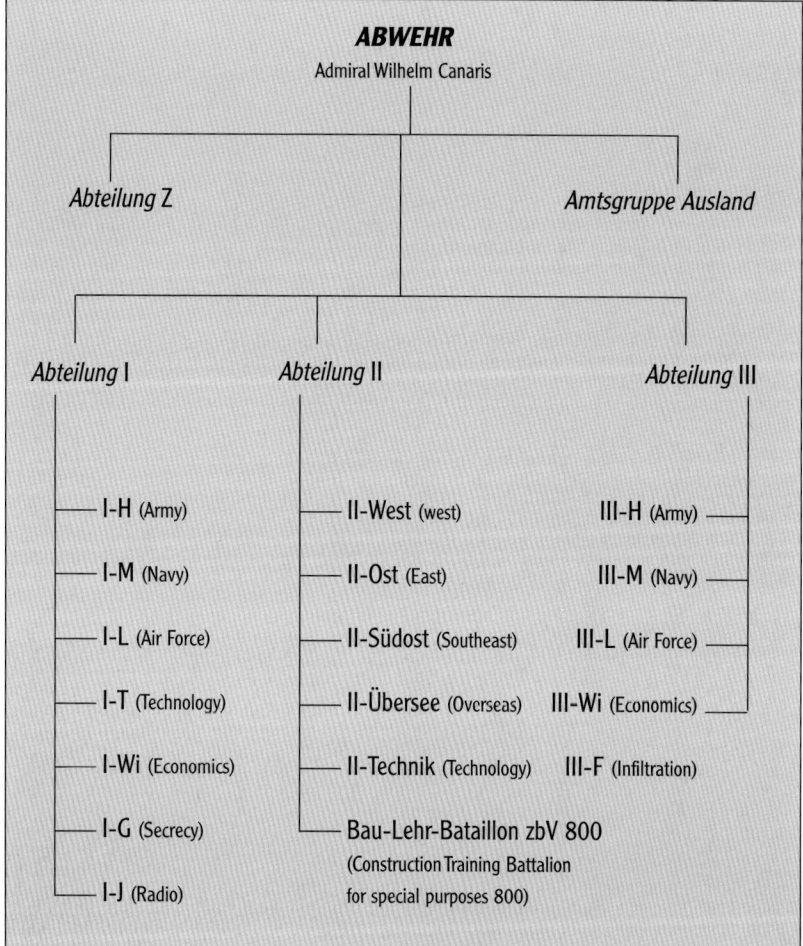

Above: The organisation of the *Abwehr*.

Above right: Lawrence of Arabia's guerrilla tactics provided the inspiration for Theodore-Gottlieb von Hippel. Here Lawrence is seen in Arab dress in Palestine. *IWM Q59314*

Right: Hippel fought with Paul von Lettow-Vorbeck (second from right in this 1913 photograph) in East Africa in World War I. Col Paul Emil von Lettow-Vorbeck (1870–1964) was not defeated in the campaign, although he surrendered in the end to British troops. Returning to Germany a national hero and highly regarded by his enemies, Lettow-Vorbeck joined the Freikorps, and successfully crushed Spartacist forces in Hamburg. But he opposed the Nazis, fell on bad times and when, after World War II Jan Smuts, his former opponent, heard that he was living in destitution, Smuts arranged for him to receive a small pension which he received until his death on 9 March 1964 at the age of 94. *via Chris Ellis*

It did establish valuable contacts in the Balkans, Portugal and Spain, where there were right-wing regimes in power with clear Nazi sympathies, but proved remarkably unsuccessful in Britain, France and the United States. Hitler had a part in this. He initially prohibited any intelligence operations against England and the restrictions were only lifted gradually in 1936 and 1937, while espionage against the United States did not begin until the two countries went to war in December 1941. *Abteilung* III under Col Egbert von Bentivegni did score some noteworthy counter-espionage coups during the war. Between mid-1941 and October 1942, for example, it uncovered and then smashed the *Rote Kapelle* (Red Orchestra), a Europe-wide spy network run by the Soviet Union that Canaris believed had cost the lives of some 200,000 German troops due to the military intelligence its operatives had collected and transmitted by radio back to Moscow. Equally, the department's bureau chief in the Netherlands, Lt-Col Hermann Giskes, conducted the *Englandspiel* (England Game) between March 1942 and November 1943 in which foreign-born British agents were captured and turned, radioing plausible but misleading intelligence back to their controllers on the other side of the Channel. The operation, codenamed '*Nordpol*' (North Pole), cost the lives of 54 other British agents, numerous Dutch resistance workers, and around 50 Royal Air Force personnel engaged in flying support missions.

However, it was *Abteilung* II that had the most aggressive role in furthering Nazi Germany's political and military ambitions, both immediately before and during World War II. Among other exploits prior to the outbreak of the conflict the department was involved in a none-too-successful disinformation campaign in Austria, where local Nazis under Artur Seyss-Inquart were demanding, and on 13 March 1938 gained, *Anschluss* (union) with Nazi Germany. More successfully, its agents promoted unrest among members of the three-million-strong *Volksdeutsche* (ethnic German) community in Czechoslovakia that was used as a pretext for Hitler's successful attempt to annex the Sudetenland region in the north and west of the country, a move that was effectively rubber-stamped by Britain and France at Munich in late September 1938. Despite the *Abwehr*'s involvement in the Czech escapade, the plan to annex the Sudetenland actually appalled Canaris as he believed, wrongly as it turned out, that the crisis would lead to a British declaration of war against Germany. For a brief period around this time he even dallied with a band of conspirators plotting to overthrow Hitler. This *Schwarze Kapelle* (Black Orchestra) comprised aristocrats, diplomats and other senior officers, including his own deputy Oster.

It was *Abteilung* II that also contained the highly secretive and specialised troops who were commonly known as Brandenburgers, men who were trained to fight in small bands in the forefront of battle and whose poorly recorded exploits, which took them to every theatre of war where German regular forces were deployed, remain shrouded in mystery. The germ of the idea for this unit dated back to the interwar period and the musings of a World War I veteran, Capt Theodore-Gottlieb von Hippel, who was subsequently to join the *Abwehr*. Like many officers in the much diminished postwar armed forces, he struggled to explain Germany's defeat in World War I and, fully expecting a second round of blood-letting, sought to uncover the means to prevent a similar outcome. Hippel's military experience during 1914–18 was in colonial East Africa, where a small force comprising no more than a few thousand German-officered local Askaris under Col Paul von Lettow-Vorbeck had outwitted much larger British-led forces and, undefeated to the end, only surrendered on 25 November 1918, when news of the Armistice finally reached them. This brilliantly conducted campaign of irregular warfare, of guerrilla-type operations, had brought significant results, not least the tying down by a comparative handful of men of thousands of enemy troops that could have been better employed elsewhere. Hippel's background with Lettow-Vorbeck made him the ideal candidate to undertake an officially sanctioned study of similar irregular operations conduct by the victorious powers, especially those of the flamboyant British officer Lt-Col T. E. Lawrence in Arabia.

Lawrence of Arabia's campaign against the Turkish forces garrisoning Arabia, Palestine and Syria between June 1916, when the British-inspired revolt by local Arabs broke out, and late October 1918, when Turkey signed an armistice, was and is regarded as a defining moment in guerrilla-style warfare. Studying the action in detail and reading Lawrence's own writings, Hippel identified several aspects of its conduct that might prove of benefit to German in any future conflict. In a strategy paralleling that of Lettow-Vorbeck, Lawrence's small force had tied down thousands of Turkish troops, had paralysed the region's scanty rail links and, unlike the totally isolated Lettow-Vorbeck, had cooperated to considerable effect with offensives by larger conventional forces,

especially during the Battle of Megiddo in September 1918. Hippel reasoned that similar forces could be employed in a conventional European war in the van of, or indeed far in advance of, an offensive. Well trained and motivated, their role would be to operate in small, highly mobile bands, to strike fast and hard at targets that were of great military value — such as enemy headquarters — or those that might be destroyed to impede attacks by regular forces, such as river or canal bridges. Stealth and surprise were vital to these hit-and-run missions, but the Brandenburgers also employed methods that came close to, and sometimes crossed, the line of internationally accepted military conduct and law. Whether by good fortune or intent Hippel's thoughts melded well with the rapidly evolving strategy of the fast-moving Blitzkrieg attacks that would bring Nazi Germany great victories between 1939 and 1941.

Hippel had the ear of Canaris, whom he considered a friend, and the *Abwehr* commander concurred with his subordinate's findings. The admiral was aware that the army's senior generals would in all likelihood oppose the formation of such a specialist unit, particularly one that was independent of them and answerable to the *Abwehr* alone, but knowing that he enjoyed Hitler's confidence and sufficient status within the OKW hierarchy, Canaris judged, correctly as events turned out, that the Brandenburgers would indeed be raised and maintained under the *Abwehr* umbrella and operate directly under the OKW. Canaris was probably less aware of the impact that simmering rivalry between the *Abwehr* and the SS, the guardians of National Socialism, would have on the fortunes of the Brandenburgers. The *Abwehr* was at heart an agency for gathering and disseminating intelligence, with each *Abteilung* having three sub-sections — air force, army and navy — and any action taken on the basis of this information was made by either the relevant branch of the armed forces or, in the case of internal security, the various local, regional and national police forces that by 1936 were effectively run by a department of the SS, the *Sicherheitsdienst* (SD/Security Service).

The SD had been founded by Heinrich Himmler in March 1934 and was responsible not only for the safety of Hitler and the wider Nazi leadership but was also tasked with safeguarding the Third Reich and National Socialism itself. Its ranks were filled with

Below: The main personnel of the *Abwehr* during the war years until it was broken up in 1944 and its duties passed over to the SS.

AMT AUSLAND/ABWEHR PERSONNEL

Commanders
Capt Konrad Patzig (1932–35)
Adm Wilhelm Canaris (1935–44)

Department	Commander	Role
Amtsgruppe Ausland	Vice-Adm Leopold Bürkner	Overt intelligence gathering
Abteilung Z	Maj-Gen Hans Oster (1938-43) Col Jakobsen (1943–44)	Administration
Abteilung I	Col Hans Piekenbrock (1937–43) Col Georg Hansen (1943–1944)	Foreign espionage
Abteilung II	Maj Helmut Groscurth (1938–39) Col Edwin Lahousen, Edler von Vivremont (1939–43) Col Wessel von Freytag-Loringhoven (1943–44)	Sabotage and subversion
Abteilung III	Maj Bamler (1933–39) Col Franz-Eccard von Bentivegni (1939-44)	Counter-espionage

Left: Admiral Wilhelm Canaris and SS-Gruppenführer Reinhard Heydrich seen before the war. From the outset there was tension between the SS and the Abwehr — although this was helped in the initial stages by the relationship between Canaris and Heydrich who had served together in the Reichsmarine.

Reinhard Tristan Eugen Heydrich was born on 7 March 1904 in Halle an der Saale, and was involved in extreme right-wing politics from an early age. A member of the Freikorps in 1919–20, in 1922 he joined the Reichsmarine, but was cashiered by a naval court in 1931 following a love affair with the daughter of a naval officer. In 1931 he joined the NSDAP and SS and was promoted by Heinrich Himmler who took him under his wing. An SS-Standartenführer by July 1932, he was promoted again to head the political department of the Munich police department in 1933 as an SS-Oberführer. He played an important part in the June 1934 'Night of the Long Knives' that disposed of Ernst Röhm and in 1936 he became chief of the Sicherheitspolizei and the Sicherheitsdienst for the whole German Reich. Three years later, Heydrich took charge of the RSHA (Department of Security). The RSHA was responsible for all official and secret police and security departments in Germany. In 1940 he became president of the International Criminal Police Commission and sought to develop spy rings in other countries — and this would bring him back into contact with Canaris again. Heydrich was fundamental to the progress of the Nazi government from anti-semitism to genocide. It was he who organised the 'concentration' of Polish Jews in ghettos and mass deportations from Germany, Austria and Poland. He chaired the Wannsee conference (20 January 1942), where the 'Final Solution' was discussed. (See also caption on page 30.)
Bundesarchiv

dedicated Nazis, not least in the person of the SD's first chief, the cold and ambitious Reinhard Heydrich. Himmler and Heydrich had already played a part in convincing Admiral Erich Raeder of the need to dismiss Patzig, an officer of the old school openly scathing about National Socialism, and were sarcastically dismissive of Raeder's choice of Canaris as his replacement, nicknaming him '*der Weihnachtsmann*' (Father Christmas) behind his back because of his white hair. Strangely Canaris and Heydrich had once been brother officers on a cruiser, the *Berlin*, until an ill-judged incident with the daughter of a shipyard director in 1931 forced the latter to resign from the service, whereupon he immediately joined the Nazi Party and shortly thereafter the SS. Promotion was rapid and in 1939 Heydrich was given command of the newly created *Reichssicherheitshauptamt* (RSHA/Reich Security Main Office), a sinister co-ordinating body of immense power that effectively controlled all of Nazi Germany's secret police.

On paper at least the *Abwehr* and SD/RSHA had clearly defined and separate areas of responsibility that should not have brought them into conflict, yet the tortuous nature of Nazi politics, not least the scheming of Himmler and other senior SS officials, ensured that relations between the heads of the *Abwehr* and SD/RSHA were at least potentially unstable, particularly as it was suspected by Himmler and Heydrich, and in some case known beyond doubt, that Canaris, Oster and other *Abwehr* members were at the very least lukewarm Nazis. Yet for a time the two bodies maintained a reasonably good working relationship and it appears that Canaris and Heydrich had a genuine friendship. In the early stages of World War II, the underlying tensions between the *Abwehr* and SD/RSHA were probably kept in check by the outstanding feats of arms of the German forces, which were undoubtedly aided by the *Abwehr* and its Brandenburgers, and the SS's unsureness as to its actual power and position within the Third Reich. Yet subsequent reversals on the battlefield, *Abwehr* intelligence failures, plotting against the Nazis by its senior figures and the eventual power of the SS combined to bring Canaris's department and its leader to their knees. Among those destined to be struck by the fallout from this struggle were the Brandenburgers themselves, but between 1939 and 1944, when Canaris and the *Abwehr* finally fell victim to the SS, they conducted some of the most daring exploits seen during the entire war.

READY FOR WAR

Below: Polish Volksdeutsche — those of German ancestry — who deserted the Polish Army to join the Nazis.

Under the direction of Col Erwin Lahousen, head of the *Abwehr*'s *Abteilung* II, Capt Theodore von Hippel was tasked with finding the recruits who would fill the ranks of the Brandenburg detachments, which would expand with increasingly rapidity between the outbreak of war in September 1939 and the invasion of the Soviet Union in June 1941. He was looking for particular types of men: those who could demonstrate hardiness, resourcefulness and self-reliance, and those who had a useful skill that could be put to a military use. Hippel was especially interested in those who had excellent language abilities and, much to the chagrin of the SS which trumpeted its racial purity, he was willing to accept pretty much anyone who fitted the bill, particularly if they could match their language expertise with a deep understanding of the customs and colloquialisms of the country or countries concerned. Hippel recognised from the outset that it was more important for Brandenburgers to blend in with their surroundings than attain the levels of racial purity demanded of early recruits to the SS. Although none initially realised he was being interviewed for highly dangerous service with the *Abwehr* rather that the regular armed forces, there was no shortage of potential candidates, and as an additional bonus they were able to supply up-to-date official documents and passes from their homelands that could be copied and would prove immensely valuable for future operations. Many of the original recruits were *Volksdeutsche*, ethnic Germans who had grown up in the recently annexed Sudetenland or lived in Poland along its border with Germany. These men, many fluent in not only German but also Czech and Polish, were brought together in the first six months of 1939. The new unit comprised just two companies with the first having the additional title of the German Company (*Deutsche Kompanie*).

As the Brandenburgers expanded, a second source of suitable manpower was the German citizens who had left their homeland to seek their fortunes and a better life elsewhere after World War I, when the country was in economic turmoil. A large number had settled in South America and Africa, but in the late 1930s they had been encouraged to return to a newly prosperous Nazi Germany. A third pool of recruits was members of other Nordic races, such as the inhabitants of Finland, the Baltic states of Estonia, Latvia, Lithuania, and — in a decision that infuriated the SS — this included people that the latter considered racially impure. These came from the Slavic nations, including ethnic Russians opposed to their homeland's regime or those fighting against domination of their lands, such as the Ukraine, that also provided a pool of *Volksdeutsche*. The Balkans also proved a useful source of men as did Nazi sympathisers spread across the nations of Western Europe. These original recruits, and all subsequent Brandenburgers, underwent intense training to learn techniques beyond those thought relevant to the ordinary soldier. Among the specialist skills taught by instructors were those appropriate for urban guerrillas and partisans operating in the countryside. Emphasis was placed on small unit skills, tracking and navigation and survival skills. As the scope for Brandenburger operations widened, these courses would be supplemented by parachute training, maritime skills and skiing. Unlike regular army units the Brandenburgers trained with live ammunition like their counterparts in the Waffen-SS. Recruits were also sent on several courses at Gut Quensee, a school established by the *Abwehr* outside Berlin to train its agents.

The first opportunity to test the validity of the Brandenburger concept and the effectiveness of the training programme came with Hitler's decision to invade Poland. Although they belonged to a comparatively new and untried outfit, the soon-to-be-Brandenburgers were given a leading and top-secret role in plans for the invasion, which was codenamed '*Fall Weiss*' (Case White). Canaris was ordered to put his men not already active in Poland on 48-hour standby on the evening of 24 August, the day after Hitler had gained the Soviet Union's acquiescence to the invasion of their mutual neighbour through the signing of a non-aggression pact. Details of the subsequent operations remain sketchy but it is known that *Abwehr* sections in three military districts in the eastern Third Reich, at Breslau and Königsberg in Germany proper and a third based in the Austrian capital of Vienna, were ordered to send an estimated 16 Brandenburger teams of *Volksdeutsche* from the Sudetenland and Poland into Polish territory before the start of the invasion. The Breslau and Vienna groups were partly charged with seizing key economic targets in eastern Poland, chiefly the coal and iron ore mines of Polish Silesia, to prevent their destruction and loss to the Nazi economy. They

Above: Hitler visits the Schöber Line during the occupation of the Sudetenland. Brandenburgers were involved in Czechoslovakia to ensure that key bridges and crossroads were kept clear for the invading German troops. *Bundesarchiv*

infiltrated these installations well before the outbreak of hostilities, stashed their weapons and took jobs as ordinary Polish workers. Closer to the invasion date members of teams codenamed 'Bisek' and 'Georgey' were dressed in Polish uniforms or civilian clothes and smuggled in high explosives intending to neutralise military targets. Brandenburgers from Königsberg in east Prussia were tasked with seizing vital bridges over the Vistula River, a key defensive line north of the Polish capital Warsaw, to prevent their destruction before the arrival of spearheads of Gen Fodor von Bock's Army Group North.

Perhaps the most significant purely military role of the ground war for the Brandenburgers was given to the group of some 34 men commanded by 2-Lt Hans-Albrecht Herzner. These were ordered to take the Jablunkov Pass in the Beskid Mountains through which ran the railway line linking Polish Silesia to German-controlled eastern Czechoslovakia. It was a vital corridor for the invasion and two divisions from Gen Wilhelm List's Fourteenth Army stood ready to drive through the pass to take the city of Cracow in the opening days of the campaign, thereby protecting the eastern flank of the main drive by Gen Gerd von Rundstedt's Army Group South on Warsaw. Herzner's men, who were mostly Polish *Volksdeutsche*, launched their cross-border attack in the early hours of 26 August in accordance with the original timetable for Case White. They caught the larger Polish garrison by surprise; there was some fierce fighting around the station at Mosty but the Poles eventually surrendered. Then one of their officers informed a puzzled Herzner that Germany and Poland were not actually at war, a fact confirmed when the lieutenant was able to contact his frantic *Abwehr* superior at Zilina in Slovakia. It appears that Hitler had a temporary loss of nerve on the eve of the attack, chiefly because on the 25th the British and Polish authorities had signed a mutual assistance pact that pledged either to come to the aid of the other if attacked by what was termed a European power but meant Germany. Canaris had attempted to halt the attack on the pass when informed of Hitler's *volte face* but Herzner lacked a radio to receive the recall order.

Below right: Hitler and Keitel. Keitel turned down Canaris's recommendation that Herzner receive the Iron Cross for storming the Jablunkov Pass.

Below: The Polish campaign: note Gleiwitz and the Jablunkov Pass in Polish Silesia.

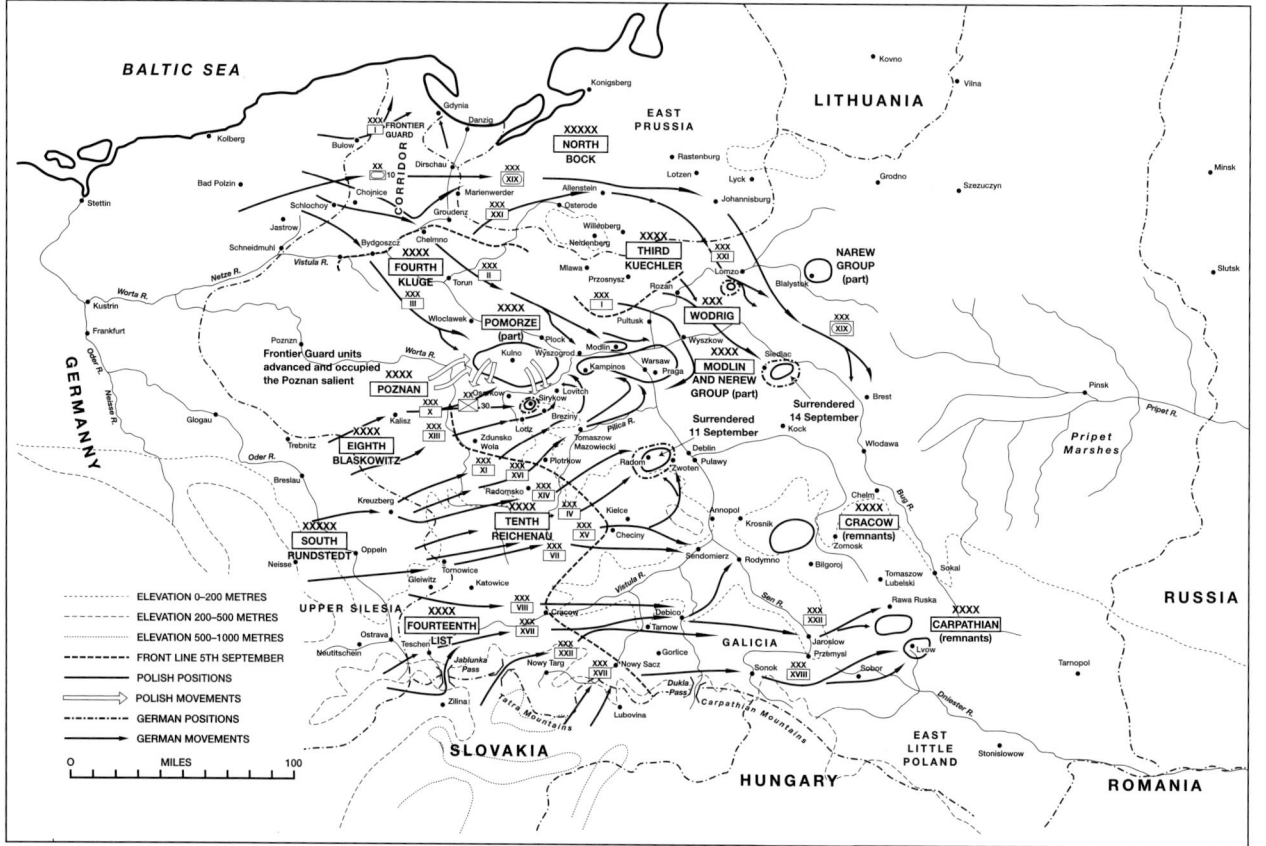

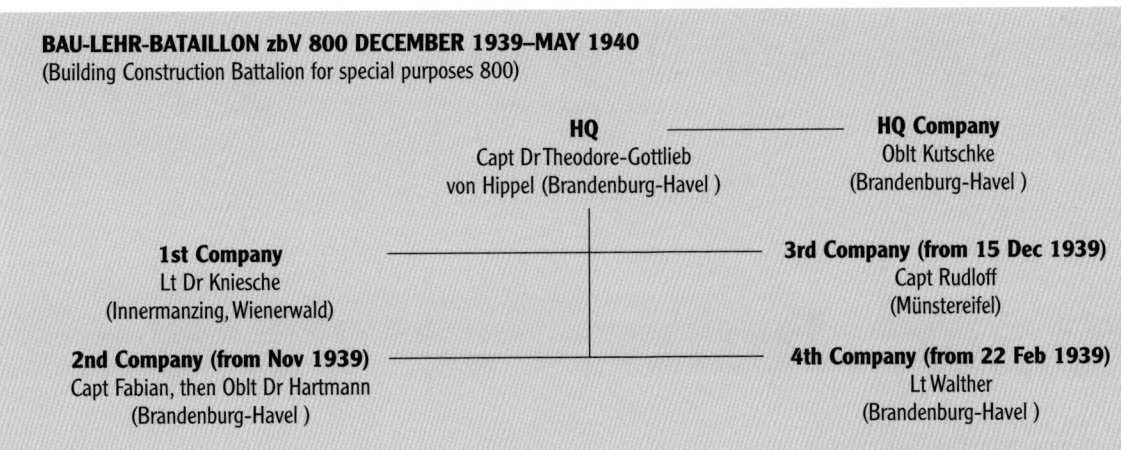

BAU-LEHR-BATAILLON zbV 800 DECEMBER 1939–MAY 1940
(Building Construction Battalion for special purposes 800)

HQ
Capt Dr Theodore-Gottlieb
von Hippel (Brandenburg-Havel)

HQ Company
Oblt Kutschke
(Brandenburg-Havel)

1st Company
Lt Dr Kniesche
(Innermanzing, Wienerwald)

3rd Company (from 15 Dec 1939)
Capt Rudloff
(Münstereifel)

2nd Company (from Nov 1939)
Capt Fabian, then Oblt Dr Hartmann
(Brandenburg-Havel)

4th Company (from 22 Feb 1939)
Lt Walther
(Brandenburg-Havel)

Despite this comedy of errors at the front, it took little time for Hitler to regain his nerve and on the night of 31 August, members of the SS acting on Reinhard Heydrich's orders engineered a border incident centred on a small radio station at Gleiwitz — in Germany but just one mile (1.6km) from the Polish frontier — as a pretext to launch the invasion. Dressed in Polish uniforms allegedly provided by the unknowing *Abwehr*, eight men under SS Maj Alfred Naujocks, a member of the SD, attacked the station, fired a few shots — picked up by its German listeners — to subdue its small staff, and began broadcasting in Polish that it was time for Poland to invade Germany. To add veracity to the ruse, Naujocks' team killed a concentration camp inmate they had brought with them dressed in a Polish uniform. Exposed for the scrutiny of the media, the wider world had little time to react to this stage-managed event for on the morning of 1 September German troops stormed into Poland and the remaining Brandenburger teams set about their various tasks. Few details are available of these operations but the coal and iron ore mines of Silesia were captured with only limited damage and units of Army Group North began crossing the Vistula with little difficulty five days after the opening of the campaign. Poland was effectively defeated with a matter of days and Warsaw surrendered on the 27th.

The Polish campaign had mostly proved the validity of Hippel's concept yet the Brandenburgers received little tangible official recognition for their efforts. Canaris did request that Herzner receive the Iron Cross for the somewhat premature storming of the Jablunkov Pass but was turned down by Gen Wilhelm Keitel, head of the OKW, on the grounds that the medal was only awarded during wartime and that Germany and Poland were not actually at war when the action at Jablunkov took place. However, the unit did receive a new title on 25 October, becoming the *Lehr und Bau Kompanie zbV 800* (Special Duty Training and Construction Company No 800). The newly activated command remained under Hippel and was established at Brandenburg-an-der-Havel for the first time. Its men began to refer to their unit as the Brandenburg Company and to themselves as Brandenburgers.

Poland had proved the Brandenburgers' value and in the latter part of 1939 the unit grew significantly so that on 15 December it was retitled *Bau-Lehr-Bataillon zbV 800*. Elements of the four-company battalion made their debut in Western Europe during the invasion of Denmark and Norway, which opened on 9 April 1940. Information is sketchy but it appears Danish-speaking Brandenburgers dressed as local soldiers captured crossings over the Grosse Belt, thereby allowing regular troops to drive into the north of the country. Similar ploys were also used by a Brandenburg detachment known as the *Nordzug* (North Platoon) during the first stages of the two-month campaign to subdue

Further units were also added within the battalion and later integrated within the unit:

Motorcycle platoon
Oblt Erwin Graf Thun

Paratrooper Platoon
Lt Dlab

North Platoon (Recovery Platoon)
Lt Zülch

West Platoon
Sgt Kürschner

Southeast Company

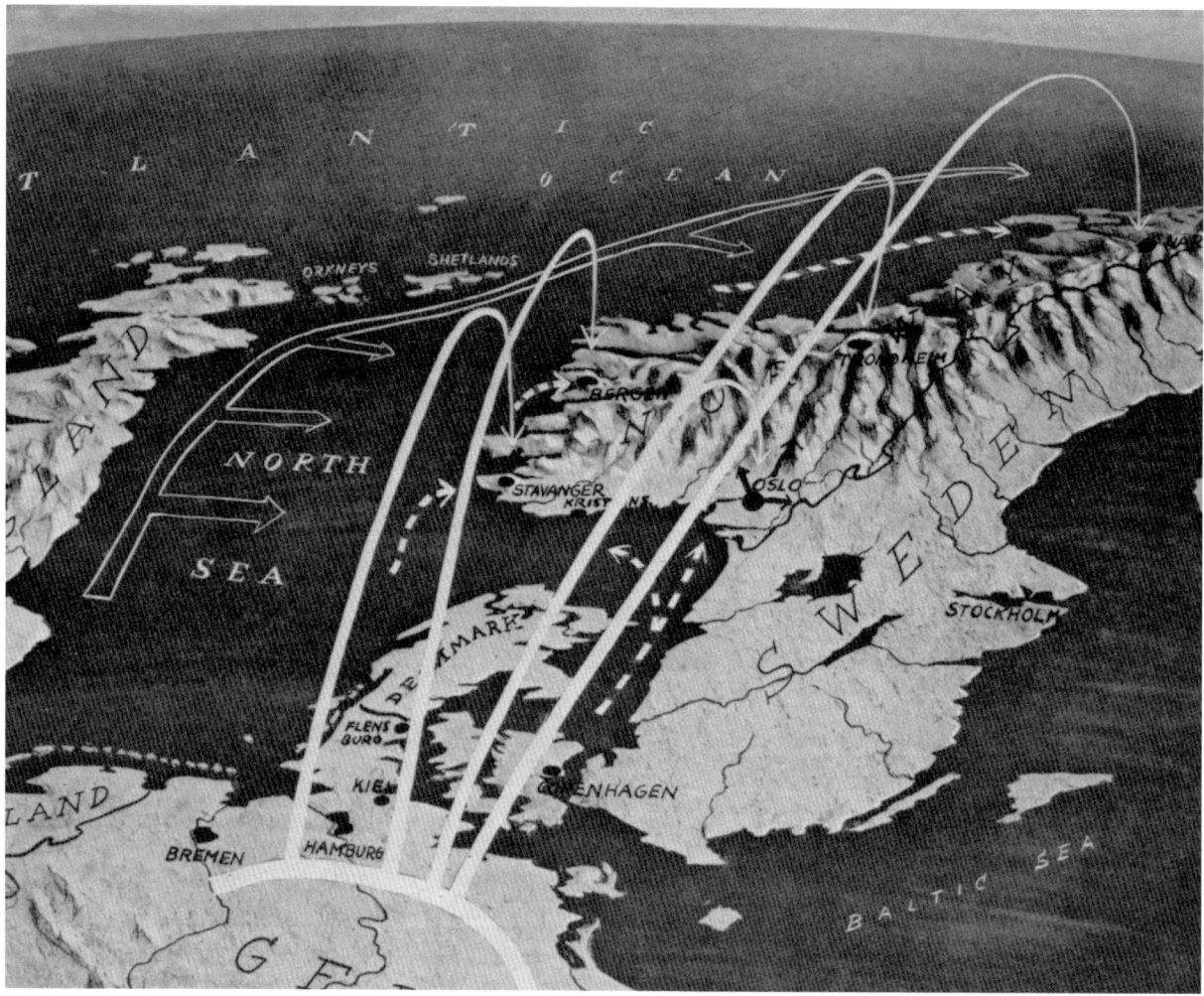

Above: This map, taken from the propaganda magazine *Signal*, shows the Nazi view of the invasion of Denmark and Norway from 9 April 1940. 'The most important points,' the article announced, 'were occupied like lightning by German troops. At the same time German forces took over the defence of Denmark against any attempts at invasion by the English.'

Norway. On 20 April it left Brandenburg for Oslo by train and was deployed to sabotage Norwegian communications. On 1 May, one of the *Nordzug*'s units flew from Trondheim to support the drive on Namsos by the 181st Infantry Division. Norway surrendered on 12 June and the *Nordzug* departed eight days later.

The campaigns in Poland, Denmark and Norway thus established a pattern that was repeated in subsequent Brandenburg operations. First, a decision was taken by the *Abwehr*'s *Abteilung* II as to whether the troops involved should wear disguises or not. Second, the extent of the disguise was settled: was it to be partial (*Halbtarnung*/semi-camouflage) with perhaps just a few items — a greatcoat and helmet, say — or should those involved go further and adopt the whole panoply of enemy's military clothing (*Volltarnung*/full camouflage)? Third, details were passed down to the relevant Brandenburger group in the field, which would determine the size of the detachment it would commit to the operation, usually between a mere handful of men to a platoon depending on the target's importance. The lessons learned by the Brandenburgers in Denmark and Norway undoubtedly proved invaluable during the main event in Western Europe — '*Fall Gelb*' (Case Yellow), the invasion of France and the Low Countries. Even before the outbreak of hostilities disguised Brandenburgers had been infiltrated into the Benelux countries to photograph and sketch potential targets, make contact with pro-Nazi sympathisers and acquire second-hand military clothing.

IN ACTION

BLITZKRIEG IN THE WEST

Fall Gelb opened at 0535 hours on 10 May with a massive attack into northern Belgium and the Netherlands by the two armies of Gen Fedor von Bock's Army Group B. This forced the Anglo-French units to move forward from their positions along the border between France and Belgium in order to meet the developing threat. Part of Army Group B, Gen Walter von Reichenau's Sixth Army, was ordered to 'advance on the line Venlo–Aachen, to cross the Meuse [in German, Maas] quickly and to pass through the Belgian defence system without delay'. To ensure that von Reichenau's forces and those of Gen der Artillerie Georg von Küchler's Eighteenth Army to the north were able to push forward at utmost speed, some 500 Brandenburgers were tasked with capturing intact key river and canal bridges. If destroyed, the momentum of the offensive would be seriously reduced.

The various Brandenburg detachments had several missions and most wore *Halbtarnung*. For example, four bridges over the Juliana Canal at Berg, Obbicht, Urmond and Stein were taken intact by 2-Lt Kürschner's *Westzug* (West Platoon) so that the 7th Infantry Division could move into Holland; between Elsenborn and St. Vith the 3rd Company took 19 out of 24 targets that had been assigned to it. However, not all of the Brandenburger operations were successful: on 10 May 2-Lt Siegfried Grabert's 2nd Platoon of the 4th Company only took one of the four bridges assigned to it; three others, those at Maaseyck over the Juliana Canal and two over the Meuse at Roermond, were destroyed.

One of the most spectacular missions was that of the 4th Company's 1st Platoon under Lt Wilhelm Walther. The 450-yard (410m) Gennep bridge, which carried the rail line running from

Below: Capt Hans-Jürgen Rudloff inspects his troops of the IIIrd Battalion after the French campaign during training for Operation 'Sealion'. *Bundesarchiv*

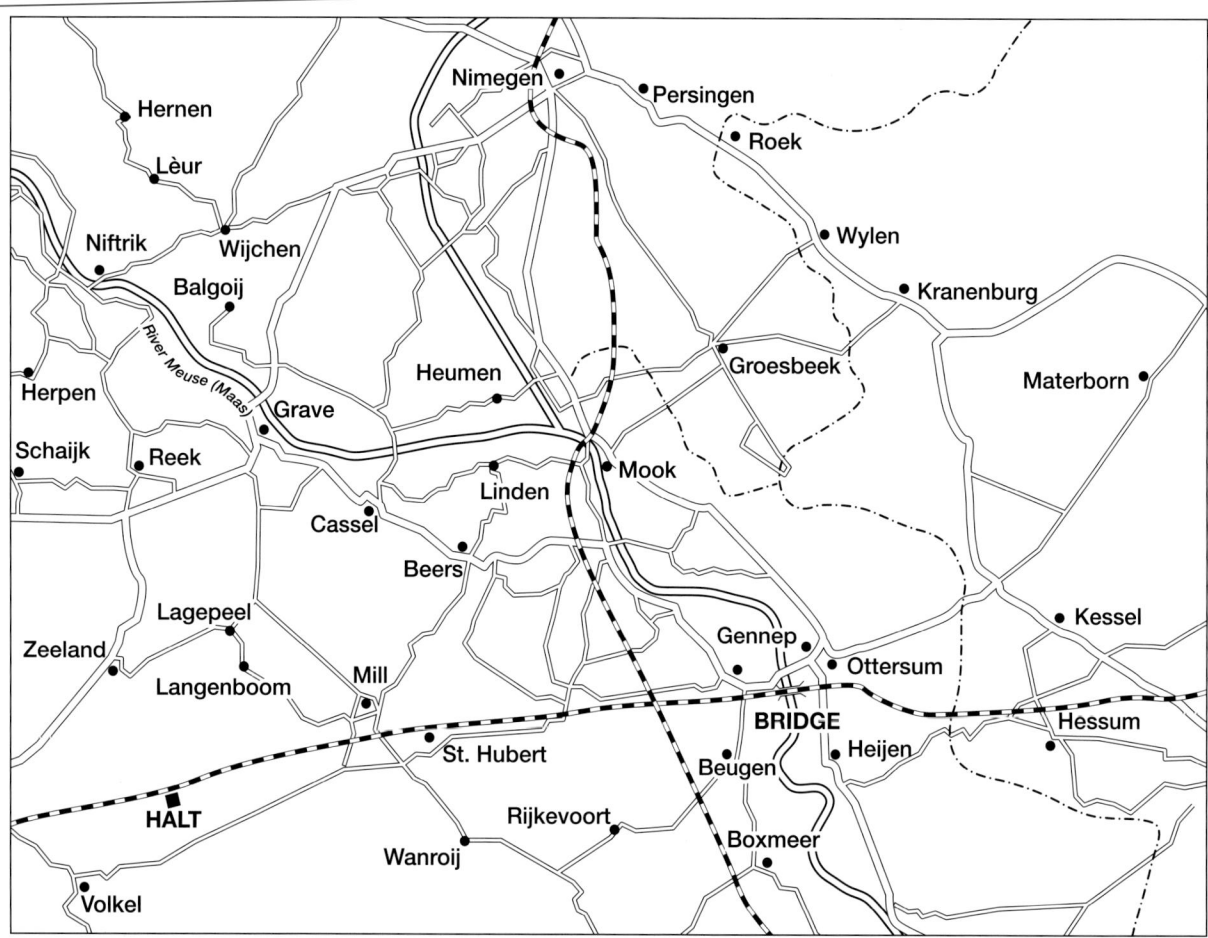

Above: Gennep railway bridge crosses the Meuse (Maas) west of the town. The halt at which the train stopped is identified between Uden and St Hubert.

Above right: Gennep railway bridge. *Bundesarchiv*

Right: The bridges over the Meuse (Maas), Albert and Juliana canals that were among the highest priorities for the German advance. Note Eben Emael at the bottom, captured by a glider-borne assault. Four bridges over the Juliana Canal at Berg, Obbicht, Urmond and Stein were taken intact by 2-Lt Kürschner's *Westzug* (West Platoon)

Goch in Germany into Holland (no longer running today), was little more than two miles (3km) from the Dutch-German border. It was of particular importance as its capture would not only permit German regular forces to cut westward through the Dutch defensive position — known as the Peel Line — before it could be properly manned, thereby splitting Holland in two, but also bring relief to the scattered paratrooper units that had landed at various points around Rotterdam and the Hague at the outbreak of the invasion. The platoon and a number of Dutch Nazis began moving to the target several hours before the main assault, crossing the Dutch border at 2330 hours on 9 May. Under cover of darkness a small party moved undetected through the low-lying ground between the Niers river and the railway embankment, crossed the road running between Heijen and Gennep, and then took cover among the scrub that covered the banks of the Meuse near the target bridge.

Shortly before dawn, some 10 minutes before main invasion began, one of four Dutch military policemen at the bridge's eastern end spied six figures — two were wearing the same uniform as the guard while the four others, less identifiable, were cloaked in long overcoats — calmly moving towards him. He and two colleagues, confused by the strange scene, were quickly overpowered as was a fourth policeman manning a telephone. One of the Brandenburgers, a fluent Dutch-speaker, now rang the western guardhouse of the bridge and reported that he had four prisoners on his hands and was sending them across for interrogation along with two guards. An exchange was made in the middle of the bridge with the four prisoners being marched off to a

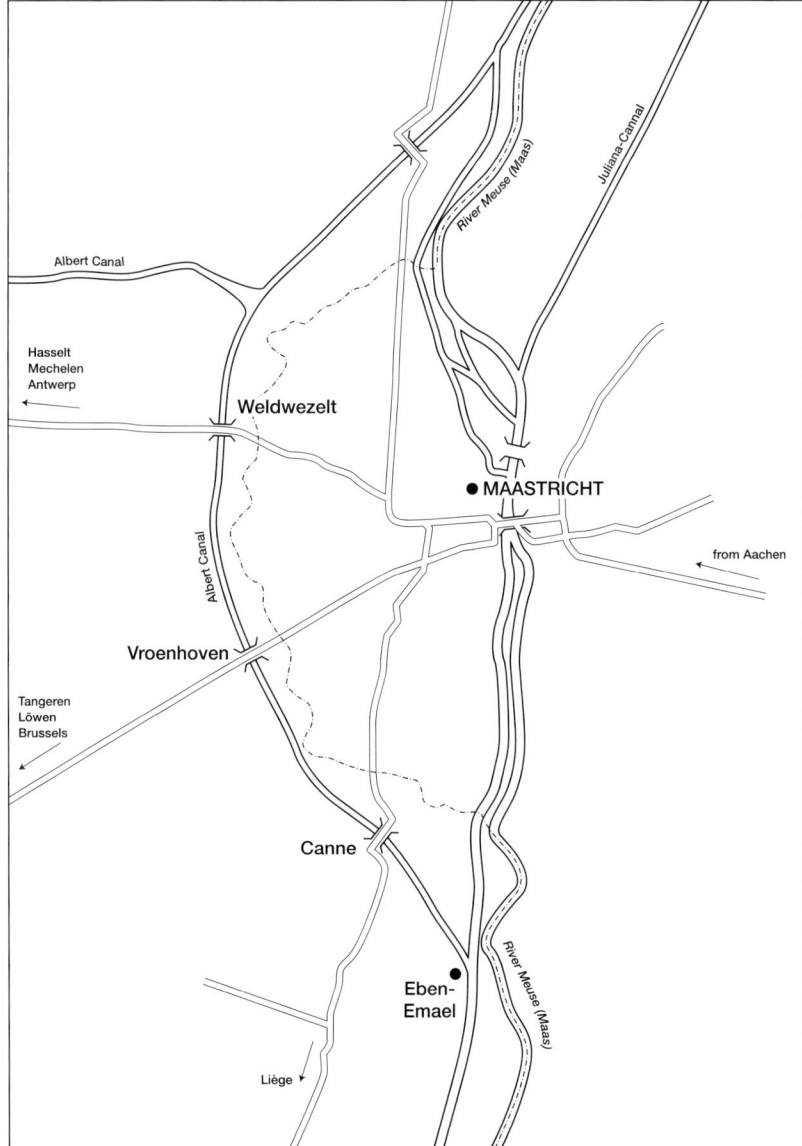

COLONEL G. J. SAS

It was a bizarre paradox that the high-risk operations conducted by the Brandenburger on 10 May 1940, during the opening phase of Fall Weiss, were very nearly compromised by one of the *Abwehr*'s own most senior figures. Col Hans Oster was Adm Wilhelm Canaris's deputy and the two men had some involvement in a plot to remove Hitler from power. Canaris was the more cautious of the two; Oster willing to take much greater risks to undermine the Nazis' war plans for the conquest of Western Europe.

Sas was the Dutch military attaché in Berlin and had regular contact with Oster. In April it appears that Oster told Sas of Hitler's imminent attacks on Denmark and Norway, information that was passed on to the Danish ambassador. On 3 May the two men met again and Oster revealed that in all likelihood both the Netherlands and Belgium would be attacked in the very near future. Finally, over dinner on the 9th Oster stated categorically that the Low Countries were to be attacked at dawn the following day. Sas hurried away and telephoned the Dutch War Office. The conversation was brief and Sas spoke the code number 210 — 200 meant the invasion of Holland and 10 referred to the date. Sas's reports of German intentions had previously been mostly discounted and later that night the head of Dutch intelligence service telephoned Sas to confirm his previous conversation. He did so, but the information was never acted upon.

The Sas affair certainly had not gone unnoticed in Germany as his conversations on the 9th had been picked up by the Nazi security services. Oster's name had not been mentioned but they were clear that Sas's information could have only come from a senior figure, one likely to be serving in the intelligence services. The *Abwehr*, the Brandenburgers parent body, was for the first of several times brought under suspicion.

Above: The Brandenburgers donned Belgian overcoats — as exemplified in this splendid photograph — to cover their uniforms. (The machine gun is a Belgian Maxim 7.65 and the rifles are 1889 Mausers.) *via George Forty*

guardhouse at its western end after a perfunctory search that failed to uncover the weapons they were carrying. Only one Dutch military policemen was now left in the middle of the bridge and the two disguised Brandenburgers returned to its eastern end. The lone Dutch sentry next spotted a train approaching from the direction of the German border but no immediate action was taken when he telephoned the information back to his superior, an aged sergeant, at the western end. German troops from the train overpowered the sentry before he could detonate the explosive charges that had been placed on the bridge. The bridge was captured intact although a few Dutch troops on the west bank did open fire briefly. They were forced to surrender when they were caught in a crossfire from the four Brandenburger prisoners who had overpowered their guards in the confusion of the train's approach and their colleagues at the eastern end of the bridge. The Brandenburgers' coup allowed the 9th Panzer Division to push forward rapidly.

After the successes of 10 May, the Brandenburgers were temporarily withdrawn from the action and sent on leave but at the end of the month their services were called upon once more. The German high command had always feared that their lightning attacks might be delayed in the Low Countries by either the Dutch or Belgians opening the sluice gates of their extensive networks of drainage canals and thereby flooding the surrounding low-lying countryside and making it impassable to German forces. Such an event had already taken place around Nieuport on the Flanders coast and it appeared that a similar fate awaited the sluice gates on the Yser River. Grabert and 12 other Brandenburgers on leave in Germany were ordered to Ghent at short notice and were informed that they had to seize the pump houses on the south bank of the Yser near the Ostend–Nieuport road bridge. With their uniforms hidden under captured Belgian Army greatcoats and benefiting from the confused and fluid situation along the Allied front line Grabert's men headed for Ostend from Ghent in a captured Belgian military bus. At Ostend a French-speaking Brandenburger discovered from a Belgian officer that his army had surrendered and that the British were in control of Nieuport and the bridge. Speed was of the essence as the British were likely to blow both the bridge and the sluice gates to cover their ongoing evacuation from the beaches at Dunkirk a few miles along the coast

The 15-mile (24km) journey to the objective from Ostend passed without a hitch, although the Brandenburgers' rate of progress was slowed by the long straggling columns of refugees they encountered. Nevertheless at around 1900 hours on the 27th they reached their target only to be hit by intense fire from British positions on the far side of the river. Grabert's team quickly debussed, removed their Belgian overcoats and made for a piece of dead ground just 50 yards (45m) from the bridge that sheltered then from the fire. Here they waited until nightfall and then Grabert and a corporal, Janovsky, who was to be awarded the Iron Cross for his part in the unfolding drama, crawled forward, freezing frequently to avoid being revealed under the glare of illuminating Very lights, and began dismantling the explosive charges they uncovered as they made their way to the opposite end of the bridge. Once across, and with the charges disarmed, Grabert signalled the other Brandenburgers to join him. A vicious close-quarters firefight developed in the darkness but the Brandenburgers were able to beat the British away from the bridge and secure the undamaged pump houses until relieved by other German units. The Brandenburgers did suffer casualties during the attack but had secured a vital bridge and prevented the flooding of the area.

The Brandenburgers had undoubtedly performed well during the initial invasion. Twenty-four hours after it had opened Hippel recorded that 42 out of 61 Brandenburger operations had succeeded. One of his men, Walther, was subsequently awarded the Knight's Cross — the unit's first — and 120 other Brandenburgers received various grades of the Iron Cross.

From May 1940 the Brandenburgers had been earmarked for considerable expansion. The original battalion was to be expanded threefold to regimental strength and as of 15 May it was decreed that the new *Lehr Regiment Brandenburg zbV 800* would be split with each of its three battalions having separate bases and areas of operations. While the staff were based in Berlin itself, the Ist Battalion under Hippel was earmarked for overseas operations and was to be stationed in nearby Brandenburg, the IInd Battalion was to be deployed to Baden-Unterwaltersdorf, Austria, for service in eastern or southeastern Europe, while the IIIrd Battalion was to establish a base at Aachen (later Düren) in the Rhineland for missions in western, northern and southern Europe. The regimental commander was named as Maj Kewisch. However, the implementation of these structural changes was delayed by ongoing military events and not fully completed until April 1941.

Above: What happened when the bridges weren't captured intact. The advance would continue but without heavy weapons or armoured vehicles — major components of Blitzkrieg. *via George Forty*

'SEALION' AND 'FELIX' — THE CANCELLED OPERATIONS

Paris was formally occupied on 14 June and the French agreed an armistice with Germany on the 22nd. England, militarily weak despite the successful evacuation from the Dunkirk beaches, now seemed ripe for invasion and on 16 July Hitler issued his Directive No 16 which related to 'preparations for a landing operation against England'. In its final form the assault, codenamed '*Seelöwe*' (Sealion), called for major landings along the coast of southeast England by elements of Army Group A, mostly based in the Pas de Calais region of northeast France. Two Brandenburger units were earmarked for

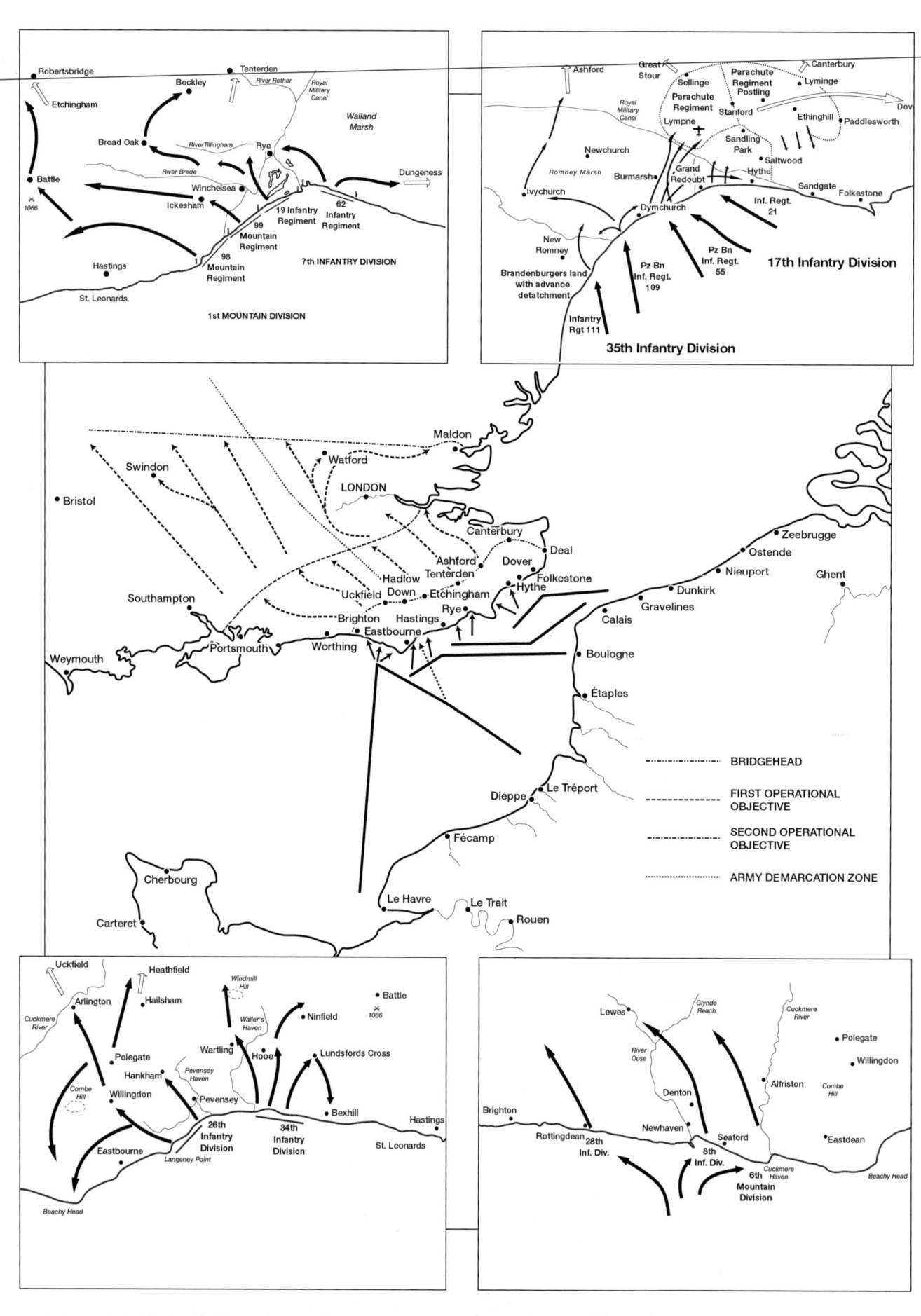

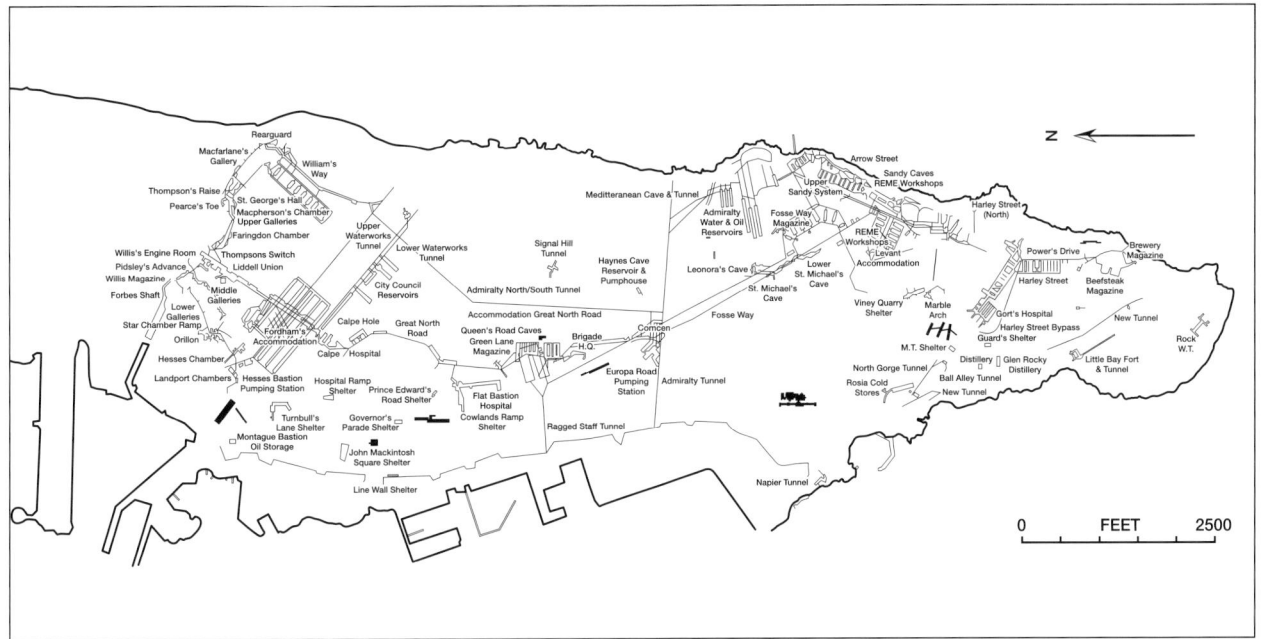

Left: Peter Schenk's analysis of the invasion plans for Operation 'Sealion' provides a blueprint of the German intentions (see page 95). The Brandenburgers of Ist and IIIrd Battalions were intended to play key roles, the former with Sixteenth Army, the latter the Ninth. Two units were allocated to 34th and 26th Infantry Divisions and were tasked with the destruction of the gun battery at Beachy Head and a nearby radio station. Two more platoons were to be with 35th Infantry Division and were tasked with the neutralisation of bases on the coast and Royal Military Canal. The most important mission was that of 4th Company — to destroy Dover Harbour's coastal batteries and prevent the harbour mouth from being blocked to the invasion fleet.

Above and Below: Operation 'Felix' planned an invasion of Gibraltar via Spain. Hitler's War Directive No 18 of 12 November 1940 laid out the ground rules, and the detailed plan called for over 65,000 men and 13,000 tons of ammunition including some 20,000 shells to silence the British batteries. With a garrison of 10,000, miles of underground tunnels (**Above**) and sufficient provisions for an 18-month siege, Gibraltar was no pushover, and Spanish co-operation was essential. However, Franco (**Below**) seen meeting Hitler on 23 October 1940 at Hendaye in southwest France (see page 24); did not agree to it, preferring to rebuild his country that had already been shattered by a protracted civil war. Hitler, his eye taken by the Italian attack on Greece and planning for 'Barbarossa', quietly shelved the idea. *IWM MH11546*

'Sealion' and, after training on the island of Helgoland, Hippel's Ist Battalion moved to the assembly point of Army Group A's Sixteenth Army just to the east of Dunkirk, while Capt Hans-Jürgen Rudloff's IIIrd Battalion assembled farther south in Normandy, close to Caen, for service with the Sixth Army. The units were tasked with specific missions: half of Hippel's men were to destroy some port facilities at Folkestone while the remainder neutralised the large rail guns that had been identified at Dungeness; the IIIrd Battalion was to make a diversionary landing to capture Weymouth to lure British forces away from major landings at Portsmouth and Plymouth. A third contingent of English-speaking Brandenburgers was attached to the Ninth Army. These were scheduled to land with the first wave wearing British uniforms and then use motorcycles to push inland rapidly to conduct various sabotage missions. 'Sealion' was an opportunity lost and never came to fruition, however, as the Luftwaffe's defeat in the Battle of Britain and Hitler's growing focus on war with the Soviet Union ensured that Germany's military resources — and the Brandenburgers — would be sent to the east.

Despite the cancellation of 'Sealion', Hitler still intended to deliver a crippling blow to Britain's war effort and on 12 November issued a directive relating to a proposed operation, codenamed 'Felix', that was to drive the British from the western Mediterranean. The aim was to persuade Spanish dictator Francisco Franco either to join the Axis alliance or to allow German troops onto his soil and then capture the strategically vital naval base of Gibraltar. Fluent Spanish-speaking Canaris, who was well-known to the Spanish leader and may have proposed 'Felix' to Hitler, had initiated preparations for the mission in early July, when he and Col Piekenbrock, the head of the *Abwehr*'s *Abteilung* I, held a meeting in Madrid with Capt Hans-Jürgen Rudloff. Canaris informed the officer that when the political preparations for 'Felix' were completed part of his battalion would be transported secretly across Spain and outside Gibraltar link up with engineers and artillery detachments that had sailed from ports in southern France. Following a brief bombardment Rudloff's Brandenburgers were to storm the British fortress relying on speed and surprise. Rudloff was not altogether impressed with the risky plan but agreed to travel to Spain to observe the objective.

Below: Major Wilhelm Walther in Greece, 1943, as CO of the Brandenburg Division's 1st Regiment.

His mission proved worthless as Hitler, who met Franco at Hendaye in southwest France on 23 October and discussed 'Felix', grew increasing doubtful that he could draw Spain into the Axis alliance. Franco argued repeatedly at Hendaye and in subsequent discussions that his country was still recovering from its recent civil war and would not be strong enough to side with the Axis for at least two years. Equally, he was unwilling to allow German troops transit through his supposedly neutral country as it would likely precipitate declarations of war on Spain. Hitler subsequently drew up secret plans for a military occupation of Spain and considered implementing them until mid-1943 but Operation 'Felix' was officially suspended within a month of the original directive of 12 November being issued.

THE BALKANS AND 'BARBAROSSA'

German influence in and domination of Romania ensured that Hitler had a free hand within a country where Ion Antonescu, prime minister from September 1940 and effective dictator from late January 1941, was pro-Nazi and willing to bend to his wishes. Canaris secured an agreement with his counterpart in the Siguranza, the Romanian intelligence service, for Germany to take over the security for much of the country's economy, chiefly its oil-producing facilities around Ploesti which were vital to Germany and likely to be a target of British sabotage squads. In October 1939 60 Brandenburgers from the 5th Company entered Romania in small groups and carried out several undercover operations to combat British sabotage efforts and they were joined in November by the 6th Company.

The Brandenburgers next military operation was at the forefront of Hitler's onslaught in the Balkans, which was prompted from October 1940 by the likely failure of the Italian offensive against Greece and the need to protect the southern flank of Operation 'Barbarossa', the forthcoming invasion of the Soviet Union. Units from the IInd Battalion saw action on 6 April 1941, the first day of Operation 'Punishment', the invasion of Yugoslavia. They were deployed, some dressed as Serbian civilians, to capture the so-called Iron Gate, a 62.5-mile (100km) long gorge on the Danube river that meanders along the border of southwest Romania and northeast Yugoslavia, to ensure that it would remain open to German traffic. (Interestingly, it was dammed in 1977 and today in parts of the Iron Gate the depth of the Danube exceeds 165yd/150m.) Men from the battalion's 8th Company under Grabert dressed in Yugoslav uniforms and successfully secured a vital bridge across the Vardar River to the west of Axiopoulos for the 2nd Panzer Division, while troops of the 5th and 7th Companies used assault boats to spearhead the crossing of the Danube near Osova. Yugoslavia surrendered on the 17th. Brandenburgers saw action in the subsequent invasion of Greece but most detachments had left the country by May.

Above: Brandenburgers dressed in Russian uniforms. *TRH Pictures*

Below: In Russia, as in the Blitzkrieg in the west, the Brandenburgers' main targets were bridges — this one over the Dvina River in Latvia was seized on 26–28 June by Oberleutnant Siegfried Grabert's 8th Company. *Bundesarchiv*

Opposite, above: Operations in the Crimea and Caucasus. Note Maikop at the bottom centre of the map.

Opposite below: Brandenburg operation against the rail line to Murmansk by the 'Hettinger' Company, August 1942, a raid discussed in Eric Lefevre's book on the division (see page 94). It was a successful raid that earned the Brandenburgers the warmest praise from Lapland Army commander Gen Eduard Dietl. The men crossed 100 miles (160km) of poor terrain, survived a Russian ambush and cut the railway line in a mission that kept them behind enemy lines for nearly two weeks.

Below: Operation 'Barbarossa'.

After the Balkans campaign the Brandenburgers were earmarked for a leading role in Operation 'Barbarossa', which officially opened at dawn on 22 June. The understrength regiment was split into three-company battalions and mostly assigned to the three army groups that had been positioned along the Soviet border. Maj Heinz's Ist Battalion companies fought with Army Group South, the IInd Battalion under Maj Paul Jacobi served with Army Group North and South, and Capt Franz Jacobi's IIIrd Battalion mostly served with Army Group Centre.

Some detachments were already within Soviet territory and many were disguised in Red Army uniforms that the Finns had captured during the Winter War of November 1939–March 1940. The Finns also provided Soviet weapons and transport to add to the veracity of the ruse. The Brandenburgers were involved in scores of clandestine operations involving the capture of bridges and crossroads to speed the Blitzkrieg and also cut telephone and telegraph lines to add to the Red Army's state of confusion. Scores of these operations took place all along the front. Typical of these was the seizure of eight bridges by the IIIrd Battalion's 10th Company to open the way for the armoured spearheads of Army Group Centre. Commanded by Lt Aretz, the company split into eight teams and, with Russian blouses over their own tunics, the men set off by truck for their targets in advance of the main attack. The greater part of the regiment was withdrawn from the Eastern Front between August and October, although two units, the 6th and 9th Companies from the IInd and IIIrd Battalions respectively remained there, fighting in the Crimea and against partisans until the following summer.

LATER OPERATIONS ON THE EASTERN FRONT

In the early summer of 1942 virtually the whole regiment was deployed to the Ukraine to spearhead the twin-pronged drive into the Caucasus and toward Stalingrad. Most of the regiment's battalions served with Army Group A, which was tasked with securing the oilfields of the Caucasus after crossing the Don River. Once again the various companies were used in a spearhead role to seize vital bridges, especially across the Don River, when the offensive began on 28 June. One of the most important was that undertaken by the IIIrd Battalion's 8th Company in support of a push by the 5th SS Panzer Division 'Wiking', the 16th

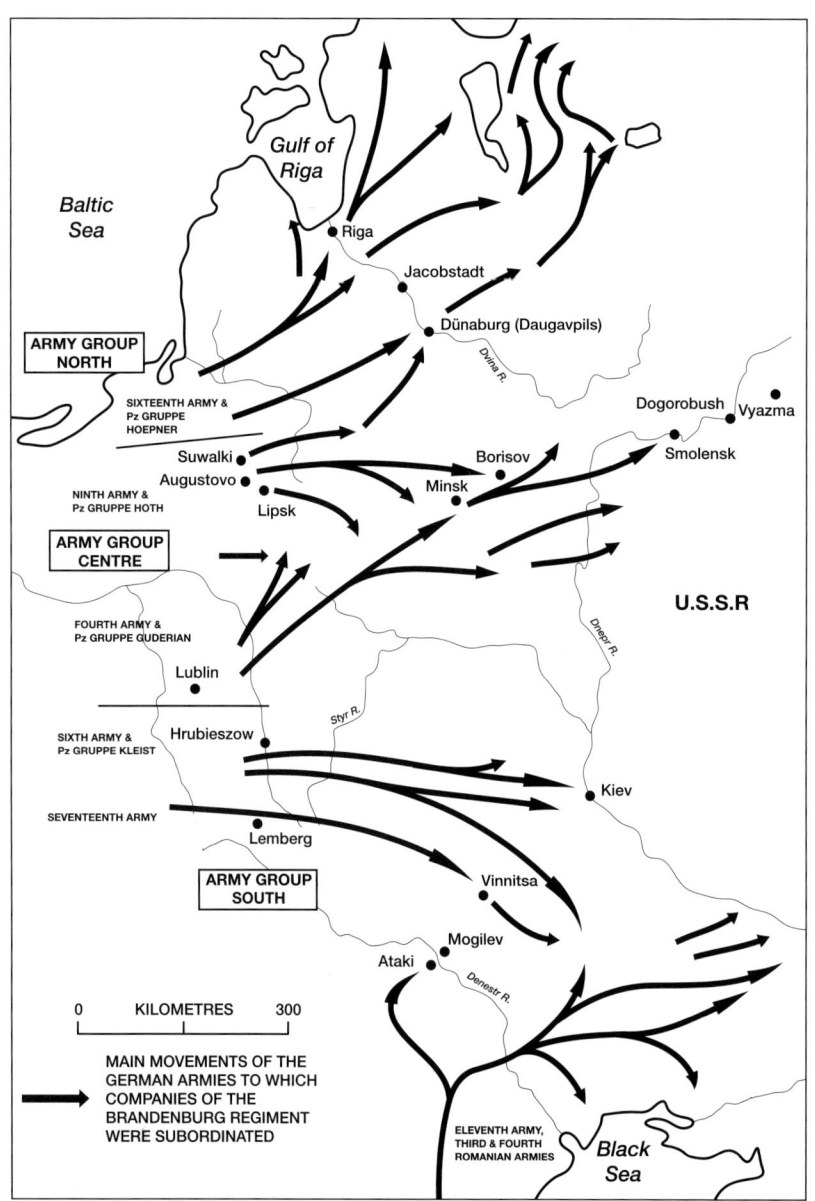

Motorised Infantry Division and the 13th Panzer Division to take the city of Maikop, an important oil-producing centre on the Kuban steppes in the northern Caucasus in August. The Brandenburgers had two detachments involved. One was a 63-man team, including many fluent Russian speakers, under Lt Baron Adrian von Foelkersam. It was to precede the attack by a long-range mission to Maikop, while a short-range operation by a single platoon under Lt Ernst Prohaska, another native Russian speaker, was tasked with seizing a bridge over the Bjelaja River across which the regular forces had to pass.

The Foelkersam detachment moved first. Dressed in NKVD uniforms they crossed the front line near Alexandrovskaja under cover of darkness on the 2nd, a week before the main attack opened, and successfully reached Maikop, where they were greeted warmly by the local NKVD commander and given billets. Over the following days, Foelkersam was taken on guided tours of the city's main installation and laid plans for a takeover. On the day of the attack, the 8th, his force split into three groups. One severed telephones and telegraph lines from Maikop to front-line units and then occupied the central telegraph office, answering any calls with the 'official' order that the city had to be abandoned. A second group under Foelkersam himself took over a strongpoint and issued false withdrawal orders to Red Army units in the immediate vicinity, while the third group succeeded in preventing the destruction of all but one of the city's oil storage tanks. On the 9th Prohaska led his team, also dressed in enemy uniforms and mounted on Red Army trucks, across the Bjelaja bridge. The appearance of apparently retreating Soviet troops sowed panic among the defenders of the bridge and, as they fled, the Brandenburgers disarmed the explosive charges that had been primed for its demolition. A spearhead from the 13th Panzer Division crossed safely and Maikop fell the same day. Foelkersam and Prohaska were both awarded the Knight's Cross for the operation, the latter posthumously.

Although the bulk of the regiment was fighting in the far south of the Eastern Front for most of 1942, some Brandenburgers saw service in the far north. The 15th Company under Lt Trommsodorf was dispatched to Finland in January to serve under Gen Eduard Dietl and established a camp near Rovaniemi. After a period of acclimatisation,

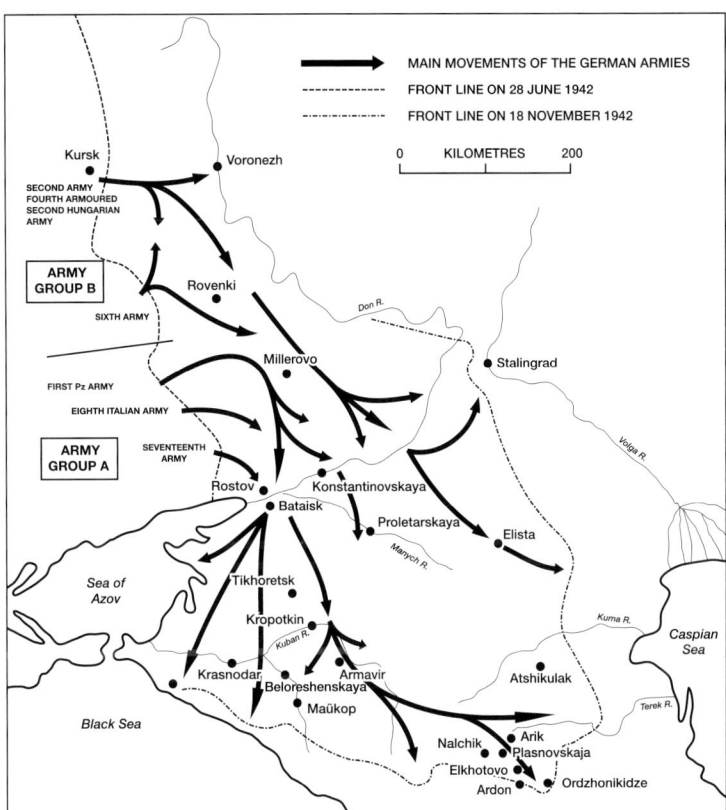

ELITE ATTACK FORCES: BRANDENBURGERS

Right: The 'Desert Fox' wasn't keen at first, but the Brandenburgers soon won his approval. The first Brandenburg units —1st and 2nd Companies of the IIIrd Battalion of Lehr-Regiment Brandenburg z.b.V. 800 —arrived in North Africa in June 1941 tasked with reconnaissance duties. Redesignated Sonderverband 287, the Brandenburgers were subordinated to Sonderstab F commanded by Gen der Flieger Felmy until Koenen arrived to take command. *via George Forty*

Below: Operation 'Salaam', the planned insertion of German agents into Cairo.

the so-called Trommsodorf Company joined a battle group that included German mountain troops and a Finnish detachment. The group's operation in late March–early April was to sever Russian supply lines running between Leningrad and Murmansk, the ice-free port, but the raid ended in failure and the Brandenburgers returned to base. Trommsodorf left — as did his replacement — and in mid-April a new officer, Lt Hettinger, arrived. After weeks of intensive training, his Hettinger Company embarked on another raid against the Leningrad–Murmansk Line on 3 August — the objective lay 100 miles (160km) behind the front line. After setting off from Kairala, the company lived partly off the

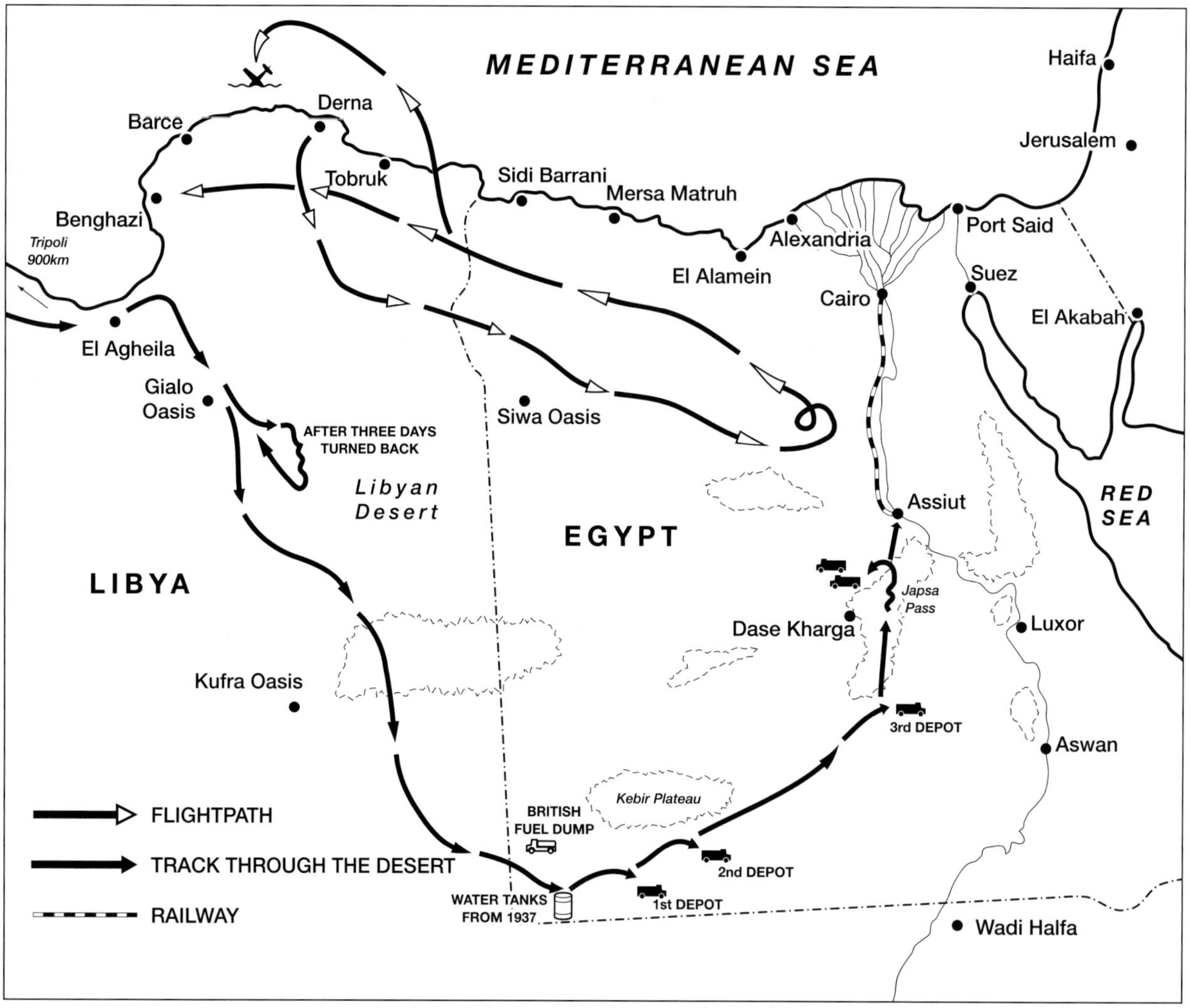

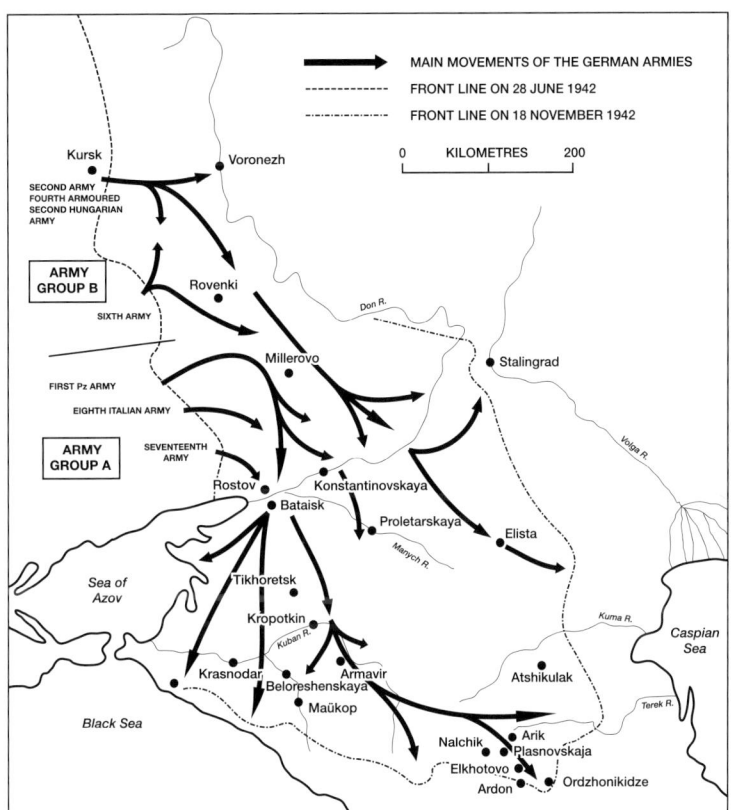

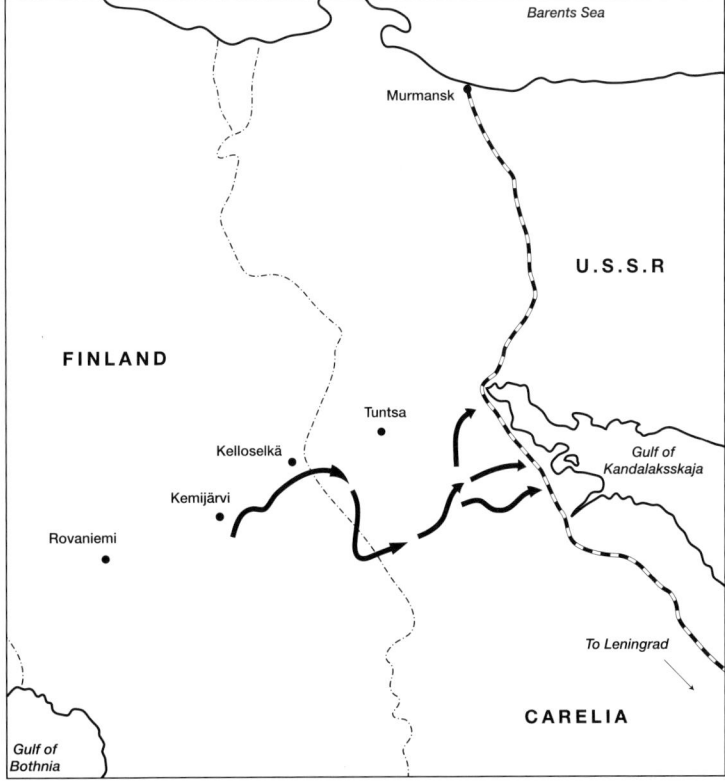

land and dodged Red Army patrols for several days. It reach the target area on the morning of the 9th and then reconnoitred the three bridges earmarked for destruction. The attack went in late on the 13th and, although sentries prevented one bridge from being destroyed, the other two were brought crashing down by explosive charges. Hettinger now retraced his steps, pursued all the way by Red Army units sent out to hunt this company down. Despite several firefights, the Brandenburgers reached Kairala late on the 16th.

THE BRANDENBURGERS IN NORTH AFRICA

Abwehr operatives had been in North Africa since from 1940 but the first large detachments appeared during June 1941 and the commitment escalated over the following months with the arrival of the Tropical Company under Lt Friedrich von Koenen. Gen Erwin Rommel was not immediately convinced of the Brandenburgers' value, but in September finally agreed to give them a free hand in intelligence-gathering, although he frowned on them wearing enemy uniforms. Brandenburgers had made two attempts to infiltrate Cairo to contact Arab nationalists who might be encouraged to openly rebel against the British. The missions, one codenamed 'Condor' in May and the second in July, both failed but in May 1942 the Brandenburgers successfully infiltrated two *Abwehr* agents into Egypt from Libya in an operation codenamed 'Salaam' (see box). However, for much of the year they conducted reconnaissance missions in the far south of the North African theatre in much the same way as Britain's SAS and Long-Range Desert Group.

A more ambitious mission under 2-Lt Helmut von Leipzig was devised in either June or July. Around 100 Brandenburgers, many fluent in a combination of Arabic, English or French, set out from Tripoli in a column of mostly captured vehicles and headed for Marzuq, an Italian garrison in southwest Libya, by way of Sabha. Their mission, codenamed 'Dora', was to conduct a long-range reconnaissance into Niger and Chad to assess the feasibility of severing the Allied supply lines that German intelligence believed ran across the interior between the Gulf of Guinea and Port Sudan. At Al-Qatrun, some 35 miles (56km) south of Marzuq, Leipzig established a forward base and split his detachment into three groups. One, under Leipzig himself, was despatched into neighbouring Algeria and struck out for the Tassili mountains in the country's far south on the border with Niger. The Brandenburgers were discovered by a French patrol and over the following days had to make a fighting retreat back across the border into Libya. The Brandenburgers escaped but four were killed by the French. The second group crossed over the Tibesti mountains in northern Chad and infiltrated the town of Bardai, only to discover that the company-strong garrison was soon to receive strong reinforcements. The decision was taken to return to Libya. 2-Lt von Leipzig's third group moved though Ghat in southwest Libya and crossed into southern Algeria, where it ran into a French-occupied village and was eventually forced to return to Algeria. The findings of 'Dora' suggested that the supply lines were only defended by comparatively small forces and could be cut by deploying a few divisions. However, Rommel had no divisions to spare and with the opening of the Battle of El Alamein in October and the 'Torch' landings in November he had more pressing matters to attend to. 'Dora' was quietly shelved.

By late 1942 the Axis forces in North Africa were in danger of being caught between two Allied forces advancing from west and east towards Tunisia. Brandenburgers were ordered to prevent British, French and US forces from reaching Tunisia before its defences could be arranged. In late October Koenen's Tropical Company left Libya for Tunisia, where it received reinforcements bringing it up to battalion strength. Their first operation, one involving 30 men, was against a bridge over the Wadi el-Kbir close to the village of Sidi Bou Baker in central Tunisia. The detachment left Bizerte airfield in three DFS 230

OPERATION 'SALAAM'

In spring 1942 the OKW ordered the *Abwehr* to infiltrate two men behind British lines in North Africa to gather intelligence that could be used by the newly arrived Afrika Korps under Gen Erwin Rommel in his drive on Egypt. A Brandenburger detachment in Libya was ordered to transport the two agents, Johannes Eppler and Gerd Sandstede, across the desert to their destination and then return to friendly lines, a round trip of some 4,000 miles (6,400km). The party was commanded by Capt Hans von Steffens, a fluent speaker of both English and Arabic, and he chose as his guide Hungarian-born Count Laszlo von Almásy, a veteran desert traveller. The plan was to use trucks to drive south down the Kufra track in east Cyrenaica to the oasis at Gialo and then motor east to reach the Yapsa Pass close to Asyut on the Nile River. From the pass the *Abwehr* agents would drive to Asiut and board a train for Cairo.

The operation began badly — within hours of setting out the trucks became stuck in soft sand and Steffens suffered a heart attack trying to dig them out. The party returned to base and made a second attempt without Steffens on 11 May. Almásy's desert experiences paid off and the team was able to reach the drop point without being discovered after 12 days even though they had to pass through checkpoints at the entrance to Yapsa. At the summit of the pass Almásy parted from the agents, who set off for Cairo, while he and his Brandenburgers retraced their steps, finally reaching safety at the beginning of June. The count radioed the completion of his mission to headquarters on the 4th but his labours proved worthless. The agents reached Cairo but British intelligence already knew of their plans and, once identified, the two men were tracked down to a houseboat on the Nile and arrested on October 14.

Above: Another *Signal* image, the caption for this portrait of Reinhard Heydrich, SS-Obergruppenführer and General of Police, Reich Protector of of Bohemia and Moravia and a strong candidate for supreme office in the future, extolled the 'chivalrous fighter as statesman, as air pilot on the eastern and western fronts and as . . . one of the best European fencers.' On 27 May 1942, Heydrich was shot by British-trained Czech resistance fighters Josef Gabcik and Jan Kubis and died on 6 June of septicaemia. As a reprisal, the SS chose a village — Lidice — and killed all male inhabitants over the age of 16 years. Meanwhile, 1,331 Czechs, among them more than 200 women, were executed in Prague.

gliders late on 26 October. After landing, Koenen reconnoitred the bridge. The Brandenburgers then trekked over 120 miles (192km) to reach friendly lines at Maknassy six days later. A second team was less lucky; it successfully destroyed a bridge near Kasserine but was intercepted and its 10 men captured. Similar operations followed in early 1943. On 18 January a detachment led by 2-Lt Luchs destroyed a rail bridge carrying the Tozeur–Sfax line over the Wadi el-Melah in southern Tunisia. Like its predecessors, the mission was successful but could not prevent the inevitable defeat of the Axis forces in North Africa. However, most of the Brandenburgers did manage to escape to Sicily by boat before the German and Italian forces surrendered in the second week of May.

THE RISE OF OTTO SKORZENY

While the Brandenburgers continued to fight on the Eastern Front and elsewhere during 1942 and 1943, the battle between the *Abwehr* and SS security service continued. A further twist in the struggle took place on 27 May 1942. Heydrich, now Reich Protector of Bohemia, was assassinated in Prague by a group of Czech agents trained in Britain. The loss of the head of the RSHA would seem to benefit the *Abwehr* in its power struggle but Himmler took charge of its operations for the next several months and filled it with SS officers, who — like himself — were dedicated to rooting out anti-Nazi plots and destroying Canaris's intelligence machine. Chief among these was Walter Schellenberg, who was a senior figure in the RSHA's foreign secret service, and Ernst Kaltenbrunner, who eventually took over the running of the various SS security services from Himmler. As these men conspired, it became increasingly clear to them that the SS should establish a special force that could rival the exploits of the Brandenburgers and step into the breach once the *Abwehr* had been discredited. In 1942 Section VI of the RSHA, which was headed by Schellenberg at the time and responsible for intelligence-gathering, began organising a force similar to the Brandenburgers but filled with members of the Waffen-SS. In April 1943, a Waffen-SS officer, Capt Otto Skorzeny, was appointed to knock the unit into shape. The new units were known as *Friedenthaler Jagdverbände* (Friedenthal Hunting Groups) after the estate outside Berlin where they were based. These units placed special emphasis on anti-partisan operations and, like the Brandenburgers, sometimes wore foreign military uniforms or civilian clothes. However, Skorzeny had little time to complete the extensive training programme he had in mind as within a few months Hitler selected him to lead a daring mission to rescue Italian dictator Benito Mussolini

Mussolini had been removed from office on 23 July 1943 in a palace coup, led by King Victor Emmanuel III, the army's high command and assorted Fascist politicians. His prestige and authority had collapsed following the Allied victory in the North African campaign in May and the subsequent invasion of Sicily, Operation 'Husky', which had opened on 10 July. By this stage of the war it had became unquestionably clear that Italy had to surrender but that it was unlikely to secure favourable terms from the Allies with

Mussolini still in power. After his arrest he was placed under close guard and over the following weeks was moved around at regular intervals by his captors, spending time at Frascati, Gaeta and the islands of Ponza and La Maddalena, before returning to mainland Italy. Hitler, who had greatly admired Mussolini in the latter's early years of power, could not let an old ally languish in captivity or possibly fall into Allied hands, and ordered that a rescue mission be undertaken. He placed the planning of the operation in the hands of the head of the Luftwaffe's paratroopers, Gen Kurt Student. The success of the mission depended on finding Mussolini and both Canaris's *Abwehr* and the RSHA's Schellenberg were ordered to find him.

The operation to rescue Mussolini was of the type that was ideally suited to the Brandenburgers, yet Hitler looked elsewhere for the men to attempt the top-secret mission and the officer to lead them into action. On 26 July he interviewed six officers from different branches of the armed forces at Rastenburg and after a brief conversion with each, selected Otto Skorzeny, like Hitler an Austrian by birth. Skorzeny flew to Italy the next day accompanied by 20 Luftwaffe paratroopers and landed at Practica di Mare airfield southeast of Rome on the coast, where around around 50 of his own troops were awaiting his arrival. Among these were Skorzeny's adjutant, SS Lt Karl Radl, a former member of the Brandenburgers. After a few false leads in August, one of which led Skorzeny to Maddalena on 26 August one hour after Mussolini had been moved by his captors, he was finally able to locate Mussolini definitively in early September thanks to his own intelligence officers and local informers. He discovered that the Italian dictator was being held on at the Albergo Rifugio, a hotel on one of the high ridges in the Gran Sasso massif approximately 60 miles (100km) northeast of Rome.

Skorzeny set to devising a plan and quickly ruled out a direct ground assault on the hotel, which could only be reached from the surrounding valley by a slow-moving funicular railway. Surprise and speed were the keys to success and he saw from high-altitude reconnaissance photographs taken from a Heinkel He111 on 8 September that a patch of seemingly flat ground close to the hotel was just large enough to land glider-borne troops. Skorzeny split his command, now with a strength of 108 men, into three parties: Skorzeny's, which was to be carried in 12 gliders, was tasked with landing by the hotel to rescue Mussolini; a battalion under Maj Mors was to secure the funicular railway station at the foot of the valley to prevent Italian troops from interfering in the rescue; a third was ordered to rescue Mussolini's wife and family who were being held at Rocca della Cominata.

Skorzeny ordered the operation to begin at 0600 hours on the 12th but the 12 DFS 230 gliders being transported to Practica del Mare from the French Riviera did not arrive until 1100 and a further delay was caused when an Allied air attack at around 1230 came close, but just failed, to destroy any of the aircraft. At 1300 hours the bulk of the armada took off for the one-hour flight to Gran Sasso except for two gliders that ran into bomb craters on the runway during take-off. The remaining gliders and their tugs climbed though clear skies, formed up and then set off for their destination. After a short

Above: Hitler had a great fellow-feeling for Mussolini, whose introduction of fascism in Italy had in many ways guided his own. The Blackshirts had gained power in 1922 — a year before the Munich Beer Hall Putsch. Thus Mussolini had been 'Il Duce' (leader) for more than ten years by 1933 when Hitler became the Führer (leader). He had already militarised Italy and engaged in expansionist policies — in 1935 he invaded Ethiopia and used poison gas to defeat the tribesmen. Initially Mussolini was unsure of Hitler but as the Nazi star began to rise, he supported the Nazis. He paid the price in July 1943, when he was arrested and imprisoned — leading to Skorzeny's mission to free him. Once freed, Hitler set up Mussolini as the leader of the Italian Socialist Republic in German-held northern Italy, and he would remain a German cipher until Axis forces surrendered in northern Italy in April 1945. Mussolini was arrested again and he and his mistress, Clara Petacci, were taken from the jail at Giulino di Messegra and lynched by the local Communist partisans. This photo is from the pages of *Signal*, where he was described as a statesman 'with the sure hand of a genius.'

Scenes from Skorzeny's daring rescue of Mussolini from the Hotel Albergo Rifugio high up in the Gran Sasso mountains on 12 September 1943. (See also colour pages 78–9.) For an excellent commentary on this rescue, many photographs taken at the time and postwar *After the Battle* issue 22 is essential reading. *All photos Bundesarchiv*

Opposite, above: A DFS 230 glider, possibly the one that Skorzeny used.

Opposite, below: From left to right — Skorzeny, dressed in a tropical Luftwaffe uniform (as were all those who took part in the operation), Mussolini and Inspector of Police Guiseppe Gueli.

Left: Rear view of the Hotel Albergo Rifugio.

Below and Below left: The rescue of Mussolini was re-enacted for the propaganda cameras by German Fallschirmjäger (Skorzeny and his team having left the area); these photographs are from the reconstruction.

time one of the tug pilots reported that he had lost contact with the two lead gliders in thick cloud and that they were nowhere to be seen, but Skorzeny ordered the mission to continue. Shortly before 1400, the planned assault time, Gran Sasso was spotted and Skorzeny ordered his pilot, Lt Meyer, to land the glider on the small patch of supposedly flat land close to the hotel, which on closer inspection turned out to be rocky and severely uneven. Nevertheless Meyer swooped toward the hotel, deployed the parachute break and made a crash-landing virtually on schedule.

Despite the danger of the rocks and boulders of the plateau, Skorzeny's glider, the first to land, skidded to a halt no more than 16.5 yards (15m) from the hotel. He led his men forward, ordering that none was to fire unless he gave the order. A lone Carabinieri sentry on guard at one corner of the hotel surrendered immediately, and the assault group led by its commander ran through an open door. A second guard, this time seated at a wireless set, was spotted and Skorzeny kicked the chair from under him and smashed the set with his machine-pistol. The band then returned outside, moved round the walls of the building and then, again with Skorzeny in the lead, scaled a 10ft (3m) terrace. Mussolini's face suddenly appeared at a first-floor window and was hurriedly waved away by Skorzeny. Brushing aside a number of Italian sentries who were quickly overpowered, Skorzeny charged into a large hallway and up a broad staircase on the right. Racing to the top he flung open the first doorway and was greeted by the sight of the dictator and two officers. These two guards were bundled aside — Mussolini had been rescued in under five minutes and no shots had been fired by either side.

While Skorzeny was rescuing Mussolini, the other gliders had come in to land but one was caught by a strong gust of wind, crashed out of control and was smashed on the rocks. The reinforcements that did land faced a brief firefight with the few Carabinieri that had not surrendered but these gave up when the Italian colonel of the garrison agreed to hang a white surrender flag from one of the hotel's windows. Skorzeny also heard that Mors's detachment had successfully captured the funicular railway station at the foot of the valley and ordered him to bring his men up to the Albergo Rifugio. Skorzeny now selected one of three pre-planned means of speedily moving Mussolini to safety. Two had already effectively failed: a surprise assault on the Aquila de Abruzzi airfield at the foot of the valley at 1600 followed by the landing of transport He111s was rejected as Skorzeny could not contact the assault group, and the plan to use a small Fieseler Storch landing close to the funicular station ended when the aircraft was badly damaged on landing. The third plan was to land a similar aircraft directly on to the plateau, a risky proposition. The pilot, Lt Gerlach,

Below: Man hanged by German anti-partisan forces in Yugoslavia, Belgrade autumn 1941. The soldiers are possibly Brandenburgers who were known to be there at the time. *via Chris Ellis*

nevertheless made a successful landing and he, Skorzeny and Mussolini took off in what was a grossly overloaded aircraft. After landing at Practica di Mare, Mussolini and Skorzeny transferred to an He111 and immediately flew to an airfield at Aspern on the outskirts of Vienna, where it was confirmed that Mussolini's family had arrived in Munich after an equally successful rescue from Rocca della Caminata. After accompanying Mussolini to Rastenburg, Skorzeny returned to Italy, where he discovered that the Gran Sasso operation was to be turned into a propaganda event.

THE FALL OF THE *ABWEHR* AND THE BRANDENBURGERS

The joint Luftwaffe–SS operation rescue was a brilliant success but, much to Student's annoyance, it was Skorzeny and his men, not the Luftwaffe, that received the accolades. Skorzeny was awarded the Knight's Cross and promoted to SS-Sturmbannführer (major) by Hitler, who recognised the enormous propaganda value of the successful rescue at a time when the German people were increasingly starved of good news from the fighting fronts. Gran Sasso also marked a decisive moment in the *Abwehr*'s — and Brandenburgers' — fall from grace and the rise of the SS and its intelligence agencies to a position of unchallenged power. Hitler had already been made aware of the *Abwehr*'s likely involvement in anti-Nazi plots, not least Operation 'U-7', by both Himmler and his senior deputies, including Schellenberg, head of the SD. 'U-7' was masterminded by Canaris's deputy, Hans Oster, and involved smuggling Jewish refugees from Germany to Switzerland. It was finally uncovered in February 1943 and Oster was subsequently dismissed from his post. Coming on top of this, the *Abwehr*'s failure to find Mussolini, deliberate or otherwise, further convinced Hitler that the organisation was at the very least unreliable if not outright treacherous from top to bottom. The *Abwehr* continued to function for several more months but both it and Canaris were completely marginalised by the SS. It was finally broken up in February 1944. Canaris was briefly ordered to keep away from Berlin and all intelligence operations were placed under the control of Himmler's SS.

The collapse of the *Abwehr* signalled the demise of the Brandenburgers as they were originally constituted. From late 1942 the unit became involved in anti-partisan activities and conventional combat roles on the Eastern Front and in the Balkans, neither of which reflected the value of its men's training or experience. Losses were high and morale undoubtedly suffered. The *Abwehr*, which was under intense pressure from the SS, also began to lose interest in the unit and it came increasingly under the direct control of the OKW. An OKW order retitled the three regiments *Sonderverbände* (Special Units) Nos 801, 802 and 803 in January 1943, and a fourth special unit, *Sonderverband* No 804, was added to the order of battle. These battalions acted as the cadre for the four regiments that would make up the Brandenburg Division from April. It was commanded by Maj-Gen Alexander von Pfuhlstein and contained the four *Sonderverbände* plus various other detachments including four tropical

Above: Lt-Gen Karl Student, Luftwaffe commander of XI Flieger Corps and nominally in charge of Mussolini's rescue. *via Chris Ellis*

Below: Hostages shot at Chabatz by anti-partisan forces (possibly Brandenburgers) in Yugoslavia as retribution for attack by Mikailovich's Chetniks, autumn 1941. *via Chris Ellis*

companies and a parachute battalion. There was also the *Küstenjäger Abteilung* (Coastal Raider Detachment) made up of volunteers from the Kriegsmarine. Little is known of its missions but its motorboats were initially based on the Dalmatian coast and subsequently took part in Operation '*Eisbär*', (polar bear) the occupation of the Dodecanese island of Cos (see map below), in October 1943 and the capture of Leros a month later (see pages 38–9). The division never fought as a single entity during 1943–4 as detachments were used where and when they were needed.

Although Brandenburger detachments conducted special operations with some noteworthy successes, particularly the occupation of Leros, the rapid expansion severely undermined their capabilities. New recruits were not of the same calibre as the first; out of 14,000 men in the division in mid-1944, for example, only 900 spoke a foreign language. To make matters worse Pfuhlstein was implicated in the anti-Nazi *Schwarze Kapelle* resistance movement that was being hunted by the Gestapo and was dismissed in April 1944 — seemingly further confirmation of the *Abwehr*'s unreliability. Pfuhlstein's dismissal, which closely followed the destruction of the *Abwehr* the previous February, ensured the Brandenburg Division would lose its role to the SS, chiefly the various forces that operated under Hitler's new favourite, Otto Skorzeny.

The Brandenburgers, now commanded by Lt-Gen Kühlwein, conducted a few special operations in the months after Pfuhlstein's dismissal. Its 1st Regiment played a supporting role in Operation '*Rösselsprung*' (knight's move), an attack on Marshal Tito's headquarters near Drvar in Yugoslavia in May (see pages 42–4 below), when it was ordered to push from Knin toward Grahovo and then move on Drvar as part of a move to cut off the partisans' line of retreat.

Below: The German attack on Cos. Defended by 1st Battalion, the Durham Light Infantry, two squadrons of RAF Regiment and the Italian garrison, Cos was a hard nut to crack. The German invading force comprised 22nd Infantry Division and two companies of Brandenburgers — 1st Küstenjäger (KJA), equivalent to the British SBS or US Navy SEALs, and a parachute company. The landings took place on 3 October 1943 and by the end of the next day the Germans were in control of the island; Lt-Col L. R. F. Kenyon, CO of the Durhams, had been taken prisoner as had nearly 1,400 British troops for the cost of 14 German dead.

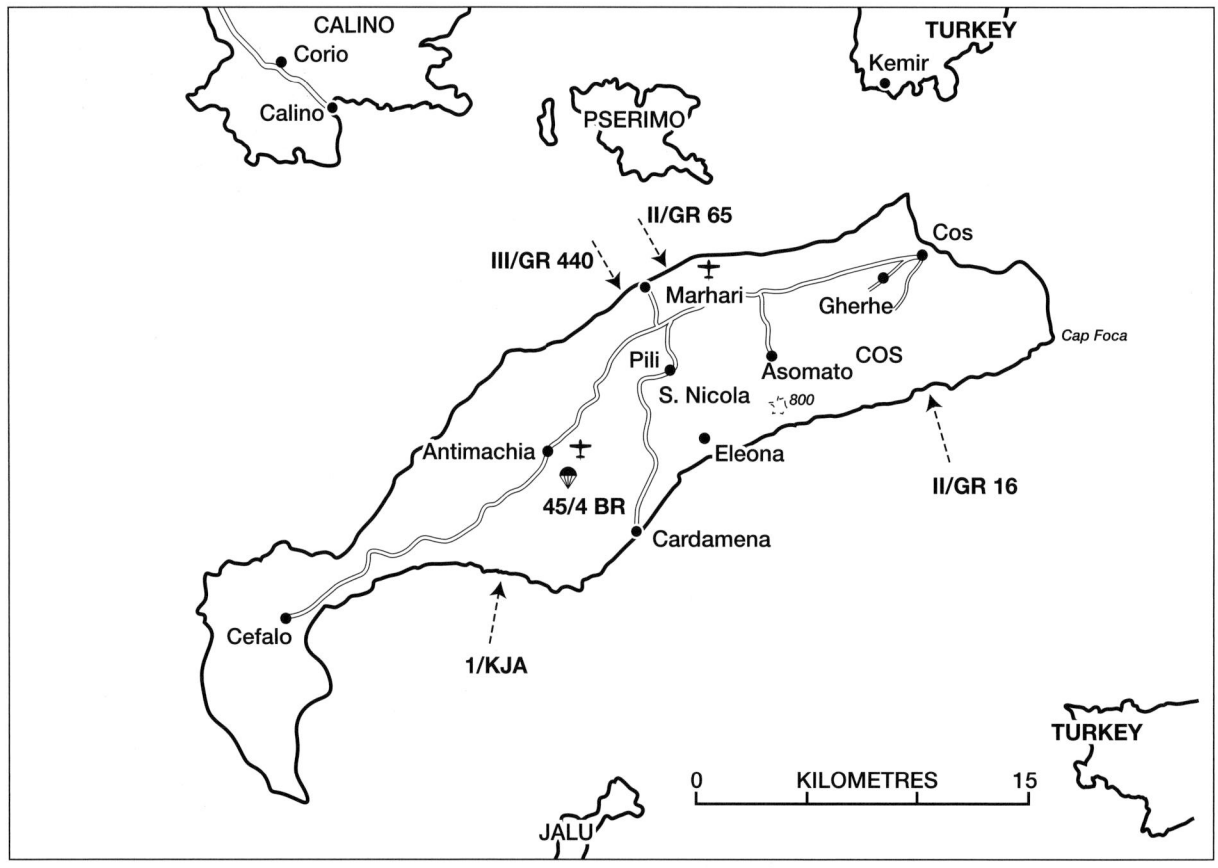

The Brandenburgers were again in action in the Balkans during the following August. The Red Army was close to Romania's borders and the country's figurehead sovereign, King Michael I, pushed forward armistice negotiations with the Soviet Union. Both he and some of his generals also suspected the pro-Nazi head of government, Prime Minister Ion Antonescu, would do little to prevent a full-blown German occupation in the event of Romania's defection from the Axis alliance. On the night of the 23rd Michael staged a coup, arresting Antonescu and his cabinet, and ordered his forces to change sides. Hitler feared the collapse of the southern sector of the Eastern Front and ordered an attack on Bucharest. Part of the Brandenburg Division's 3rd Regiment, some two company and support elements, along with its parachute battalion were ordered to the capital. Their role was twofold: to occupy Otopeni airport and rescue two generals and their staffs who had been surrounded by their former Romanian allies at their command post, Waldlager I, near the airfield.

The first Brandenburgers arrived by air at midday on the 24th and quickly began securing Otopeni. Over the following hours more Brandenburgers were flown into Bucharest in huge Messerschmitt Me323 Gigants and by about 2000 hours Waldlager I had been reached. After some tense negotiations, the generals and staffs, along with a Brandenburger escort, were given permission to head for the Yugoslavian border. However, the Romanians reneged on the deal and the generals, their staff and the majority of the Brandenburgers were surrounded and forced to surrender. Most were handed over to the advancing Red Army.

Despite these commando-style operations the transformation of the division continued. It was officially retitled the Panzergrenadier Division Brandenburg on 8 September but some 350 Brandenburgers objected to the new role and joined Skorzeny's units. After a period of reorganisation the new division's scattered units were assembled at the Mauerwald camp, East Prussia, in mid-December and henceforth served as a wholly conventional force, mostly on the Eastern Front. In the latter stages of the conflict it fought as part of the Grossdeutschland Panzer Corps, which also included the Grossdeutschland Panzergrenadier Division and the Luftwaffe's Hermann Göring Panzer Division.

The Panzergrenadier Division Brandenburg under Maj-Gen Hermann Schulte-Heuthaus joined the newly formed corps on 12 January 1945, and was immediately flung into action around Lodz in Poland. It was forced to retreat westward by the pincer attacks of the Red Army until by the end of the month it was holding positions along the Neisse River north of Görlitz. Between late February and mid-April the division fought bitter battles on the Neisse between Muskau and Steinback but was eventually forced to retreat in Czechoslovakia, where its men surrendered or escaped westward in the final days of the war.

Above: German forces landing on Cos. The German actions in the Dodecanese were the last significant use of the Brandenburgers who performed with distinction. Unfortunately, the aftermath of the invasions was the execution of most of the Italian personnel on the islands — over 100 officers were slaughtered on Cos; nearly 5,000 Italian soldiers had been systematically executed on Cephalonia in late September. The German commander, was executed on 20 May 1947 in Athens for these crimes. *via Chris Ellis*

OPERATION 'LEOPARD'/'TYPHOON' — THE CAPTURE OF LEROS

Italy's surrender in September 1943 left a power vacuum on the Dodecanese islands in the Aegean Sea that both Britain and Germany attempted to fill. The British hastily gathered together a small force and by early October had control of eight Dodecanese islands and Samos to the north of the group. One of their key positions was Leros, a seaplane base protected by several coastal batteries defended by around 9,000 British and pro-Allied Italian troops by early November.

Although the British had moved quickly, German troops still held the large islands of Crete and Rhodes, as well as mainland Greece, and Hitler, who feared that the Dodecanese would be used as bases for landings in the Balkans, ordered the lost islands retaken. Although the Germans had few ground troops for the operation, they did enjoy air superiority and the British, heavily committed on the Italian mainland, had few reserves available to bolster their garrisons.

Cos was the first German target and it fell easily after landings, on 3 October that involved the 1st Company of the Brandenburg Division's *Küstenjäger Abteilung*. Leros was targeted in mid-November and the Brandenburg Division provided the same coastal company as fought on Cos as well as part of its 4th Regiment's 15th Parachute Company and detachments from the 1st Regiment's IIIrd Battalion for the invasion, which was initially codenamed 'Leopard' (this was changed to *'Taifun'* — Typhoon — on 2 November). The operation opened on 12 November after major attacks by the Luftwaffe on the various batteries. The guns were not destroyed. The parachute company plus similar Luftwaffe units were recalled after running into intense antiaircraft fire over their landing zone, while an invasion flotilla heading for Gurna Bay was also beaten back by fire from coastal batteries. Initially only the eastern task force was able to secure two small footholds at Alinda Day close to Leros town. The paratroopers tried again and this time secured a defensive perimeter on Rachi ridge between the two bays. In the east the Brandenburgers were also able to land at Pandeli Bay to the south of Leros town and after a hard climb gain a foothold on Mount Appetici that they were temporarily unable to exploit.

The battle was stalemated but on the 13th German reinforcements reached the island to prevent the British destroying the scattered bridgeheads before they could be expanded. On the 14th and 15th Brandenburgers beat off several British counterattacks and the following day the 1st Regiment's IIIrd Battalion arrived. Going straight into action they captured Mount Meraviglia, site of the British headquarters to the south of Leros town, on the 17th and organised resistance collapsed.

IN ACTION

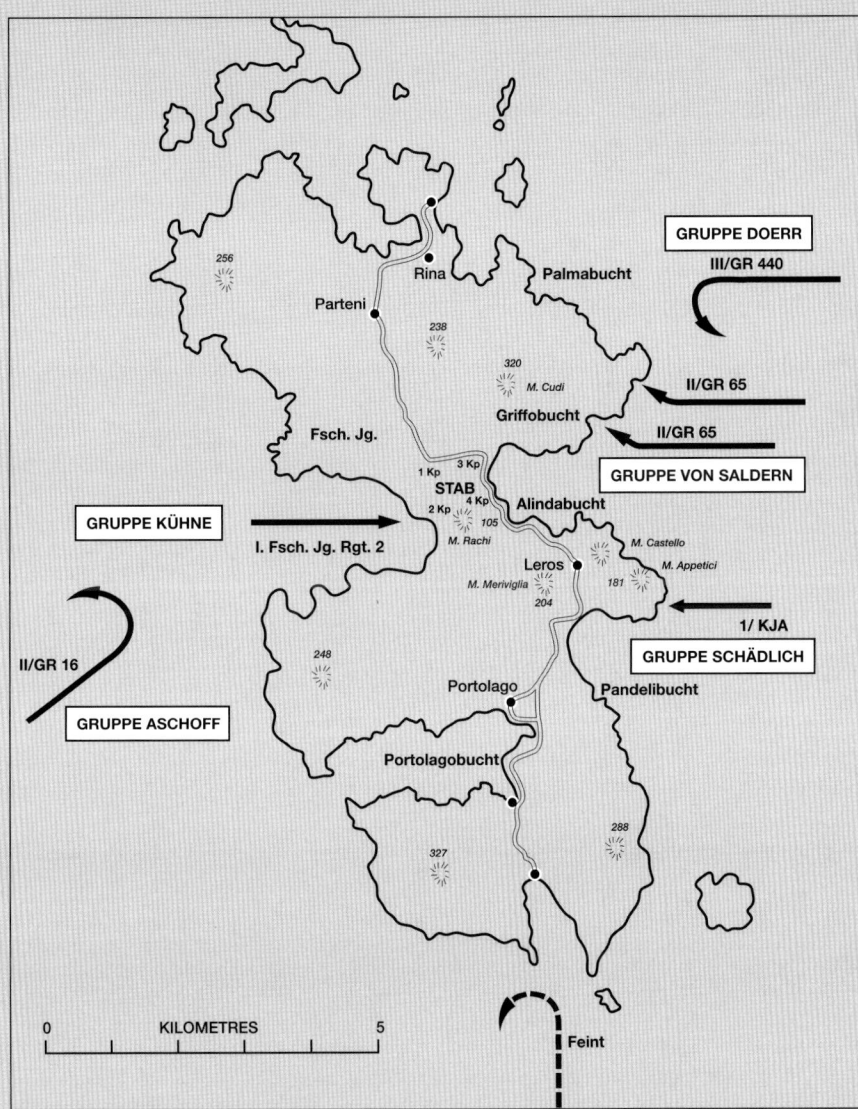

Far left: Bombs exploding near village of Portolago on Leros during the German invasion of 12 November 1943. *via Chris Ellis*

Left: The five invading groups. The Brandenburg Küstenjäger (KJA) were under the command of Lt Hans Schädlich.

Below left: British and Italian prisoners after capture on Leros (they totalled 8,850). *via Chris Ellis*

Below: Brig RAG Tilney (right) commander of the British garrison after the capture of Leros, being interviewed by German commander Gen Friedrich-Wilhelm Müller (left), CG of 22nd Infantry Division, on 16 November 1943. Müller was executed on 20 May 1947 in Athens for war crimes. *via Chris Ellis*

BRANDENBURG-LEHR-REGIMENT zbV 800 MAY 1940–DECEMBER 1942

HQ (Berlin)

- **1st Battalion** (Brandenburg Havel)
  - HQ Company
  - 1st Company
  - 2nd Company
  - 3rd Company
  - 4th Company
- **2nd Battalion** (Baden-Unterwaltersdorf)
  - 5th Company
  - 6th Company
  - 7th Company
  - 8th Company
- **3rd Battalion** (Baden-Unterwaltersdorf)
  - 9th Company
  - 10th Company
  - 11th Company
  - 12th Company
- 17th Special Company — Created in April 1941
- Light Engineer Company — Created in February 1942 from the 4th Company
- Signals Company — Created in January 1941
- V-Leute* Company — Created in spring 1940
- Training Company — Created in April 1941
- Interpreter Company — Created in spring 1940

*V-Leute = Vertrauensleute = intelligence agents

BRANDENBURG DIVISION APRIL 1943–SEPTEMBER 1943

DIVISION HQ
- Divisional Commander: Gen von Pfuhlstein
- GSO1: Maj Frankworth
- Ia: Capt Wüllberg (until 31/5/43)
- IIa & Division Adjutant: Capt Pinkert

- **1st BRANDENBURG REGIMENT**
  3 x battalions, each of 3 or 4 companies, 11 in total (one disbanded summer 1943)
- **2nd BRANDENBURG REGIMENT**
  3 x battalions, each of 3 or 4 companies, 11 in total (two disbanded summer 1943); 1 x Light Gun Battery (formed 1944)
- **3rd BRANDENBURG REGIMENT**
  3 x battalions, each of 4 companies, 12 in total (one disbanded summer 1943)
- **4th BRANDENBURG REGIMENT**
  3 x battalions, each of 3 or 4 companies, 11 in total
- **TRAINING REGIMENT**
  1 x battalion based at Brandenburg-Havel
  1 x Gebirgs battalion based at Baden nr Vienna
  12 x battalions created in 1944
  'Alexander' Legionnaire Battalion
- **SIGNALS BATTALION**
  5 x companies
- **KOENEN'S TROPICAL UNIT**
  4 x companies
- **COASTAL RAIDER BATTALION**
  4 x companies based at Langenargen, Lake Constance
- **PARACHUTE BATTALION**
  4 x companies based at Stendal
- **14th COMPANY**
  later redesignated 16th Company
- **15th LIGHT COMPANY**
  Parachute Company

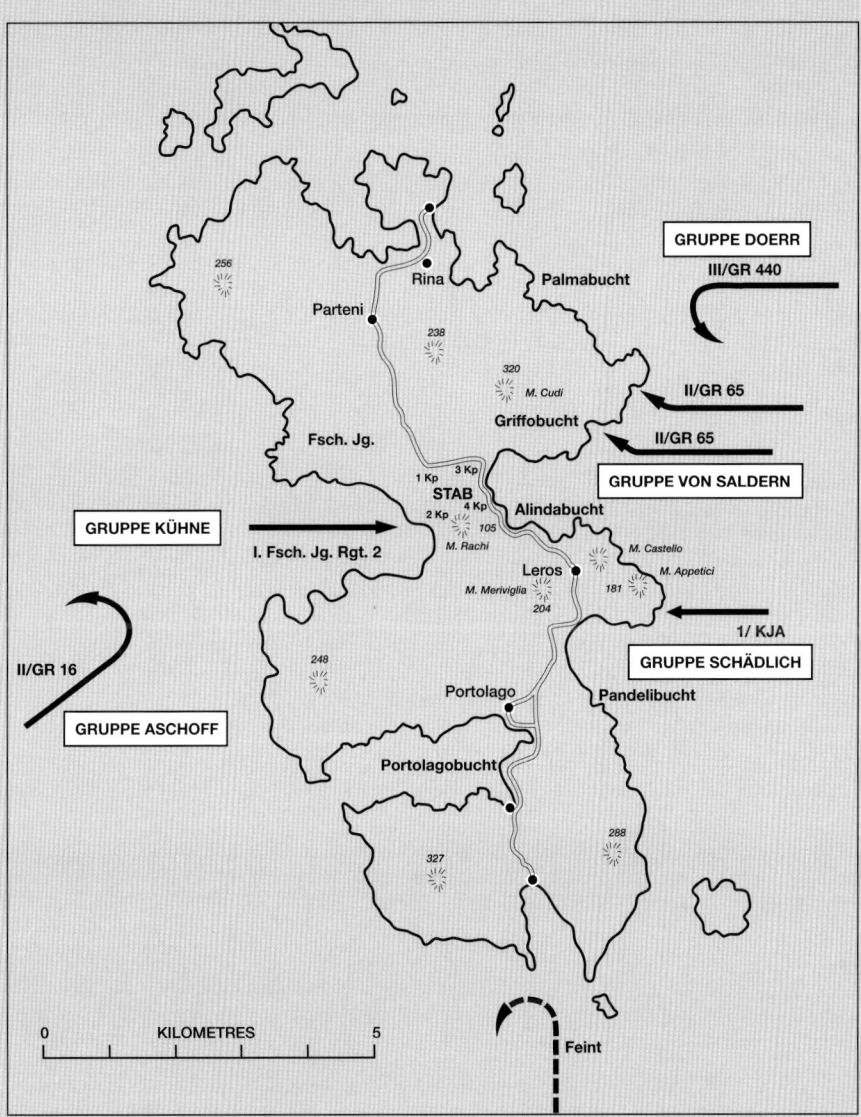

PANZERGRENADIER-DIVISION BRANDENBURG FROM SEPTEMBER 1943

- **Division HQ**
  - HQ & HQ Company
    - Machine Gun Platoon
    - Motorcycle Platoon
    - Flak Platoon (self-propelled)
    - Mortar Platoon
  - Mapping Detachment (mot)
  - Military Police Detachment (mot)

- **1st Jäger Regiment**
  - HQ & HQ Company
    - HQ Platoon
    - Signals Platoon
    - Motorcycle Platoon
  - Panzergrenadier Battalion (half-track)
    - HQ
    - Supply Company (mot)
    - 3 x Company (half-track)
    - Heavy Company
      - Staff Platoon
      - Mortar Platoon
      - Light Infantry Gun Platoon
  - Jäger Battalion (mot)
    - HQ
    - Supply Company
    - 3 x Company (mot)
    - 2 x Heavy Company (mot)
  - Heavy Infantry Gun Company (SP)
  - Pioneer Company (mot)
    - HQ (half-track)
    - 4 x Platoon (half-track)

- **2nd Jäger Regiment**
  - HQ & HQ Company
    - Staff Platoon
    - Signals Platoon
    - Motorcycle Platoon
  - 2 x Jäger Battalion (mot)
    - HQ
    - Supply Company
    - 3 x Company (mot)
    - 2 x Heavy Company (mot)
  - Heavy Infantry Gun Company (SP)
  - Pioneer Company (mot)

- **Artillery Regiment**
  - HQ & HQ Company
    - Battalion
      - HQ & HQ Battery (SP)
      - Flak Battalion (SP)
      - 2 x Light Howitzer Battery (SP)
      - heavy Howitzer Battery (SP)
    - Battalion
      - HQ & HQ Company (mot)
      - Flak Platoon (mot)
      - 3 x Light Battery (mot)
    - Battalion
      - HQ & HQ Company (mot)
      - Flak Platoon (mot)
      - 3 x Heavy Battery (mot)

- **Pioneer Battalion**
  - HQ & HQ Company
  - 2 x Company (mot)
  - Company (self-propelled)

- **Panzerjäger Battalion**
  - HQ & HQ Battery
  - Sturmgeschütz Staff Platoon
  - 2 x Sturmgeschütz Company
  - Panzerjäger Company (mot)
  - Panzerjäger Supply Company (mot)

- **Signals Battalion**
  - HQ
  - Telephone Company
  - Radio Company
  - Signals Supply Column (mot)

- **Panzer Regiment**
  - HQ & HQ Company
    - Signals Platoon
    - Pioneer Platoon
    - Flak Platoon (SP)
  - Panzer Maintenance Company
  - 2 x Battalion
    - HQ & HQ Company
    - 4 x Panzer Company
    - Flak Company (SP)
    - Supply Company (mot)

- **Reconnaissance Battalion**
  - HQ
    - Armoured Car Platoon
    - Signals Platoon (mot)
  - Armoured Car Company (half-track)
  - 3 x Reconnaissance Company (half-track)
  - Reconnaissance Supply Company

- **Army Flak Battalion**
  - HQ & HQ Battery
  - 2 x Battery (mot)
  - Light Flak Battery
  - Flak Section (self-propelled)
  - Searchlight Section

- **Supply & Support Units**

As the Brandenburgers' fortunes declined in the second half of the war, Skorzeny's stock continued to rise. In late 1943, after the rescue of Mussolini, he was ordered to oversee a large expansion of the SS's special forces that were effectively to replace the Brandenburgers. He was authorised to raise No 502 Special Services Battalion and took recruits from every branch of the armed forces, including the Brandenburg Division. Indeed, Baron Adrian von Foelkersam led a deputation of 11 Brandenburger officers that were eventually permitted to join Skorzeny's troops by a reluctant Canaris in November after months of fractious argument. He also had the 500th SS Parachute Battalion placed under his direction and took on even more wide-ranging roles. Skorzeny was involved in the development and deployment of specialist naval forces, chiefly midget submarines and frogmen, and worked closely with Kampfgruppe 200, the Luftwaffe's special operations unit, on developing a piloted version of the V1 rocket. Various schemes were hatched involving Skorzeny's forces. These included sabotage raids against oil pipelines in the Middle East, a scheme to use frogmen to block the Suez Canal and an attack on the Russian oilfields around Baku on the shores of the Caspian Sea. None of these raids reached fruition, partly because by the beginning of 1944 Germany was facing more immediate threats, especially on the Eastern Front and in the Balkans.

OPERATION '*RÖSSELSPRUNG*' — THE ATTACK ON TITO'S HEADQUARTERS

By this stage of the war the Yugoslav partisan leader Tito had command of a force numbering perhaps 250,000 men and women and controlled to some degree probably a third of Yugoslavia, mostly its mountainous rural areas. German forces had made frequent attempts to destroy the partisans beginning in September 1941 and, although they had scored some significant successes against Tito's originally weak forces, by early 1944 it was apparent that a further blow had to be stuck against the partisans before they could gather strength from supplies provided by the western Allies, chiefly Britain, and the ongoing collapse of the pro-German Ustasa government in the puppet Independent State of Croatia. Germany lacked the resources to launch a major offensive against the partisans because of growing crises elsewhere, so plans were laid to launch a surgical strike against Tito's headquarter's complex, which lay at Drvar in western Bosnia, either to kill or to capture the partisan leader. Skorzeny was dubious about the operation's chances of success for two reasons: because of its complexity and because he feared that the partisans had got wind of the plan. (He feared this with justification: they had!) Nevertheless, his SS 500th Parachute Battalion, was ordered to take part in the operation, which was codenamed *Rösselsprung* (knight's move). The plan called for ground units to approach Tito's sprawling headquarters complex from various directions while the parachute battalion dropped on the camp killed or captured Tito and then fought off the partisans until relieved.

Intelligence about Tito's precise whereabouts came from Brandenburgers, who had been operating clandestinely among the local population since before the fifth major sweep against the partisans, which opened in May 1943 and dragged on through the following summer. Shortly before the beginning of *Rösselsprung* in May 1944, they discovered that he was based in a cave at Bastasi some three miles (5km) from Drvar, and a deserter later indicated that he was guarded by around 350 partisans. It soon became apparent to Skorzeny, who had recently arrived in Yugoslavia, that *Rösselsprung* was common knowledge among local civilians and, therefore, also among the partisans. Despite this security lapse, preparations for the raid continued. The parachute battalion's commander, SS Lt Rybka, was forced to abandon the plan for a single landing because

Below: Hitler and Skorzeny.

Left: Ion Antonescu (1882–1946), Romanian marshal and dictator, served in World War I and in early September 1940 became premier of Romania. Completely pro-Nazi he forced King Carol to abdicate in favour of Carol's son, Michael, and two months later joined the Axis powers. Antonescu gave Hitler virtual control over the Romanian economy and foreign policy, allowed anti-Semitic pogroms and joined in the war against Russia on 22 June 1941. In August 1944 King Michael had Antonescu and his cabinet arrested and joined the Allied side. Antonescu was executed for war crimes in 1946. Romania was important to the Nazis because of its oil supplies, particularly around Ploesti, and because a number of Romanian divisions were fighting alongside the German forces. In an attempt to retrieve the situation the Brandenburgers were sent in to Bucharest. *TRH Pictures*

Below: The unit chosen for the Romanian mission (see page 39) was part of the 3rd Regiment. They were transported to Otopeni airport on 24 August in Messerschmitt Me323 Gigants (as here) — but the mission was to end badly for the Brandenburgers. After securing Antonescu and his staff they were surrounded by Romanian troops and forced to surrender.

of shortages of gliders and transport aircraft. He was, therefore, forced to split his battalion: the first wave, some 320 men, was split into several detachments and each was allocated a specific target within the complex. The 100 men of Panther Group was tasked with the most important, that of seeking out Tito in his personal headquarters, known as the Citadel. The others were to destroy the various military missions from Britain, the Soviet Union and the United States that were attached to the headquarters or smash communication links with the various partisan bands operating in the area. The second wave was to help out where necessary.

The 55-minute flight to the target area began shortly after dawn on 25 May and the paratroopers began jumping over Drvar and the Citadel, the target areas, from the low-flying Junkers Ju52 transports shortly before 0700 hours. Twenty seconds later the first men were on the ground and secured a perimeter into which the troops aboard DFS 230 gliders could set down. In Drvar there was limited opposition and several groups secured their objectives with few casualties but at the Citadel itself Panther Group was pinned down by the partisans, taking heavy casualties from numerous well-sited defensive positions. Rybka ordered the rest of his command to aid Panther Group but it soon became apparent that his lightly equipped men were running low on ammunition while the partisans were rushing more and more units to the battlefield. By 0930 hours the paratroopers were no longer fighting to capture the Citadel but were battling to hold out until reinforcements could arrive. The second wave of paratroopers arrived but landed in an area swept by machine-gun and mortar fire. Losses were high but the survivors among the original 300 or so linked up with Rybka. Around midday, the paratroopers launched another attack against the Citadel but it ended in failure with their commander wounded.

The loss of Rybka confirmed the battalion's plight. It was virtually surrounded by a large — and getting larger — number of partisans, was increasingly desperate for resupply, and had seen no sight of the battlegroup from 373rd Division that was supposed to relieve it. In the late afternoon the order was given to fall back from the hill on which the Citadel lay and regroup in Drvar, particularly around the town's cemetery. Harassed by the partisans, the final paratroopers did not reach its foot until around 2200 hours and then headed for the town. Throughout the night the partisans launched several attacks against the cemetery, the last coming at dawn on the 26th. Daylight allowed the Luftwaffe to bomb and strafe the partisans, who gradually fell back, and saw the arrival of troops from the 13th Regiment of the 7th SS Mountain Division Prinz Eugen. The

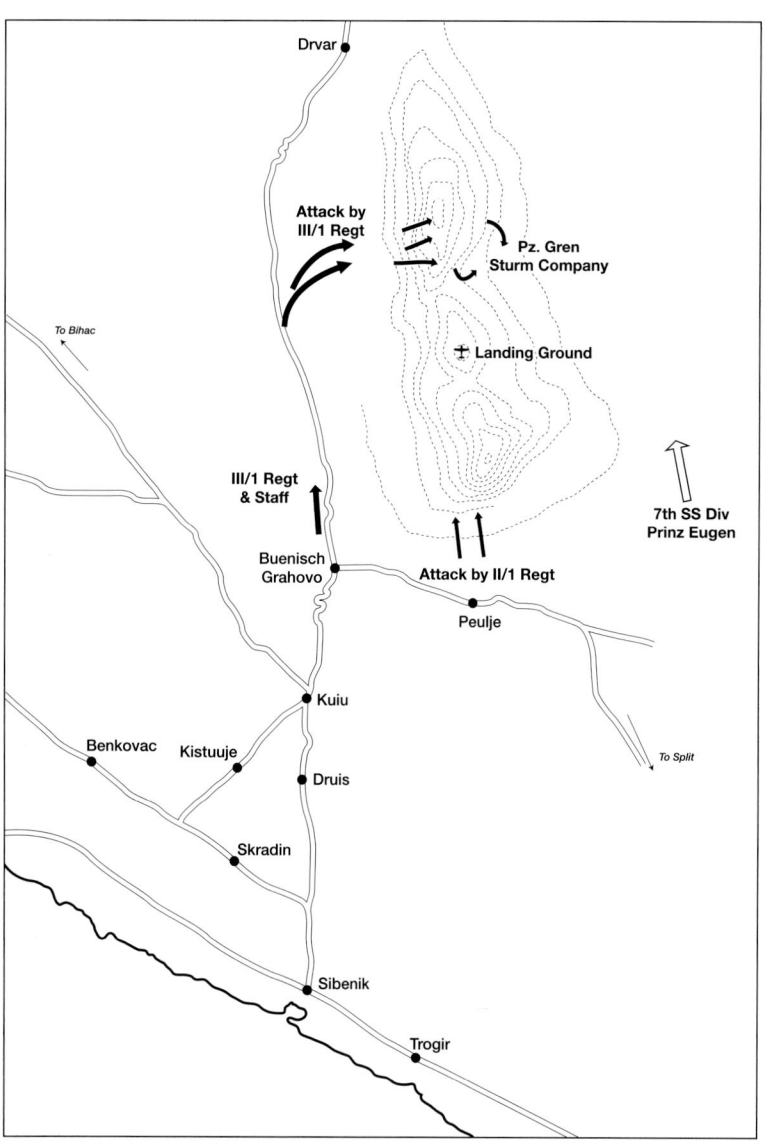

Below: Brandenburger movements during Operation 'Rösselsprung', May 1944.

paratroopers' ordeal was finally over but it was clear that their mission had failed; Tito, although slightly wounded, had escaped the trap and the parachute battalion had been effectively destroyed as a fighting force. It would be reconstituted but was ultimately destroyed fighting the Red Army on the Eastern Front.

OPERATION *'PANZERFAUST'* — SKORZENY IN HUNGARY

On 10 September 1944 Skorzeny attended various briefings at Rastenburg and in the evening attended an informal post-dinner conference with Hitler and a handful of of other leading Nazis. Talk drifted to discussion of the worsening situation along the whole length of the Eastern Front and the ongoing defection of Germany's eastern allies. The Soviet summer offensive had thrown the German forces out of western Russia and had reached the line of the Vistula River in Poland by August, while to the north Finland had agreed a truce with the Soviet Union on 4 September. In the Balkans, Romania was virtually overrun the Red Army; Bulgaria had defected from the Axis alliance on the 8th; Romania was about to fall to the Red Army after having capitulated on 23 August, and German troops in Greece and Yugoslavia were falling back to avoid encirclement in the southern Balkans. Hitler also suspected that Hungary was again looking for a way out of the war; he had already sent his troops into the country the previous March after intelligence reports had indicated that the Hungarian regent, Admiral Miklós Horthy, had contacted both the western Allies and the Soviet Union to discuss armistice terms. Although Horthy had been browbeaten by the German occupation, by September Soviet forces were arrayed on the east Hungarian border and the regent was again sending out peace feelers. Hitler, who feared the loss of Hungary's oilfields and grain supplies as well as the possible cutting off of 70 divisions fighting in the Balkans, correctly suspected that Horthy was again contemplating secret discussions with the Allies and ordered Skorzeny to prepare a mission to install a pliant puppet regime to ensure that Hungary would go on fighting.

Below: SS-Sturmbannführer Otto Skorzeny and SS-Obersturmführer Adrian von Foelkersam shown in Budapest in October 1944 after Operation *'Panzerfaust'*. *Bundesarchiv*

What Hitler had suspected in that September discussion with Skorzeny was confirmed on 15 October, when Horthy made a radio broadcast to the Hungarian people announcing that a preliminary armistice had been agreed with the Soviet Union four days before. The takeover operation had been devised in the immediate aftermath of the Rastenburg meeting. Travelling incognito as a Doctor Wolf, Skorzeny arrived in Budapest on 12 September and quickly discovered that the chief Hungarian negotiator was the regent's own son, Niklas, and that he had regular meetings with Yugoslavian intermediaries selected by Marshal Tito. Skorzeny, who had infiltrated some of his own men into the capital, decided to aid the Gestapo by capturing Niklas Horthy the next time he met the Yugoslavians in Budapest. If Niklas Horthy were in German custody, Skorzeny reasoned, his father might break off the armistice negotiations. The plan, was codenamed 'Mickey Mouse' and, after one aborted attempt, finally took place on 15 October. Skorzeny's company waited in a side street close to the building where the meeting was to take place, while he parked his car in the square on which the target stood. Gestapo officers were already in the building, on the floor above the meeting room, and others were to enter from the square shortly

Above: Belgrade is liberated by the partisans on 20 October 1944 — the name derived from the *partidas*, Spanish guerrilla bands that had harassed Napoleon during his invasions of Spain and Russia. Their importance to the Allied cause cannot be overlooked. In 1943, at a time when two German divisions were defending Sicily against the combined might of Britain and the United States, seven German divisions were being mauled by Tito's partisans. It is unsurprising, therefore, that the Germans spent so much time trying to kill Tito. *TRH Pictures*

Right: The German retreat from Greece and the Balkans in 1944.

Left: Tito (1892–1980) was born Josip Broz, the son of a Croatian blacksmith. He fought in Russia with the Austro-Hungarian army in World War I and then served with distinction in the Red Army during the Russian civil war of 1918–20. A prominent union organiser, he was imprisoned as a political agitator 1929–34, but in 1941 he emerged as a leader of the Yugoslav resistance after the defeat and occupation of Yugoslavia by the Axis powers. In spite of the opposition of the Yugoslav government in exile, which supported the Serbian resistance leader Mikailovich and his Chetniks, adopting the name Tito, Josip Broz welded together a force primarily of communists, although there were many non-communists, bedfellows in part because of the appeal of Tito's dream of a federated Yugoslavia but also because of Tito's character. Unknown at first to the outside world (partly because of Mikailovich), in 1941, when Hitler's forces took the Balkans, the head of the outlawed Communist Party of Yugoslavia was a shadowy figure; there was so much confusion about his identity that some people thought the name Tito stood for a terrorist organisation. On the ground, however, there was no doubt about who Tito was. A brilliant guerrilla tactician and a forceful, charismatic personality, by 1943 Tito headed a large army and controlled a sizable part of Yugoslavia, centred in Bosnia. He fought alongside his men supported from the start by the Soviet Union, and from 1944 by Britain and the United States. In November 1944 he liberated Belgrade. In March 1945 he became head of the new federal Yugoslav government, going on to execute Mikailovich, depose King Peter II, proclaim a republic and rule dictatorially until his death.

The Germans tried many times to kill Tito (including the Brandenburgers' attempt by Operation *'Rösselsprung'*): 'He was always encircled,' remarked Heinrich Himmler, 'and the man found a way out every time.' *TRH Pictures*

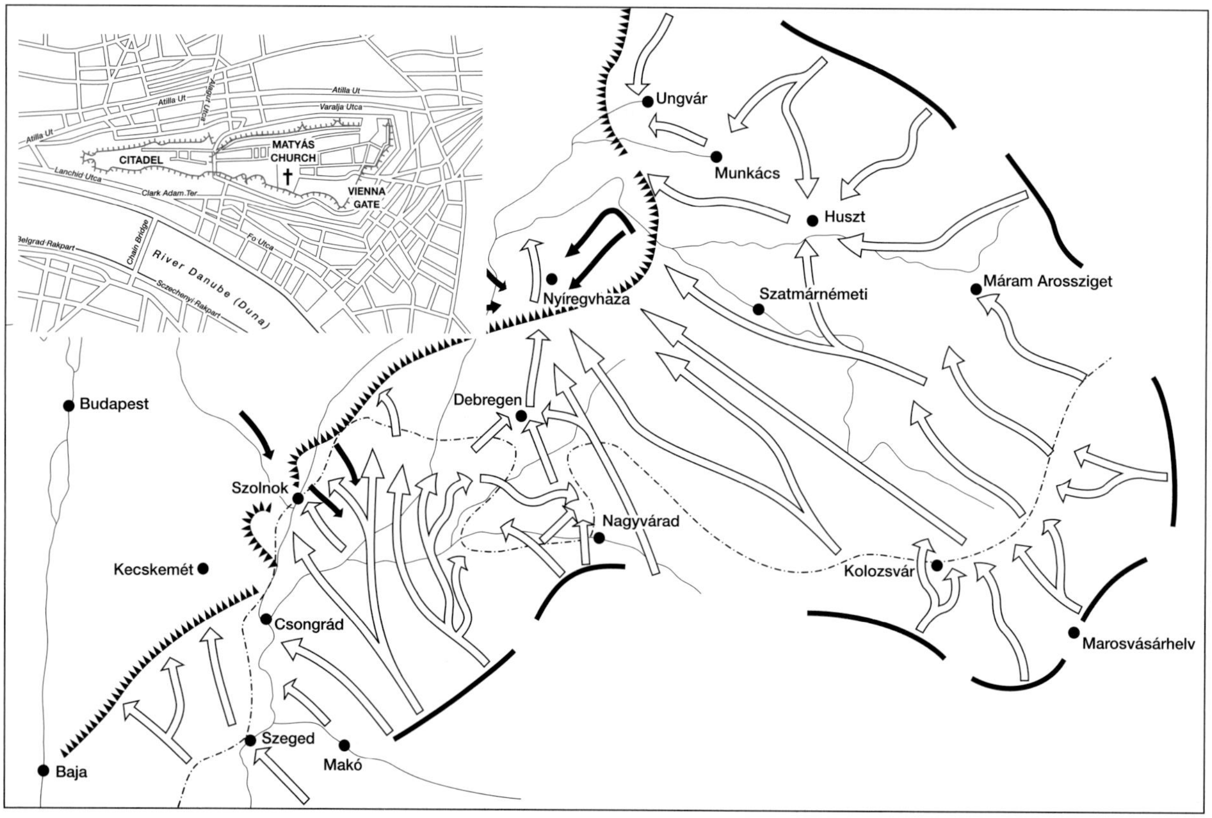

ELITE ATTACK FORCES: BRANDENBURGERS

after 1000 hours to make the arrests. The first Gestapo man entered on schedule but the second aroused the suspicion of the Hungarian guards parked outside the entrance and was shot. Skorzeny immediately went into action, calling for his detachment in the side-street to join him as a vicious but brief firefight broke out with Hungarian troops hidden in buildings along the sides of the square. As this ended the Gestapo men and Skorzeny brought Horthy and a second Hungarian conspirator out of the building wrapped in large rugs to hide their identity and bundled them into a truck. The captives were taken to a convenient airfield and flown out of Hungary to spend the remainder of the war as 'guests' of the Germans.

'Mickey Mouse' had taken just ten minutes and over the next few hours Skorzeny waited anxiously for the regent's reaction. It came later that afternoon, at 1400 hours, when Horthy made the radio announcement that revealed the ongoing peace negotiations with the Soviet Union and that hostilities would cease with immediate effect. Clearly Operation 'Mickey Mouse' had not had the desired result but Skorzeny responded rapidly. He contacted the recently arrived commander of the nearby German troops, SS Gen Erich von dem Bach-Zelewski, and persuaded him to throw a cordon around the strongly defended Castle Hill, the regent's official residence and location of many other government buildings. Bach-Zelewski, who had recently razed Warsaw to the ground, suggested that similar action against Budapest would bring the Hungarians to heel, but Skorzeny wanted a subtler approach. The general's troops were to surround Castle Hill and make obvious but leisurely moves to lay siege to the government complex. While the Hungarians were occupied by this ruse, he would launch a surgical strike to apprehend the regent with a small detachment. The operation was codenamed 'Panzerfaust' after the German single-shot disposable anti-tank rocket-launcher.

Skorzeny's main assault team, a mixture of Waffen-SS paratroopers and his own Mitte battalion, was supported by four Panther tanks and a number of Goliaths — remote-controlled tracked explosive devices that were to be used to clear any barricades (see pages 74–5).

At dawn the next day, Skorzeny's detachment formed up close to Castle Hill and then followed the winding road to the complex's Vienna Gate. The attack was supported by a battalion of naval cadets from the Wiener-Neustadt Kriegsakademie, which advanced though garden's on the citadel's southern slope, a platoon of Skorzeny's own Mitte battalion moved on the western side supported by a pair of Panthers, while a platoon of the 600th SS Parachute Battalion advanced through a tunnel to reach the Hungarian Ministries of War and Home Affairs. A Luftwaffe paratrooper battalion acted as a reserve. Skorzeny feared that mines might delay his progress but this proved unfounded as the Hungarians had removed them in an attempt to defuse the tense situation but the detachment reached the citadel without arousing undue suspicion and, crashing through a barricade, entered its central square. As a firefight developed, Skorzeny made his way to the commandant's office and demanded that he surrender the citadel immediately. Ten minutes later the sounds of battle died away, leaving German forces in charge of all of the main government buildings. Skorzeny discovered that the regent was already in the custody of SS Lt-Gen Karl Pfeffer-Wildenbruch. 'Panzerfaust' was a brilliant coup and cost the lives of just four German troops, with a further 12 men wounded. Hungarian casualties were equally low, just four dead and 12 wounded. The regent's abdication was swiftly announced and Skorzeny later accompanied him on the train journey that took him into German captivity. A new government under a pro-German prime minister, Count Szalasi, was formed. One of its first acts was to rescind the armistice proclamation, ensuring that Hungary remained in the Axis camp until the last days of the war.

Left: Waffen-SS troops — probably 7th SS Gebirgs Division Prinz Eugen — in Split after retaking the town from partisans in 1943. Note the ancient Renault R35 tanks. The fighting in Yugoslavia against Tito's partisans was tough, uncompromising and studded with atrocities.

Below left: The Russian troop positions at the time of 'Panzerfaust', and (inset) Castle Hill in Budapest.

BUDAPEST 1944
The scene of one of Skorzeny's most brilliant triumphs, the effect of Operation 'Panzerfaust' was only to delay the inevitable. The Russians were on the doorstep, and Hungary would fall to them, no matter who was in power. The Soviet army completed the encirclement of the city on Christmas Eve 1944. Up till then the city had survived the war largely intact: during the 108-day siege, most of it would be destroyed. Pest, on one side of the Danube, was liberated by Soviet troops first, on 14 January 1945, while Buda held out for another month against the Soviet advance. The taking of the Royal Castle and the caves beneath it was a massacre. When it was over, the population of Budapest had fallen to 833,000 some 28% less than in 1941. Only a quarter of the buildings were intact.

Above: The *leichter Ladungsträger* SdKfz 302/303 Goliath. See pages 74–5 for technical details. *IWM B5115*

Below: A Goliath team prepares to set their vehicle on its way. First the two-wheel trailer is detached. *via Chris Ellis*

OPERATION '*GREIF*' — SKORZENY AND THE BULGE

Skorzeny's stock was riding high with Hitler after the swoop on Budapest and the Führer summoned him to an awards' ceremony at Rastenburg, his headquarters hidden deep in the forest of East Prussia, on 22 October. The commando leader was raised to the rank of SS-Obersturmbannführer (lieutenant-colonel) and was also briefed on his part in the forthcoming Operation '*Wacht am Rhein*' ('Watch on the Rhine'), better known as the Battle of the Bulge. Hitler was planning an all-out blow against the Allies marshalled along the west German border and the plan was to deploy the best of his remaining troops in the wooded Ardennes, from where the fall of France in 1940 had been engineered, and unleash them against the understrength, green and exhausted US troops holding a sector of the front stretching from Monschau in Belgium southward to Echternach in Luxembourg. After the initial breakthrough, which it was hoped would drive a wedge between the US forces and the British to the north, the German spearhead was to swing to the northwest and strike out for Antwerp, the most important forward supply port held by the Allies. Crucial to the plan was the need to seize bridges over the River Meuse (Maas) between Liege and Namur and roughly half way between the first point of attack and final objective. Speed was of the essence and Hitler had devised a plan to take the bridges by subterfuge, by deploying a special unit of men with US equipment and wearing GI clothing. Skorzeny was informed that he had to raise and lead this new force, which was designated the 150th Panzer Brigade, and that it would be deployed on the northern wing of '*Wacht am Rhein*' as part of Gen Sepp Dietrich's Sixth SS Panzer Army. Hitler also stressed that the target bridges had to be secured no more than 24 hours after the opening of the offensive, which was initially scheduled for early December but was later pushed back to the 16th.

According to Hitler's original timetable Skorzeny had little more than five weeks to find sufficiently competent English speakers and train them for their part in 'Wacht am Rhein', which was codenamed Operation '*Greif*' (Griffon). Within a few days of the meeting, he sent Gen Alfred Jodl, chief of staff of the OKW, a list of his requirements, which included some 3,300 men to form the three battalions that would be the core of the 150th Panzer Brigade. OKW passed the request on to Oberkommando West (Ob West), the body responsible for the the conduct of the direct war in Western Europe, on 25 October and it in its turn sent the order down the chain of command to the various army groups in the theatre. In a worrying breach of security, the repeated requests sent to the army groups were intercepted by the Allies but it appears the information was not acted upon as their high command doubted that Germany was militarily capable of launching a major offensive on the Western Front.

Skorzeny soon became aware that little US equipment was finding its way to his new command and on 2 November he contacted Ob West's chief of staff, Lt-Gen Siegfried Westphal, to demand a greater effort. A week later Ob West sent out orders to the army groups under its command to provide the captured Allied uniforms, small arms, ammunition and heavier equipment that Skorzeny had requested, including 15 tanks, 20 self-propelled guns, 20 armoured cars, 120 trucks, 100 jeeps and 40 motorcycles. The operation to gather the war matériel was codenamed '*Rabenhügel*' (Raven's Hill) and each army group was allotted a particular quota of tanks and jeeps. Army Group B had to provide five tanks and 30 jeeps, Army Group G eight tanks and 20 jeeps and Army Group H two tanks and 50 jeeps. The equipment was supposed to be delivered to the panzer brigade's training base at Grafenwöhr but it quickly became apparent to Skorzeny that his targets were not being met. He complained to Ob West on the 21st but matters did not improve to any extent and he had to improvise by hastily transforming German equipment. The silhouettes of Panther tanks were modified by the addition of steel turret plates cut to give them the profile of US M10 tank-destroyers (see colour section, pages 70–1) but most of the other German heavy equipment received nothing more than an overall coat of US olive drab camouflage paint and the Allied white star recognition symbol stencilled to their superstructures. A report sent to Ob West in late November revealed that the 150th Panzer Brigade roster of equipment totalled just 57 jeeps, 74 trucks and two armoured cars, a third of which were in poor condition and needed overhauling by the unit's mechanics. Two Shermans had turned up but both proved unserviceable and, most bizarrely, Skorzeny also received considerable quantities of former Polish or Russian equipment. US uniforms also proved a problem as the brigade was short of 1,500 steel helmets and many of the uniforms were summer rather than winter issue.

Skorzeny was also having problems finding suitably qualified men to take on the role of US troops. Language experts scoured the German armed forces for suitable candidates but after two weeks their efforts were less than impressive. Ten men, mostly sailors, were discovered who had a high proficiency in American English and a good command of slang; 30 to 40 more were found to speak convincingly but had little or no knowledge of slang; around 150 men spoke English to an adequate degree, and some 200 had studied English at school during their youth. Skorzeny was dubious as to their value and later remarked that, 'In practice it meant that we might as well just mingle with the fleeing Americans and pretend to be too flurried and overcome to speak.'

The difficulties of locating suitable men and equipment impacted on Skorzeny's original mission for the panzer brigade and he had to scale down his plans: rather than having three battalions he would have to make do with just two. Each was supposed to

THE IMPACT OF *EINHEIT STIELAU*
It is difficult to assess the military value of the English-speaking *Stielau* detachments during the Battle of the Bulge. It seems that the scale of their operations has been exaggerated, partly because of Skorzeny's own embellishment of the facts and partly because nervous US troops frequently reported incursions by German soldiers that were subsequently attributed to *Stielau* groups. Equally an enemy soldier wearing partial US clothing was a not uncommon sight in the winter of 1944–45 due to the increasingly wretched and poorly quality uniforms provided, if at all, by German manufacturers. Skorzeny provided some details of *Stielau* activities but many other details are based on personal recollections from US soldiers and local civilians. For example, one Belgian civilian reported overhearing a German-speaking US officer at Lingueville on 16 December; the following day US Sgt Edward Keoghan reported being stuck in a traffic jam outside Malmédy and a conversation with a MP who stated that the roads signs had been switched to send US troops in the wrong direction; and Sgt John Myers recorded a *Stielau* team being killed at Poteau on the 18th after betraying themselves through their ignorance of the subtleties of US Army unit designations. One of the *Stielau* men claimed they were from Company E of a cavalry unit when in fact cavalry units used the term troop. It is also a matter of official record that one three-man team was captured at Aywaille on the 17th after giving the wrong password. In his own writing Skorzeny states that the last *Stielau* team was sent through US lines on the 19th after which they reverted to wearing German uniforms as the element of surprise had been lost.

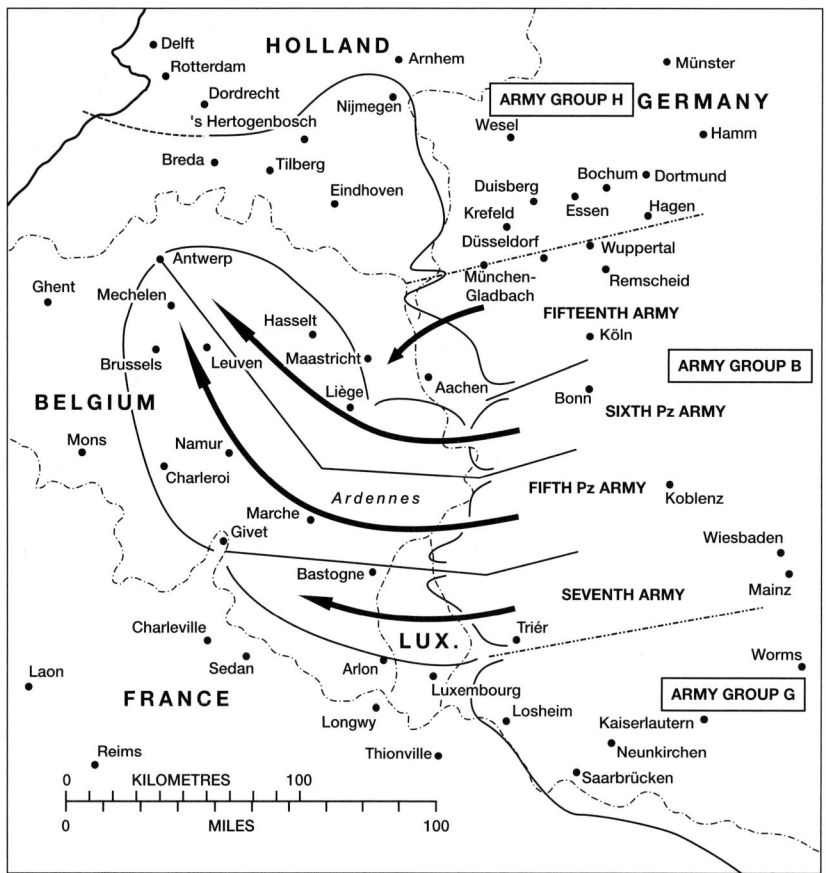

Above: Hitler's plan — push through the Ardennes to Brussels and Antwerp, split the Allied armies into two and finish them off individually.

Above right: Within a few hours of meeting Hitler on 22 October, Skorzeny sent Gen Alfred Jodl, chief of staff of the OKW, a list of his requirements. Jodl passed it down the chain of command on 25 October and did little to pursue the matter. The result was that Skorzeny had nowhere near sufficient men, vehicles or supplies to undertake his mission. *via George Forty*

Below right: On 2 November Skorzeny contacted Ob West's chief of staff, Lt-Gen Siegfried Westphal seen here in the Western desert, to demand a greater effort. It took a week before Ob West sent out orders that Skorzeny should be provided with the equipment he had requested. By this time there was absolutely no chance that he would be able to complete his mission. *via George Forty*

consist of four infantry companies, a company of armoured cars, a single AA platoon and a company of tanks. The 1st Battalion was allocated 22 PzKpfw V Panthers, and an additional company of Panzergrenadiers, while the 2nd Battalion was to be provided with 14 StuG IIIs. Additional units attached to the brigade also included a company of engineers, bridge-building detachments and a battery of self-propelled guns. However, It soon became apparent that even these plans were overly ambitious and at the last minute Skorzeny was again forced to reorganise the men and equipment he had available. Finally assembled at Grafenwöhr were 2,500 troops, some 1,200 from the army, 800 from Luftwaffe ground units and 500 from the Waffen-SS — a total of 800 men short of his original figure — and the organisation of the brigade was modified for the second time, resulting in three battle groups. SS Lt-Col Willi Hardieck took charge of Kampfgruppe X, Kampfgruppe Y was placed under Capt Scherff, and Kampfgruppe Z devolved to Lt-Col Wolf. In their final form each battle group comprised three infantry companies, two panzergrenadier platoons, two mortar platoons along with engineer, signals and mechanical detachments. Kampfgruppen X and Y also received additional armour in the shape of five Panthers modified to look like M10s and five StuG III assault guns respectively. Each battle group was assigned to one of the main assault divisions of Dietrich's Sixth SS Panzer Army.

The shortage of top-grade English speakers had also resulted in a rethink. The best were formed into a commando detachment known as *Einheit Stielau* (Unit Stielau), which would be the most 'American' of Skorzeny's forces, but as none of these recruits had any experience of such missions, all had to undergo a period of brief but intensive training in explosive and radio transmission as well as learning about US rank badges and drill. Some were sent to prisoner of war camps at Küstrin and Limburg to improve their English and get up to speed on US slang. *Einheit Stielau* was split into several small detachments each with a specific task. Some were formed into teams of five or six to carry out sabotage missions against ammunition depots, bridges and fuel dumps; others, usually three or four men in jeeps, were to head for the Meuse to reconnoitre the way forward and at the same time spread alarm and confusion among US units they met. Finally, detachments of three to four men were assigned individually to the divisions for which the panzer brigade was acting as a spearhead. Their chief role was to undermine the US command structure by destroying radio stations, issuing false orders and severing telephone wires.

As the date for Operation '*Wacht am Rhein*' approached, Skorzeny finally revealed the brigade's role to his three battle group commanders on 10 December. He stated that they had to take intact at least two of three bridges over the Meuse at Amay, Andenne and Huy. In the first hours of the attack they were to keep pace with but travel slightly behind the leading elements of the main assault divisions to preserve the special unit's anonymity until they had reached an area known as the Hohes Venn — a line running approximately southwest to northeast centred on the small town of Spa about 20 miles (32km) from their start point around Losheim and a similar distance from the Meuse to the northwest. Once the Hohes Venn had been reached the three groups were to strike out on their own along parallel routes and, travelling under cover of darkness, reach the bridges within six hours. Skorzeny stressed that to ensure the success of the operation Hohes Venn had to be reached on the first day of 'Wacht am Rhein' and the bridges secured early on the second.

Shortly after this briefing the brigade moved out of its camp at Grafenwöhr and, travelling only at night to avoid detection, arrived at Münstereifel on 14 December. Two days later the offensive opened at 0530 hours and the three Kampfgruppen advanced in conjunction with the lead elements of three divisions of Gen Hermann Priess's 1st SS Panzer Corps — Brig Wilhelm Mohnke's 1st SS Panzer Division Leibstandarte Adolf Hitler, the 12th SS Panzer Division Hitlerjugend and the 12th Volksgrenadier Division — to which they had been attached. Skorzeny accompanied his brigade's Kampfgruppe X, which was detailed to operate with a battle group under Lt-Col Jochen Peiper drawn from the Leibstandarte. The attack called for the utmost speed yet quickly became bogged down due to the appalling weather and the area's poor roads and weak bridges that could not cope with the mass of vehicles that the German were trying to pass down them. The greatest bottleneck was around the Losheim Gap, virtually on the offensive's startline, and it was here also that Kampfgruppe X suffered the loss of its commander, Hardieck, who fell victim to a mine. His replacement was

Above: A PzKpfw V Panther tank tries to get past a column of halftracks in the snowclad Ardennes, higlighting vividly the chaos resulting from traffic congestion. In the end a combination of lack of men and equipment, chronic traffic jams and bad weather meant that Panzer Brigade 150 was forced to fight in a conventional role. *RAC Tank Museum via George Forty*

Above right: The Brandenburgers' war in the west had started with the Meuse (Maas) bridges in 1940: the bridges were also the intended targets for Skorzeny's commandos during the Battle of the Bulge. This map, based on one produced by the air reconnaissance office, shows the information about the bridges known to the Germans on 12 December — the dates identify the most recent photos available. When Hitler briefed Skorzeny he emphasised the need to seize bridges between Liege and Namur.

a former Brandenburg officer and Knight's Cross holder, Baron Adrian von Foelkersam, now a captain in the Waffen-SS. Matters did not improve over the next few hours and it was rapidly becoming clear to Skorzeny that the collapse of the original timetable was critically undermining Operation '*Greif*'. He might have had an even gloomier prognosis of the deteriorating situation if he had been aware that key documents relating to '*Greif*' had been captured near Heckhuscheid by elements of the US 7th Armored Division.

Skorzeny acted to retrieve the situation during a night meeting on the 17th at the headquarters of the SS Sixth Panzer Army. He asked for, and was granted, permission to reform his three scattered battle groups as a single force and attach them to the 1st SS Panzer Division, which was currently headquartered at Ligneuville. The 150th Panzer Brigade was ordered to assemble there and participate in the division's general attack towards the still-distant Meuse. Its chief objective was to take Malmédy, a key position where two roads, one running north–south and the other east–west, met. Capture of the small town a few miles to the north of Ligneuville would threaten the western flank of the divisions of Maj-Gen Leonard Gerow's USV Corps holding the Elsenborn Ridge to the east that were blocking the advance of the Hitlerjugend and also aid Kampfgruppe Peiper, which was struggling to maintain the momentum on its assigned route of advance some way to the south of Malmédy. Skorzeny planned his assault on the basis that Malmédy was weakly held — one of his commando teams had briefly entered the village during the 17th to discover its defenders were just a few US engineers — but did not know that the position had later received reinforcements in the shape of the US 30th Infantry Division's 120th Infantry Regiment and the 99th Infantry Battalion. To Skorzeny's annoyance he had to draw up a plan of attack on 20 December on the basis that his Kampfgruppe Z would not reach the brigade's two other battle groups in time because of the clogged roads. Consequently only Kampfgruppe X, attacking from

IN ACTION

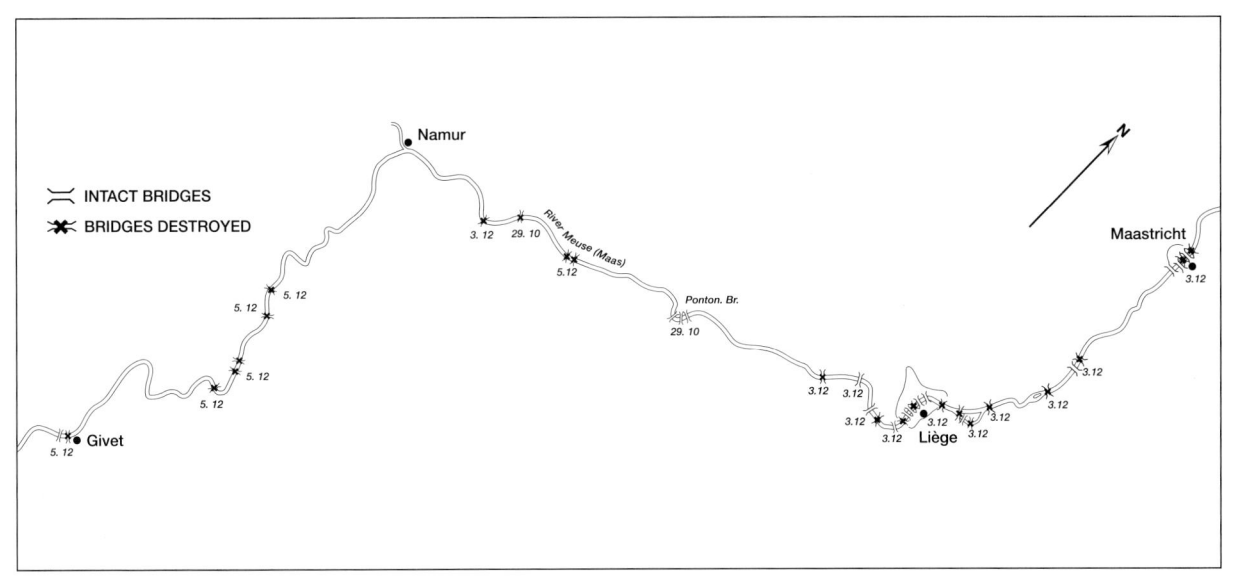

150th PANZER BRIGADE DECEMBER 1944

Brigade HQ ──── **Einheit Stielau**
(SS-Obersturmbannführer Otto Skorzeny)   detachments

Kampfgruppe X
(SS-Obersturmbannführer Willi Hardieck
then SS-Hauptsturmführer Adrian von Foelkersam)

- 1 x Panzer Company (5 x PzKpfw V Panthers)
- 3 x Infantry Companies
- 2 x Panzergrenadier Platoons
- 2 x Anti-Tank Platoons
- 2 x Heavy Mortar Platoons
- 2 x Engineer Platoons
- 1 x Signals Platoon

Kampfgruppe Y
(Capt Scherff)

- 1 x Panzer Company (5 x Sturmgeschütz III)
- 3 x Infantry Companies
- 2 x Panzergrenadier Platoons
- 2 x Anti-Tank Platoons
- 2 x Heavy Mortar Platoons
- 2 x Engineer Platoons
- 1 x Signals Platoon

Kampfgruppe Z
(Lt-Col Wolf)

- 3 x Infantry Companies
- 2 x Panzergrenadier Platoons
- 2 x Anti-Tank Platoons
- 2 x Heavy Mortar Platoons
- 1 x Engineer Platoon
- 1 x Signals Platoon

Above: A Sturmgeschütz III of Kampfgruppe Y, abandoned beside the N32 at Géromont. Pictured on 15 January, while US troops remove a booby trap, note the Allied markings. *US Army*

Above right: GIs of 393rd Infantry Regiment, 99th Infantry Division, digging in on Elsenborn Ridge on 19 December – before the snows came – and came – and came! *US Army via George Forty*

Below right: Sturmgeschütz III — Kampfgruppe Y had five that went into action on the 21st, running into the 120th Infantry on the N32. *via George Forty*

Below: One of Kampfgruppe X's five disguised Panthers. *La Gleize Museum*

Ligneuville, and Kampfgruppe Y, pushing on Malmédy from Baugnez, were committed to the pincer attack. The third battle group would be held in reserve if it arrived in time. The advance was scheduled to begin early on the 21st and Skorzeny hoped that speed and surprise would make up for his unit's depleted strength and lack of heavy artillery. Once again, as at Heckhuscheid, his plans were compromised when one of his men was captured on the afternoon of the 20th and revealed that Malmédy was earmarked for attack the next day.

Kampfgruppe Y moved off from Baugnez under cover of night early on the 21st, advancing down one of the region's better roads, the N32, but soon ran into the alert outposts of the US 120th Infantry Regiment. Hit by tremendous artillery fire the group's attack stalled and it soon withdrew back to its start line. Kampfgruppe X, which was led by five disguised Panthers and two infantry companies, moved forward from Ligneuville along the Route de Falize and, after passing through Bellevaux, ran into positions held by the 120th's 3rd Battalion to the west of Malmédy at 0430 hours. The battle group now split in two. The greater part turned left and advanced down a small road that led to a bridge over the Warche River, while the smaller portion pushed directly on to Malmédy along the Route de Falize. The troops heading for the bridge set off US-laid trip wires that sent illuminating flares into the dark sky, revealing the silhouettes of the accompanying Panthers. The tanks immediately opened fire but US tank destroyers, firing from the cover of a house close to the bridge, checked the German armour. The accompanying panzergrenadiers made a rush for the house but the 30 men inside, members of the 291st Engineers and Company K, 120th Regiment, beat them off after a vicious close-quarters firefight. However, the attack on the house allowed the Panthers to resume their advance and one gained a position on the bridge where it was able to kill the crews of the US tank destroyers. As the battle around the Warche bridge developed, the other element of the battle group was facing an equally tough struggle. Led toward Malmédy by its own Panthers, the remainder of Kampfgruppe X was halted by a minefield sown at the foot of a railway embankment. One of the tanks soon brewed up and the accompanying panzergrenadiers launched several unsuccessful attacks to dislodge the defenders, Company B of the US 99th Infantry Battalion. The fight ebbed and flowed but the German troops were finally forced to retire under a heavy barrage from US artillery based on high ground to the north of the Werthe river. Using shells fitted with the newly developed proximity fuse set to airburst, they caused several casualties among the panzergrenadiers.

By around 1030 hours the early morning fog that had clouded the two battlefields around Malmédy cleared, allowing the US forces at the Warche bridge and on the railway embankment to see each other for the first time. Aided by the clearer weather the US artillery continued its deluge of shells, firing some 3,000 rounds by the time the action ebbed away over the next few hours. The Panther holding the bridge was destroyed and the others found it impossible to make any headway. Skorzeny, watching the deteriorating situation from high ground on the Route de Falize, saw that the game

Right: It is easy with hindsight to write off the Ardennes offensive as the squandering of German reserves that would have been better spent in defence of the Reich. Indeed, the Battle of the Bulge took the eyes away from the vicious battles going on in the Hürtgen Forest — attritional warfare that favoured the defenders. Nevertheless, counterattack was part of German military doctrine, and there was no doubting the quality of their troops nor their commitment to the cause — as evinced by this group. It is a well-known, probably posed, photograph from a sequence showing troops from the 2nd Company, SS-Panzergrenadier Regiment 1. *US Army*

Opposite, Above: The confusion created by the 'Greif' teams was widespread and far reaching: everyone took much more care to identify units and individuals when they could. Here US 84th Infantry Division MPs check vehicles at the Baillonville crossroads in Marche, Belgium. *US Army via TRH Pictures*

Opposite, Below: In the end the offensive simply dissipated Germany's meagre resources and hastened the end of the war. *US Army*

Below: This photograph shows two German soldiers looting dead US troops (note the lack of boots on corpse at left). *US Army*

IN ACTION

was up and the surviving Panthers were ordered to cover the withdrawal of the panzergrenadiers. By mid-afternoon Kampfgruppe X was back at the start point on the high ground south of the Werthe with its commander, Foelkersam, nursing a painful wound in his posterior. Skorzeny had also been wounded by a shell splinter that caught him in the face as he returned to the Leibstandarte's headquarters at Ligneuville to discuss the deteriorating situation at Malmédy. The wounds inflicted on Skorzeny and Foelkersam did not prevent one final push on Malmédy by Kampfgruppe Y in the early hours of the 22nd but the advance soon bogged down in the face of resistance from the 120th Regiment. Members of the 291st Engineers also added to the difficulties facing the attackers by blowing the Warche bridge as well as a rail bridge over the N32, which severed the main road east of Malmédy, and a second railway bridge that crossed the Route de Falize. Skorzeny returned to the battlefront on the 23rd after having had his wound dressed but quickly recognised that the Meuse bridges were permanently beyond the reach of his battered command, particularly as Allied reinforcements were being rushed to the area.

The panzer brigade's involvement in *'Wacht am Rhein'* ended when it was relieved by the 18th Volksgrenadier Division

Key players in the Ardennes in 1944:

Opposite, Above right: SS-Gruppenführer Hermann Priess commanded Ist SS Panzer Corps, to which Skorzeny's *Kampfgruppen* were attached.

Left and Below: Two photographs of Joachim 'Jochen' Peiper. The first (**Left**) shows him as an SS-Sturmbannführer at Kursk in 1943 while commanding the IIIrd Battalion of Leibstandarte's 2nd SS Panzergrenadier Regiment in one of the crucial Eastern Front battles. In the other, autumn 1944, photograph (**Below**) he has been promoted to SS-Obersturmbannführer. He wears a black SS Panzer uniform and a Knight's Cross with Oakleaves. Note the 'Leibstandarte' cuff title. Kampfgruppe X was detailed to operate with a Leibstandarte battle group under Peiper. *TRH Pictures*

Opposite, above left and Below left: SS-Obergruppenführer und Gen der Waffen-SS 'Sepp' Dietrich, commander of Sixth SS Panzer Army. He is seen here wearing the Waffen-SS winter dress and his Knight's Cross with Oakleaves. He would go on to become one of only two members of the Waffen-SS to be awarded the Diamonds to add to the Oakleaves and Swords. A rough, tough 'bully boy', who lacked military knowledge, he was nevertheless a brave and fearless individual, much respected by his troops. *RAC Tank Museum via George Forty*

on the 28th and pulled back to Schlierback to the east of St Vith. It then moved by train to Grafenwöhr and was disbanded with the troops being returned to their original units by 23 January 1945. Skorzeny's force had had a brief existence, little more than three months, and had been in action for just under two weeks. It had a casualty rate of around 15 percent, mostly victims of Allied artillery strikes or the air attacks that intensified once the low cloud over the battle area began dispersing on the 23rd. The deception plan had involved several groups of men dressed in US uniforms and the last of these penetrated behind Allied lines on 19 December after which the element of surprise had been lost, the opposing US units alerted and the remainder reverted to wearing German uniforms. It is difficult to quantify the impact of '*Greif*' as much of the evidence is anecdotal. The teams undoubtedly added to the panic and uncertainty that gripped some US forces in the first days of the offensive and the rumour that their actual target was Eisenhower did restrict the Allied supreme commander's freedom of action as security was built up around him. The man who had started this rumour, L/Cpl Wilhelm Schmidt, was captured at Aywaille on 17 December with the two other members of a *Einheit Stielau* commando group, Oberfähnrich Günther Billing and Cpl Manfred Pernass, after failing to provide the right password. After a military trial, the three men were shot by

ELITE ATTACK FORCES: BRANDENBURGERS

Above: The end of the 'Bulge'. A column of German prisoners passing a US Third Army tank. *US Army via George Forty*

Above left: A Tiger II passes a long line of Americans taken prisoner at the start of the offensive. *US Army via George Forty*

Left: American generals gather at 12th Army Group headquarters, Bad Wildungan, Germany, 12 May 1945. Gen Dwight D. Eisenhower, with some of his most senior American generals including, front row left to right, William H. Simpson (CG US Ninth Army), George S. Patton, Jr (CG US Third Army), Carl A. Spaatz (CG USATAF), Eisenhower (Supreme Commander), Omar N. Bradley (CG 12th Army Group), Courtney M. Hodges (CG US First Army), Leonard T. Gerow (CG US Fifteenth Army). It was Gerow's V Corps that held the Elsenborn Ridge and bore the brunt of the attack by Kampfgruppe Peiper and the Hitlerjugend Division. *US Army via George Forty*

Right: The massacre of Malmédy is revealed. The events of 17 December 1944 would lead to a war crimes trial in which Skorzeny and his men were convicted but later acquitted. While there were undoubtedly premeditated atrocities during the Battle of the Bulge, it is difficult to say what triggered the events at Malmédy. *US Army via TRH Pictures*

firing squad on the 23rd at Henri-Chapelle (see photo on page 68) and their fate was shared by 15 other men of the *Stielau* teams, who were executed at either Henri-Chapelle or Huy.

SKORZENY'S LAST BATTLES

Germany's military situation deteriorated rapidly after the collapse of '*Wacht am Rhein*' but Skorzeny was still called on for special missions, although many of his forces were committed to conventional ground operations and would be bled white by the time of Germany's surrender. In January 1945 he sent several groups of Russian-speaking Germans and Russian turncoats deep behind the advancing Red Army to aid trapped German units attempting to reach friendly territory. Several teams were flown deep behind the Soviet lines into the western Soviet union in aircraft operated by KG 200, but most disappeared without trace and only one eventually linked up with a 2,000-strong group of troops from several units under the command of Lt-Col Scherhorn.

Skorzeny requested that Scherhorn make his way to some frozen lakes some 200 miles (320km) from Minsk, from where the trapped men could be airlifted to safety. It took Scherhorn several weeks to reach the lakes but there was no rescue as Germany lacked the aircraft and fuel to undertake such a long-range mission on the scale required.

At the end of January Skorzeny was ordered to assemble his forces around Schwedt on the Oder River to block the massive Soviet offensive toward Berlin. The fighting was vicious and consumed the greater part of his command by the end of February. As the Third Reich crumbled further in the final spring of the war Skorzeny returned to Berlin on 8 March and was ordered to destroy the Remagen bridge over the Rhine that had been captured by US troops the previous day. He immediately returned to Friedenthal and asked for volunteers from among the ranks of his Danube Frogman Group to destroy the bridge with explosive charges. They tried but failed with many dying from wounds or drowning after contracting frostbite in the bitterly cold waters of the Rhine.

Skorzeny was awarded the Knight's Cross with Oak Leaves in late March, when he spoke briefly to Hitler for the last time, and was then ordered to travel to Vienna to oversee the creation of the so-called Alpine Redoubt. The half-hearted scheme to establish this final centre of resistance was overtaken by Hitler's death and Germany's surrender, events that marked the end of the career of the 'most dangerous man in Europe' and Germany's special forces in World War II.

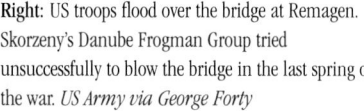

Right: US troops flood over the bridge at Remagen. Skorzeny's Danube Frogman Group tried unsuccessfully to blow the bridge in the last spring of the war. *US Army via George Forty*

Below: The 'Greif' commandos managed to create a good deal confusion and panic – but any Germans found driving jeeps could expect trouble. *US Signal Corps*

IN ACTION

INSIGNIA, CLOTHING & EQUIPMENT

Right: Tactical signs associated with the Brandenburgers: 1 Divisional Signals Battalion. 2 The sign of the Koenen Tropical Company. 3 Divisional vehicle marking combining Brandenburg eagle with Grossdeutschland Panzer Corps helmet. 4 Parachute Battalion.

Below right: The Brandenburgers and Skorzeny's SS commandos wore standard uniforms most of the time. Here Skorzeny sports the collar patches of an SS-Sturmbannführer; note the Nazi eagle and swastika badge worn by the SS on left upper arm; other uniformed bodies wore it on the left breast. *Bundesarchiv*

Below: Brandenburg Division cuff title.

Neither the Brandenburgers nor Skorzeny's various commands were notably different from other German units in terms of the uniforms worn or the equipment carried as standard. Most photographs of the Brandenburgers show them wearing standard army clothing and insignia. However, due to the nature of their more clandestine operations they did make use of unusual German equipment and clothing that was far from standard issue among the Wehrmacht.

BADGES AND INSIGNIA

The Brandenburgers and Skorzeny's units wore standard issue clothing and insignia, as would be found among regular army or Waffen-SS forces. When not wearing foreign military dress or civilian clothing, the Brandenburgers were remarkably similar to any other German soldier with the exception of a cuff title. This was worn on on the lower left sleeve of the tunic and consisted of a band of dark green cloth with silver-grey thread, which was used for piping above and below the title *Brandenburg* rendered in gothic script. The title was worn throughout the war and Brandenburgers were still identifiable as such even when incorporated into the Grossdeutschland Panzer Corps in the final part of the war. The Panzergrenadier Division Brandenburg also had a distinctive field sign That was painted on to vehicles. This comprised a stylised eagle, the emblem of Brandenburg, superimposed on a white M1943 helmet shown in profile — the field sign of the Grossdeutschland Division. By linking the two insignia it indicated that the Panzergrenadier Division Brandenburg was part of the Grossdeutschland Panzer Corps.

INSIGNIA, CLOTHING & EQUIPMENT

1

2

3

4

Right: Captured Germans (in this case probably *Greif* commandos) in Allied uniforms could well be shot as spies. *IWM PL 68548*

Below: American MPs tie Unteroffizier Manfred Pernass to the execution stake at Henri-Chapelle at dawn on 23 December 1944. Pernass and two other members of Skorzeny's *Einheit Stielau* – Oberfähnrich Günther Billing and Corporal Wilhelm Schmidt – were captured together wearing US Army uniforms and were subsequently executed together.
US Army via TRH Pictures

CLOTHING

There was nothing especially unique or unusual about the uniforms wore by either the Brandenburgers or Skorzeny's special forces. As is often the case, there was probably some relaxing of the strict dress regulations that were adhered to in more conventional units. There was undoubtedly greater variety in the case of the various Brandenburger detachments, some of which wore German paratrooper kit, tropical issue uniforms and clothing associated with mountain units. In general a detachment's specialisation, mission or area of operation would determine what clothing was appropriate. On Leros in late 1943 the Brandenburger paratroopers wore Luftwaffe tropical kit, while anti-partisan groups in the Balkans were seen in the cold-weather uniforms normally associated with mountain and Jäger units.

One area in which both the Brandenburgers and Skorzeny's forces were virtually unique during World War II was in the wearing of enemy uniforms, particularly in the case of the former, when conducting combat missions. Between 1939 and 1942 the Brandenburgers certainly wore them in Poland, Denmark, the Low Countries, North Africa and the Soviet Union and may have done so in the Balkans, but thereafter this ruse appears to have been little used by them. Skorzeny's men mostly famously wore foreign uniforms in one operation, that of the 150th Panzer Brigade and the *Stielau* detachment during Operation '*Wacht am Rhein*' in late 1944, but undoubtedly wore the military uniforms of other states as well as civilian clothes. Skorzeny himself went undercover during Operation '*Panzerfaust*' in 1944 and in his memoirs he records his troops wearing both Hungarian and civilian dress in the final weeks of the war.

Uniforms were sourced in several ways. The Brandenburgers bought Dutch uniforms in second-hand shops or made use of supplies captured by the Finns from the Red Army during the Winter War of 1939–40, while Skorzeny's forces in the Ardennes simply wore uniforms found in captured US supply dumps by other German troops. In the Brandenburgers' case the deceptions were mostly successful and for Skorzeny's men rather less so. It is wrong to believe that wearing the enemy's uniform effectively makes the wearer liable to summary execution. This is not the case in military law as a soldier may wear a captured uniform but only becomes liable to summary justice if he fights in it. Evidence indicates that at least on some occasions, Brandenburgers took off enemy greatcoats and headgear before going into action in the German uniforms worn beneath, but it seems equally likely that they also fought in partial or total enemy kit. We also know that Skorzeny's men in the Ardennes wore partial or complete US uniforms. The subtlties of this fine distinction in international military law were often lost in the heat of battle or simply unknown to ordinary front-line soldiers. It is well documented that 18 of the *Stielau* detachment were captured, tried and executed by firing squad for wearing US uniforms, although doubts have been cast over the legitimacy of the court's decision as it seems that in certain cases the men had not used their weapons. Nevertheless, German special forces captured in complete enemy uniforms were treated as spies and therefore liable for the death penalty.

The Brandenburgers and Skorzeny's commandos had very little specialised equipment. However, in the Ardennes in December 1944 Panzer Brigade 150 was intended to be equipped with Allied vehicles. In the event these proved difficult to get hold of; indeed, Skorzeny's intended allocation of 15 tanks, 20 SP guns and 20 armoured cars ended up being five Sturmgeschütz IIIs with Allied markings and five PzKpfw V Panthers made to look like Allied M10 tank destroyers by the addition of sheets of armour plate — as illustrated in this artwork which has been given US 10th Tank Battalion, 5th Armored Division markings.

INSIGNIA, CLOTHING & EQUIPMENT

Above: This Panther/M10 – coded 'B10' – shows how well disguised they were by use of appliqué plates, track links and Allied markings. *La Gleize Museum*

Below: 'B5' with 10th Tank Battalion, 5th Armored Division markings was knocked out by Sergeant Francis Currey who was awarded the Medal of Honor for his bravery on 21 December. *La Gleize Museum*

WEAPONS AND EQUIPMENT

Both Skorzeny's men and the Brandenburgers were generally lightly equipped for their operations and the small arms and few heavier support weapons they used on the majority of their missions were little different from the standard issue found in more conventional units. During their early spearhead missions between 1939 and 1942 the Brandenburgers went into action with nothing more than small arms and grenades, while Skorzeny's men appear to have been increasingly equipped with heavier machine

guns and mortars, as was the case with the 500th SS Parachute Battalion during its raid on Tito's headquarters during 1944. As the Brandenburgers expanded, they, too, received heavier equipment. In 1944, for example, the 3rd Battalion of the division's 2nd Regiment formed a light gun company. The Panzergrenadier Division *Brandenburg* was, of course, much more heavily equipped, including tanks and self-propelled guns, although it is doubtful that it ever fought at full strength given the parlous nature of Germany's armed forces in the final stages of the war.

Both the Brandenburgers and Skorzeny received items of foreign equipment. There is little firm evidence, but its seems like that they on occasion fought with the enemy's small arms. This was undoubtedly the case with Skorzeny's *Stielau* detachments during the Battle of the Bulge as these English-speaking units needed enemy small arms to complete their disguise as US troops. It is much more certain that they both regularly used foreign transport as seen by the Brandenburgers' use of Red Army trucks on the Eastern Front during 1941 and 1942 and Skorzeny's deployment of dozens of US jeeps during Operation '*Wacht am Rhein*'. The use of heavier vehicles, tanks and the like, is more debatable. All that can be said for sure is that Skorzeny tried to get US armour for Operation '*Greif*' but little was provided — just two unreliable Shermans that were not taken into action. If Skorzeny required heavier equipment for a mission it was usually provided by other units in his area of operations as was the case with the handful of Panther tanks that served under him during the coup in Budapest.

Occasionally the German special forces did receive items of equipment that were at the cutting edge of World War II technology. One of the best examples was the deployment of the Goliath during Operation '*Panzerfaust*'. This was a small tracked explosive device with the rhomboid profile of a World War I British tank (see pages 74–5). The device was powered by a petrol or electric engine and steered to its target by a trailing wire. Once the objective had been reached, the Goliath's 200lb (90kg) explosive charge could be detonated by remote control. It had a range of approximately 700 yards (640m) and a top speed under ideal conditions of around 10mph (16kph). The Goliath was not a great success. Its lack of range, slow speed and high profile meant that many were knocked out before reaching their intended target. During '*Panzerfaust*' Skorzeny intended to use the Goliath company attached to his command to destroy barricades but it seems they were not need as the faster-moving tanks could destroy or crush the obstacles more quickly.

Both the Brandenburgers and Skorzeny's men did make considerably more use of aircraft in their operations than conventional units. Among the types used were the Fieseler Fi156 *Storch* (Stork), a small short take-off and landing aircraft normally used for reconnaissance work and the transport of generals on the battlefield, but also deployed by Skorzeny to whisk Mussolini away from Gran Sasso in 1943. Normally carrying a pilot and passenger, the Stork entered service in 1937 and some 2,550 were produced. It had a top speed of around 110mph (176kph) and a range of 230 miles (368km).

Gliders were also deployed by the special forces, most commonly the DFS 230. Produced by the German Research Institute for Gliding, this was a fabric-covered machine with a tubular fuselage. It carried a pilot, co-pilot and 10 troops or one ton of equipment. The troops sat astride a wooden bench down the centre of the fuselage when in flight and deployed through two doors, one port and one starboard, on landing. The pilot and co-pilot exited through the removable forward perspex windscreen. The DFS 230 could be towed at a maximum speed of 100mph (160kph), usually by Junkers Ju52 transports, and once released descended at a rate of around 240ft (75m) per minute, although the special forces often approached the landing zone at a much steeper angle for a shorter landing, as Skorzeny did during the Mussolini rescue mission. The

PREVENTING FRIENDLY FIRE DURING 'WACHT AM RHEIN'

As both the men and equipment of the 150th Panzer Brigade and the *Einheit Stielau* were disguised entirely — or at least in part — to represent the US Army, Skorzeny recognised that there was a real danger of his units being fired on by their own side as their missions placed them at the leading edge of the attack and even behind the front line. He attempted to minimise this risk in a number of ways. First, Skorzeny's men were ordered to paint white dots on objects such as houses and trees to mark their route so that follow-on forces would know that somewhere in front of them were units belong to Skorzeny's command. Second, the vehicles used in Operation '*Greif*' were marked by a small yellow triangle at the rear as a field recognition signal. Third, while on the move and not in action his armoured vehicles, tanks and the like, were to keep their guns pointing in a particular direction. Fourth, the men were to wear pink-red or blue scarves and quickly remove their steel helmets if they made contact with German forces. Finally, torches fitted with red or blue filters were to be flashed as a means of identification at night.

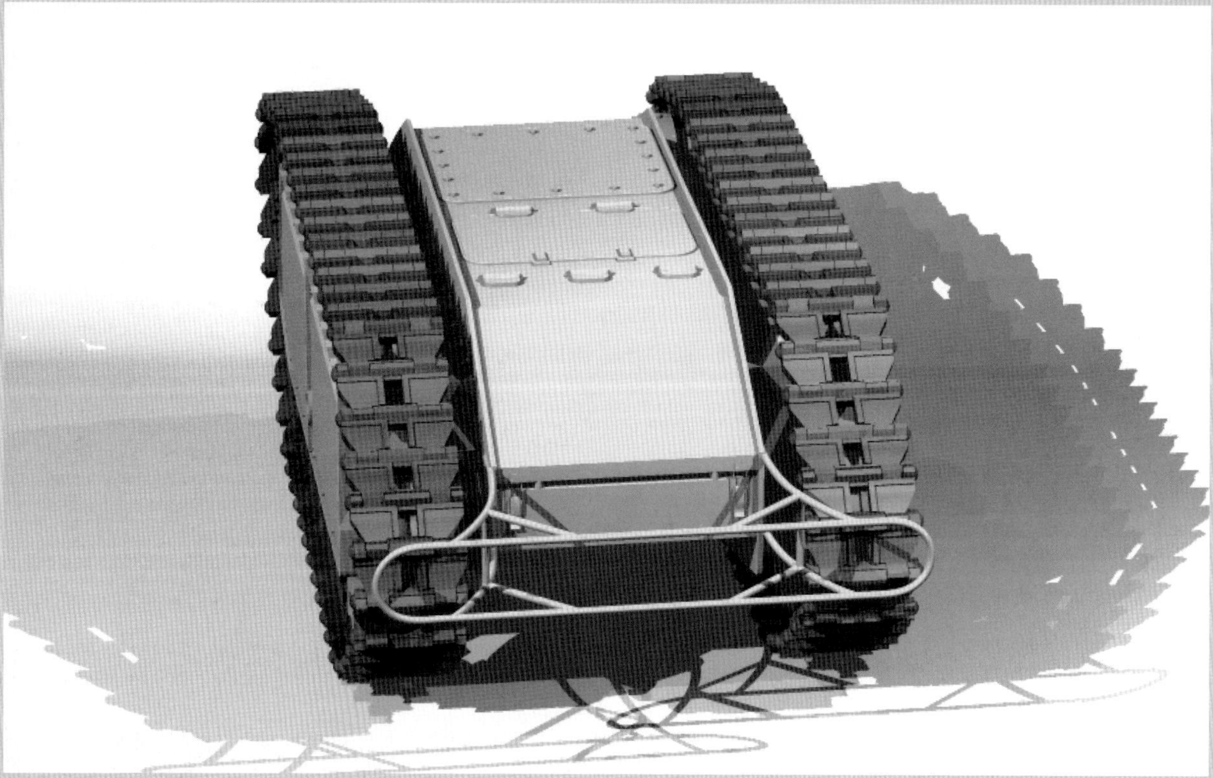

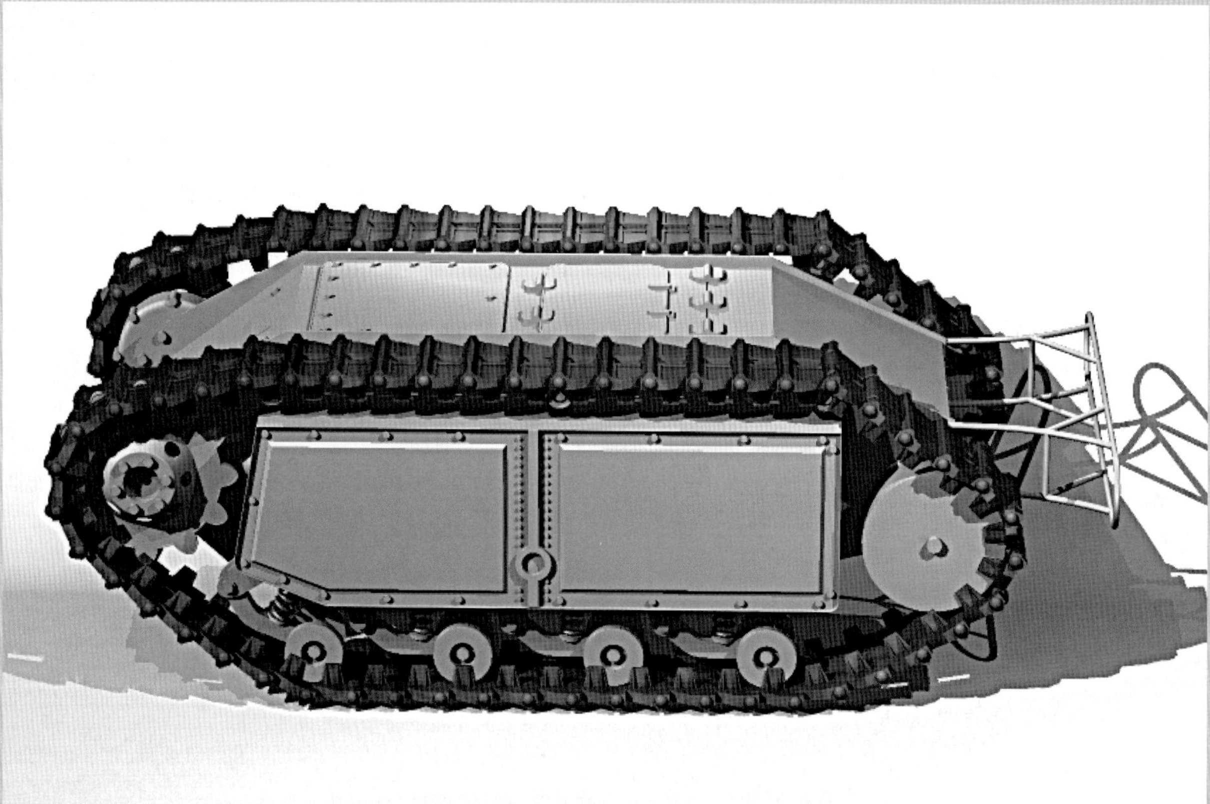

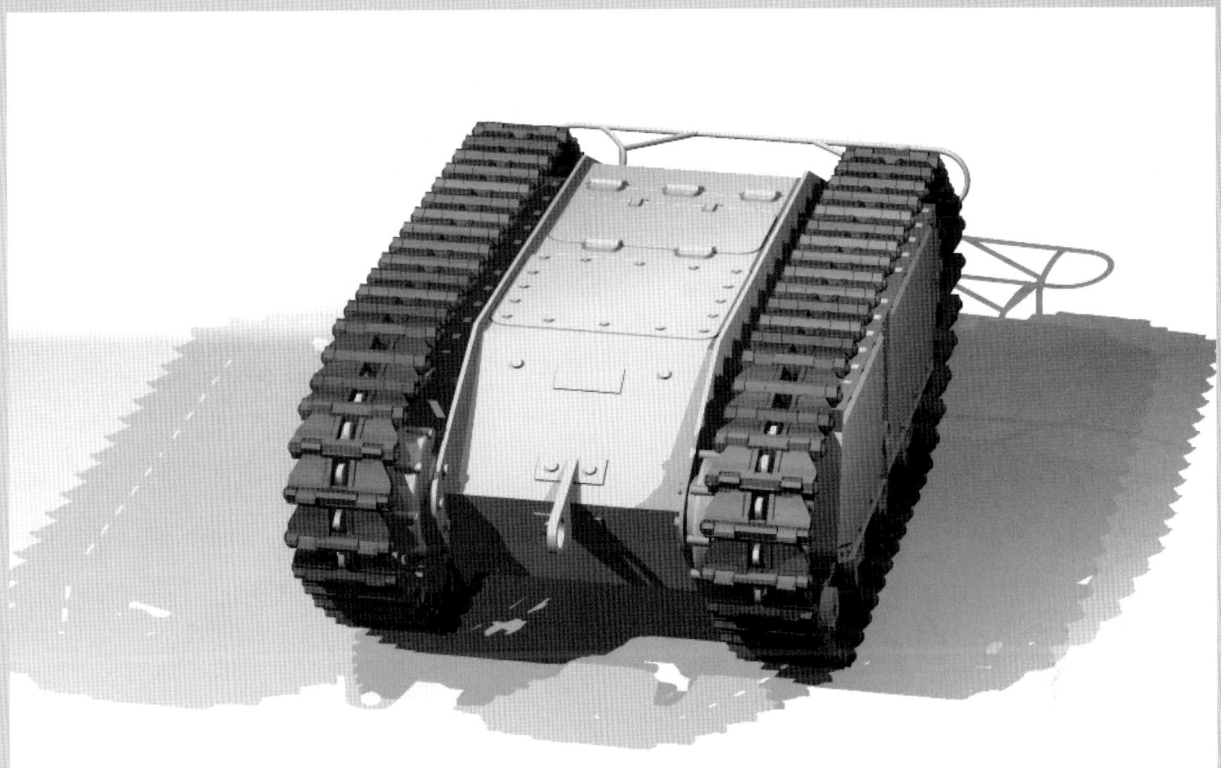

GOLIATH

The *leichter Ladungsträger* SdKfz 302/303 Goliath was an expendable remote-controlled tracked demolition charge was produced from 1942 to supersede the earlier *Minenräumwagen* (mine-clearance vehicle).

The Goliath was transported to the scene of action by a purpose-built two-wheeled trailer that could be pulled by two men or towed behind a vehicle. The attachment points are the holes in the centre of each side sponson and the bracket on the centreline of the hull front. The vehicle was remotely controlled via a three-strand cable that unwound from a drum in the rear compartment of the hull. (Two strands for guidance; one for detonation.) This led out via a slit opening through a guide cage that prevented the cable snagging on the tracks during tight turns. The compartment forward of this contained the electrical equipment for control and detonation, whilst at the front of the vehicle was the explosive charge — 60kg (132lb) — covered with a belt-down hatch. The side sponsons contained the batteries and two Bosch 2.5kW electric motors each connected via a short drive shaft to the transmission unit behind each sprocket.

There were three versions of the Goliath. Borgward and Zündapp produced 2,560 *E-motor* (electric-motor) SdKfz 302s between April 1942 and January 1944. It was succeeded by the V-motor (petrol-engined) SdKfz 303A. This was cheaper to produce and the more efficient petrol engine increased speed and range with a heavier payload of 75kg (165lb). This was the main production version and Zündapp and Zachertz produced 4,602 units between April 1943 and September 1944. This was in turn replaced in production by the SdKfz 303B in November 1944. Also petrol-engined, it was slightly larger than the 303A and could carry a charge of 100kg (220lb). By the end of the war 325 of this version had been built making a grand total of 7,487 of all types.

The main distinguishing feature between the electric and petrol-engined versions are:

a) top plate flat on 302; raised air intake on 303
b) three return rollers on 302; only two on 303
c) disc idler on 302; spoked idler on 303

	SdKfz 302	SdKfz 303A	SdKfz 303B
Weight (kg)	0.37	0.37	0.43
Length (m)	1.5	1.62	1.63
Width (m)	0.85	0.84	0.91
Height (m)	0.56	0.60	0.62
Speed (km/hr)	10	12	12
Range	650m of wire usually carried on drum		

Brandenburgers flew to some targets in the DFS 230 during the Tunisian campaign in 1943 and also apparently used the 24-ton Messerschmitt Me323 *Gigant* (Giant) glider on one occasion — the unsuccessful raid into Bucharest in 1944. Capable of carrying up to 120 troops, a tanks or 20 tons of supplies, this monster had to be towed by three tugs but the arrangement proved unsatisfactory. Consequently, rockets were fitted to aid the tugs during take off but these made little difference to the instability of the combination and later versions of the Gigant were converted to powered aircraft by the fitting of six engines. Some 200 Gigants were built but the design, the largest glider aircraft of the conflict, was generally unsatisfactory.

Although Skorzeny did have some involvement in naval special forces, his units mostly avoided amphibious warfare. This was not the case with the Brandenburgers, who established their own coastal raider battalion. Evidence is scarce but this battalion, which mostly served in the Adriatic and Aegean, was equipped with various sizes of powerful assault craft for carrying troops into action. At a lower level, it is known that the detachment that destroyed rail bridges on the Murmansk-Leningrad line in August 1942 made use of kayaks commandeered from pleasure boat businesses on Berlin's Wannsee that were fitted with small outboard motors for the raid. Some Brandenburgers were alarmed that they came in a range of rather bright colours — red, blue and orange — but they were used in the attack.

Above: Fieseler Storch liaison and observation aircraft as used on the Mussolini mission — although rather too small for the final number of passengers. *via George Forty*

Above left: Brandenburgers training for Operation 'Sealion' at Büsum in August 1940. Note the inflatable life jackets but otherwise standard equipment. *Bundesarchiv*

Left: The Germans used the DFS 230 assault glider from the start of the campaign in the west. The most famous escapade using DFS 230s was the capture of Fort Eban Emael on 10 May 1940. Its last significant use was delivering Otto Skorzeny's force for the rescue of Mussolini. *Bundesarchiv*

Centre left: Practice makes perfect — the Brandenburgers spent a great deal of time honing their skills ensuring that everyone knew what to do and when to do it.

Far left: The attack on Norway was spearheaded by lightly equipped Brandenburg and other special units. Note the number of hand grenades carried by these Marines. *Photo from* Signal *magazine.*

INSIGNIA, CLOTHING & EQUIPMENT

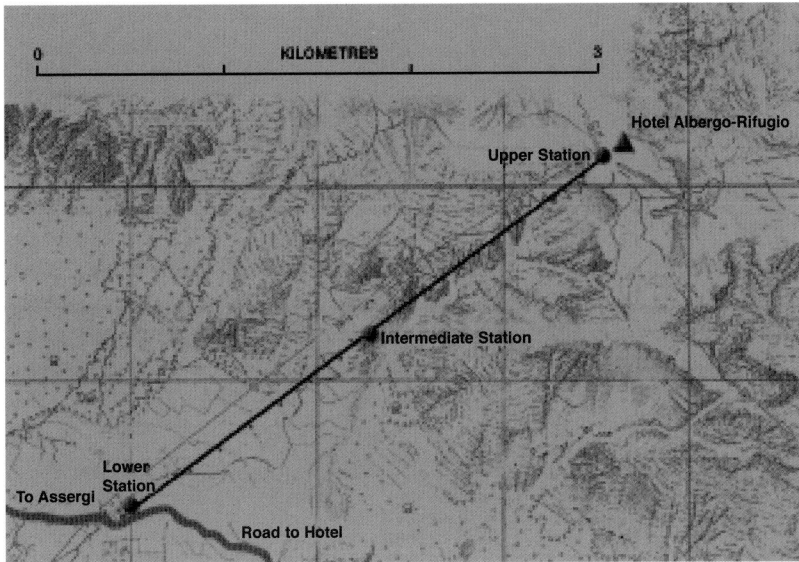

The freeing of Mussolini
This artwork shows (**left**) the mountain-top location of the hotel in which Mussolini was held and the take-off run of the Storch with (**above**) details of the funicular railway that ran up the Gran Sasso and (**below**) the location of the hotel in relation to Rome and central Italy.

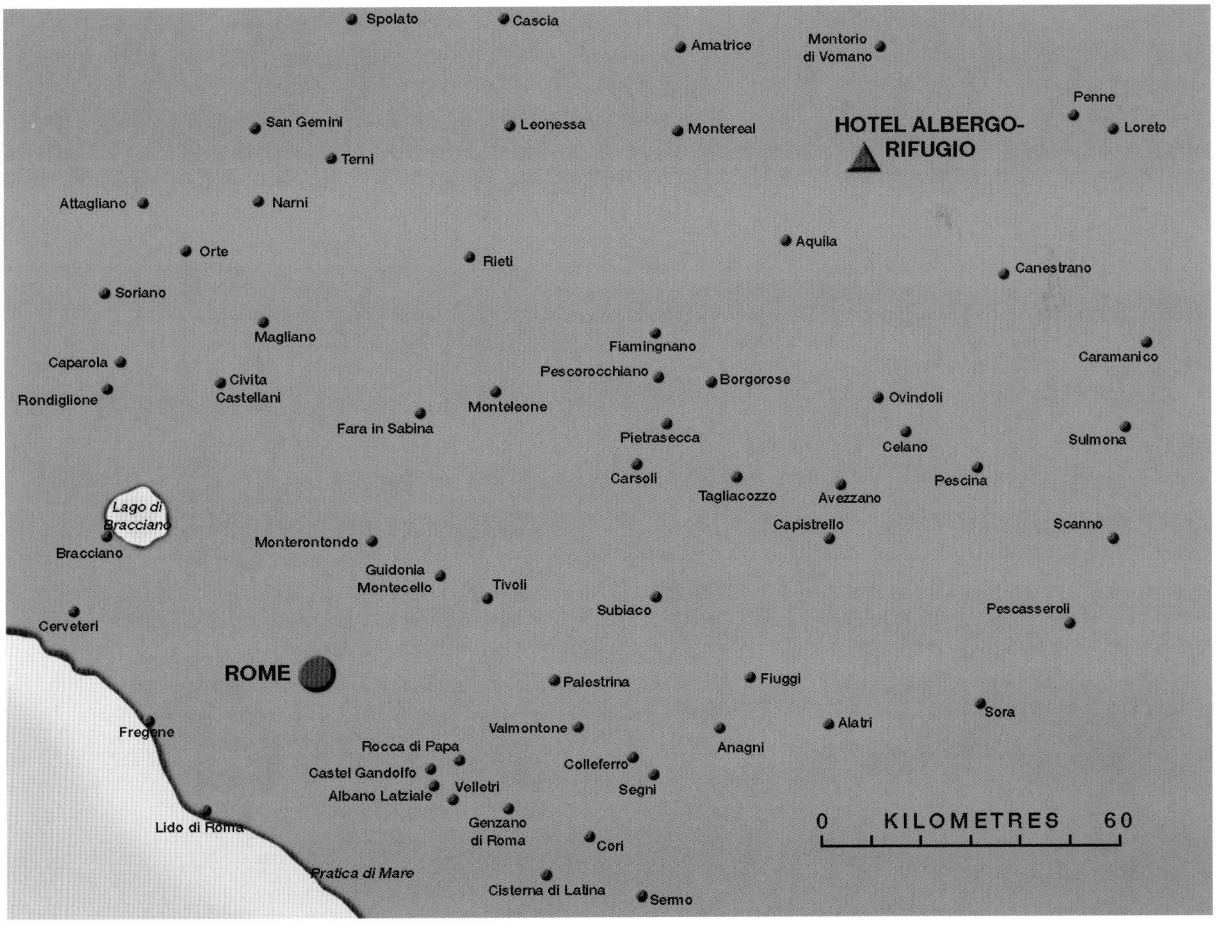

171

PEOPLE

WILHELM CANARIS (1887–1945)

Above: Admiral Canaris, who was head of the Abwehr from 1935. He did not devise the idea for the Brandenburg type of armed units and he was not entirely convinced of their usefulness, but nevertheless he accepted the idea. *Bundesarchiv*

Born into the family of a wealthy industrialist, Canaris joined the Imperial German Navy as a cadet in 1905 and during World War I served on board the *Dresden,* which fought in the battles of Coronel and the Falklands in November and December 1914. The cruiser escaped destruction but was eventually scuttled off Juan Fernandez on 14 March 1915, and Canaris made a daring escape back to Germany, avoiding internment and British agents on his trail. Canaris subsequently gained a reputation as an excellent intelligence officer during missions for the navy in Spain during 1915 and 1916, and in the final two years of the war he was a U-boat captain. In the interwar period he was a member of the military tribunal that tried the murderers of left-wing revolutionaries Karl Liebknecht and Rosa Luxembourg, who were killed during an attempted revolution in Berlin during January 1919. Over the following years he held several positions including that of captain of the predreadnought battleship *Schlesien* and was appointed head of the *Abwehr* in January 1935. He was responsible for organising military support for Francisco Franco during the Spanish Civil War. Between 1938 and 1940 Canaris was promoted vice-admiral and then admiral and made head of both the *Abwehr* and *Amt Ausland*. During this period the Brandenburgers were raised with his agreement

The admiral grew increasingly disillusioned with Hitler and from around 1938 became linked to various anti-Nazi resistance movements. The extent of his involvement is unclear but it seems he himself was opposed to any plans to kill Hitler and focused his efforts on protecting those around him who were more actively involved in anti-Nazi plots. Nevertheless Canaris was temporarily suspended from duty in February 1942 for aiding Jews to escape death in Germany by smuggling them to Switzerland. In March 1942 the *Abwehr* suffered two further blows: one of its officers, Paul Thümmel, was arrested and murdered by the Gestapo for supplying top secret information to Britain and the Soviet Union, and a British raid that successfully captured key parts of a German radar system at Bruneval on the north coast of France so enraged Hitler that he turned on the admiral and demanded to know why the *Abwehr* had singularly failed to uncover Britain's radar secrets. Henceforth the SS's intelligence and counter-espionage department took over much of the *Abwehr*'s work and Canaris appears to have sunk into apathy and despair.

Although the Gestapo suspected that he was negotiating with the Allies through neutral countries, the final blow came with the defection of an *Abwehr* officer in Istanbul, Erich Vermehren, to the British in early 1944. On 18 February, Hitler ordered the *Abwehr* dissolved, but Canaris was not arrested or imprisoned, merely temporarily suspended from duty until June when he was made chief of the department for economic warfare. The admiral was not directly involved in the July bomb plot to assassinate Hitler but one of those who was made mention of Canaris's name while being interrogated. Subsequent investigations discovered his personal diaries, which expressed strong anti-Nazi sympathies, and further details of his involvement in previous plots. Arrested, tried and convicted, he was taken to Flossenbürg concentration camp in Bavaria and executed on 9 April 1945.

HANS OSTER (1888–1945)

Oster was dismissed from the army because of an unacceptable love affair, but his fortunes improved when he joined the *Abwehr* in May 1933 and gained the confidence of its chief, Admiral Wilhelm Canaris. Canaris was able to engineer Oster's readmittance to the officer corps and made him his deputy in 1938. Oster was utterly opposed to Hitler and the Nazis and became involved in several conspiracies to remove him from power. In 1938 he joined an unsuccessful attempt to remove Hitler, and while some of the conspirators advocated that Hitler be simply deposed, Oster believed passionately that he had to be assassinated to break his grip over the will of the German people. Oster's position became less secure as the *Abwehr*'s fortunes declined and those of the SS rose but he continued to plot Hitler's downfall. In February 1943 he provided explosives for Col Henning von Tresckow, who with fellow officers planned but failed to kill Hitler when he visited Army Group Centre's headquarters at Smolensk. Oster was sacked a few weeks later after the Gestapo had found definitive evidence of his involvement in 'U-7' — an *Abwehr*-run operation that between late September and early December 1942 spirited away Jewish refugees from certain death in Germany to neutral Switzerland. His fate was sealed when he became implicated in the July 1944 bomb plot against Hitler. Arrested on 21 July, he was tried and conviction of treason and finally executed at Flossenbürg concentration camp on 9 April 1945.

Above: Hans Oster.

ADRIAN VON FOELKERSAM (1914–45)

Born on 20 December 1914 in St Petersburg, Russia, the son of a Baltic German admiral who had served in the Russian Tsarist Navy and fought against the Japanese in the Russo-Japanese war of 1904–5, Adrian Baron von Foelkersam could speak fluent Russian, English and German and studied economics at universities in Berlin and Vienna. He joined the Brandenburgers in 1939 and took part in many operations. His greatest achievement — and the one for which he was awarded the Knight's Cross (on 14 September 1942) — was during the capture of the Maikop oilfields in the Caucasus when he was a lieutenant with the Ist Battalion of the Brandenburg Regiment. He and his men — 62 Baltic and Sudeten Germans, nicknamed the 'wild bunch' — disguised as Soviet troops, prevented the destruction of the oilfields by retreating Soviet forces. Using Red Army trucks and NKVD (Russian secret police) uniforms they infiltrated the Soviet lines and ran into a large group of Red Army deserters. Foelkersam persuaded them to return to the Soviet cause and this gave him the credentials he needed when he reached Maikop.

Pretending to be a Major Truchin from Stalingrad, Foelkersam convinced the Russian general commanding the area that he was who he said he was; the general even gave him a personal tour of the city's defences. On 8 August, with the German army near, the Brandenburgers used grenades to simulate an artillery attack and knocked out the communications centre. Foelkersam then convinced the Russian defenders to withdraw and the German army was able to enter the city without a fight the next day.

Below: Lt Adrian Baron von Foelkersam, seen wearing his newly awarded Knight's Cross. *Bundesarchiv*

When the Brandenburgers were formed into the Brandenburg Division and made part of the Grossdeutschland Panzer Corps, von Foelkersam — along with many other Brandenburgers — joined Skorzeny's new SS commando unit. Skorzeny accepted him with alacrity and he was promoted Oberleutnant, based at the unit's Friedenthal training ground where Skorzeny had set up his HQ.

Skorzeny's first mission — an attempt to kidnap Marshal Pétain — was cancelled; the second was the precursor to Operation '*Rösselsprung*' — the attack on Tito's headquarters (see pages 42–5) to kill or capture the Yugoslav partisan leader. Initially planned to involve only a small squad of men dressed as partisans, the plan escalated into a major operation, which involved the Waffen-SS 500th Parachute Battalion and other Army and Waffen-SS units. With little security, the partisans soon got wind of the operation and in the end Skorzeny and Foelkersam were lucky to escape with their lives.

Shortly afterwards Foelkersam was involved in the reaction to the 20 July Bomb Plot. During the confusion of the first few hours after the attempt on Hitler's life, Skorzeny and his men were among the many who stood firmly against the conspirators. Foelkersam was assigned to guard the SS intelligence building.

He took part in Skorzeny's brilliant Operation '*Panzerfaust*' (see pages 45–9) at the forefront of the action and his relationship with Skorzeny was further strengthened when Foelkersam became his adjutant.

During the Ardennes offensive Skorzeny's Panzer Brigade 150 was split into three Kampfgruppen — X, Y and Z (see pages 50–64) — and after the death of Kampfgruppe X commander SS-Obersturmbannführer Willi Hardieck, whose vehicle struck a land mine, Foelkersam took over the command. Kampfgruppe X took part in the actions around Malmédy, Ligneuville and Belleveux and engaged the US 3rd Battalion, 120th Regiment west of Malmédy.

With the failure of the Ardennes offensive Foelkersam went east again with SS-Jagdverband Ost, which was briefly under Skorzeny's command. As SS-Hauptsturmführer and Chief of Staff, Foelkersam asked for and was given the command of the unit. He had personal reasons for fighting the Russians — his brother had been captured by the Red Army and his wife and young daughter were living in the east near Posen. However, he did last long in his new command: he was killed by a head wound on 21 January 1945 near Hohensalza.

He was promoted posthumously to the rank of SS-Sturmbannführer and on 5 February received the *Ehrenblattspange des Heeres* (Roll of Honour clasp of the German Army).

Below: The Roll of Honour clasp of the German Army was instituted by Adolf Hitler on 30 January 1944 for exceptional bravery, that didn't quite reach the level required for the Knight's Cross. Over 4,500 had been awarded by war's end. Adrian Baron Foelkersam was awarded his pothumously.

THEODORE-GOTTLIEB VON HIPPEL

As has already been discussed in Origins and History (pages 9–10), the legacy of German Gen Paul von Lettow-Vorbeck's superb guerrilla war in East Africa made a profound mark upon one of his junior officers, a young captain named Theodore von Hippel. Finding a place in the German intelligence community after the war, Hippel proposed utilizing small, elite units to penetrate enemy defences before hostilities or offensive actions had begun. However, the idea ran afoul of the stiff-necked Prussian sense of honor. Hippel persevered, however, and when he became an officer in the war ministry's intelligence agency, the Abwehr, his ideas finally found a home.

Under Admiral Wilhelm Canaris, the German high command allowed Hippel to do what he had proposed — and thus the Brandenburgers were formed. Hippel scoured Germany's borders to find Slavs or other ethnic groups to ensure recruits had language skills. Hippel ran the show to begin with but then became commander of the Ist

Battalion. Promoted major in September 1940 he was involved in training for Operation 'Sealion', but during the preparations for 'Sealion' he had to quit the Brandenburgers in October 1940 after an incident related at length in Eric Lefevre's *Brandenburg Division* (see Bibliography page 94) that led to his court-martial. He and his men had been ordered to take an oath that they would undertake any mission proposed to them by the OKW. This went against the principle that the Brandenburgers' missions were voluntary and Hippel was not prepared to accept this. His argument was that it was dangerous enough to be sent into enemy territory — often in the enemy uniforms. Capture in almost every case would mean execution for spying. The only way to achieve this was by using volunteers who could refuse a mission if it seemed to be suicidal. He lost his job for refusing to administer the oath — which, interestingly, never was administered. He was replaced initially by Maj Kewisch, then von Aulock before Lt-Col Paul Haehling von Lanzenhauer became CO on 28 November 1940. Lt Wilhelm Walther took over command of Ist Battalion.

OTTO SKORZENY (1908–1975)

Above: Skorzeny in custody after his capture in Austria on 16 May 1945. He was a university student in Vienna and it was during these days that student duelling was prevalent. It was during the tenth of his fifteenth duels that the famous scar on his left cheek was incurred and would give rise to the nickname 'Scarface'. *US Army*

Skorzeny was born in Vienna, Austria, to a father who was an engineer. While studying to follow in his father's footsteps at the Technical University in 1926–31 he gained the duelling scars that would later earn him the nickname 'Scarface', joined the right-wing Freikorps movement of mostly ex-soldiers and became a member of the Heimwehr local defence force. In 1930 he joined the emerging Nazi Party and immediately before the outbreak of World War II worked as a business manager for a building contractor. In 1939 he joined the IInd Reserve Battalion of the SS's Leibstandarte Adolf Hitler, the Führer's personal bodyguard, which was stationed in Berlin Lichterfelde. Skorzeny saw service during the invasion of France in 1940 and the attack on the Soviet Union in 1941, when he won the Iron Cross, Second Class. For much of 1942 he was stationed in Berlin as an engineering officer with a reserve regiment but in the autumn secured a post with 3rd SS Panzer Division Totenkopf. In April 1943 he transferred to Section VI of the *Reichssicherheitshauptamt*, the state security department of the SS. The section was headed by Walter Schellenberg and was responsible for political and, increasingly,

Above: SS Oberststurmbannführer Otto Skorzeny became Hitler's favourite commando after rescuing Mussolini.

military intelligence-gathering. The previous year it had established the Oranienberg special training course to raise the SS's equivalent of the Brandenburgers and Skorzeny was ordered to find and train recruits. These became known as the *Friedenthaler Jagdverbände* (Friedenthal Hunting Groups) after their base, a park and hunting lodge close to Berlin.

Skorzeny's rise to public fame opened with the rescue of Italian dictator Benito Mussolini in September 1943. He was specially selected to conduct the mission by Hitler and thereafter became one of his favourites. Skorzeny was permitted to expand his special forces and he gained some control of various specialist weapons, such as the Kriegsmarine's midget submarines, and the Luftwaffe's Kampfgruppe 200, which carried out special airborne missions. The Führer's faith in him was further confirmed during the 1944 bomb plot. On 20 July Skorzeny was on a Vienna-bound train stopped in the Berlin suburb of Lichterfelde when news of the coup attempt reached him. He immediately retraced his steps to the Bendlerstrasse, home of the Oberkommando der Wehrmacht, and set about aiding officers loyal to Hitler who crushed the plot. Skorzeny continued to carry out special operations until the end of the war, mostly memorably in Budapest during the following October and in the Ardennes in December. In the final months of the conflict he organised attacks by frogmen on Remagen bridge, conducting operations on the Eastern Front and attempted to organise Werewolf resistance bands in the so-called National Redoubt in the Bavaria Alps.

Skorzeny was arrested by US troops near Steiermark on 15 May and in September 1947 was tried for war crimes by a US military court at Dachau. The charges, relating to the murder of US prisoners at Malmédy in the Ardennes, were not proved and Skorzeny was acquitted. After working for the historical section of the US Army for a brief period he was rearrested by the postwar German authorities but escaped from a prison camp near Darmstadt in July 1949 and eventually fled to Spain where he enjoyed the protection of dictator Francisco Franco and adopted the cover name of Robert Steinbacher. Outwardly a business man in the import-export trade and real estate, it is believed that Skorzeny also founded a secret organisation known as *Die Spinne* (The Spider) that was supported by undiscovered funds from the Third Reich and aided around 500 former SS men in Germany to escape justice by mostly fleeing to South America.

ALEXANDER VON PFUHLSTEIN (1899–1976)

Born on 17 December 1899 in Danzig, Alexander von Pfuhlstein joined the German Army as a Fähnrich on 29 March 1917. He was promoted to lieutenant on 14 December 1917 and fought with 4th Grenadier Regiment. He rejoined the army when the Nazis came to power as a staff officer — the GSO Ia (operations) with 19th Infantry Division — in 3 November 1938 serving there until 10 January 1940 during which, on 1 June 1939, he was promoted lieutenant-colonel. The division took part in the Polish campaign fighting at first in the area around Zina Wolda where it took heavy casualties during the crossing of the river Warta and, later, the Vistula. Involved in the assault on Warsaw, after Poland surrendered the division was one of the units occupying the city until transferring to the west — the lower Rhine — in December. The 19th Division attacked across the Meuse in May 1940 but Pfuhlstein wasn't with them. He had transferred to become GSO Ia of 58th Infantry Division on 15 March 1940. This division,

COMMANDERS OF THE BRANDENBURG DIVISION, 1943–45	
Brandenburg Division zbV 800	
Maj-Gen Alexander von Pfuhlstein	1 April 1943–10 April 1944
Lt-Gen Fritz Kühlwein	10 April 1944–15 September 1944
Panzergrenadier Division Brandenburg	
Lt-Gen Fritz Kühlwein	15 September 1944–16 October 1944
Maj-Gen Hermann Schulte-Heuthaus	16 October 1944–8 May 1945

as part of XXIII Corps, advanced through Luxembourg and France to Verdun before moving south to Toul. It spent the rest of 1940 in Belgium designated part of the third wave of Operation 'Sealion' before the unit moved east, to Poland, in spring 1941. It would serve on the Eastern Front for the rest of the war, as part of Army Group North, attacking through Riga and Pleshkov in June 1941 and besieging Leningrad. Von Pfuhlstein became commander of the IInd Battalion of Infantry Regiment 18 on 1 March 1941 and then commanded Infantry Regiment 77 from 29 July 1941 to 2 March 1942, being promoted colonel on 1 February 1942. He became commander of Infantry Regiment 154 on 1 March 1942 serving with that unit until the autumn. It was as commander of IR154 that he won the Knight's Cross on 17 August 1942 in the Demjansk Pocket.

Pfuhlstein took over command of the newly created Brandenburg Division on 1 April 1943 and was involved in its change from a special operations unit to a much larger division — of 14,000 men. He was promoted major-general on 1 July 1943, but although during his time as commander the division took part in some notable actions — such as the occupation of Cos and Leros (see pages 36–7) — the writing was on the wall for the Brandenburgers, whose cause was not helped when Pfuhlstein was implicated in the anti-Nazi *Schwarze Kapelle* resistance movement. He was dismissed after just over a year in command on 10 April 1944 and discharged on 14 September 1944. He died on 20 December 1976 having lived postwar in Bad Homburg near Frankfurt am Main.

FRITZ KÜHLWEIN (1892–1976)

Pfuhlstein's position was taken by Lt-Gen Fritz Kühlwein, who assumed command of the division on 10 April 1944. Born on 29 November 1892 in Hatten/Weissenburg, Fritz Kühlwein entered the pre-World War I Reichsheer as a *Fahnenjunker* — a candidate for a regular commission — on 17 July 1912. He joined Infantry Regiment 97 as a lieutenant on 18 February 1914 and fought on the Eastern Front, particularly around Dünaburg (Daugavpils) in southeast Latvia, on the Western Dvina River. In December 1917 the regiment was transferred to the west to take part in Ludendorff's spring offensive, fighting around the Somme and Ancre. Part of the thrust that reached Noyon, the regiment would fight hard defensive battles as the Spring Offensive ground to a halt and the Allied armies started the offensive that would bring them victory. The regiment was disbanded on 19 September 1918.

Kühlwein's served in the Reichswehr — the standing army of the Weimar Republic and opening years of the Third Reich — being promoted lieutenant-colonel on 1 August

FROM COMPANY TO DIVISION
Bau-lehr-Kompanie zbV 800 'Deutsche Kompanie'
Founded on 25 October 1939.

Bau-Lehr-Bataillon zbV 800 'Brandenburg'
On 15 December 1939, the company was enlarged to become a battalion of four companies, a motorcycle platoon, a paratroop platoon. Other specialised units were later attached (see page 15).

Lehr-Regiment zbV 800 'Brandenburg'
On 12 October 1940, the battalion was enlarged to become a regiment of three battalions with attached special companies (see page 40).

Lehr-Division zbV 800 'Brandenburg'
Between late 1942 and January 1943, the regiment was transformed into a division (see page 40), with specialised units such as von Koenen's Tropical Company.

Panzergrenadier-Division 'Brandenburg'
From 13 September 1943, the unit was no longer used for special operations and was organised along standard lines (see page 41).

Other Units
In summer 1942, the *Küstenjäger-Kompanie* was formed, the equivalent of the Special Boat Service.

Arabische Brigade
A volunteer force, fighting from 1940 onwards in Lebanon, Syria, Iraq and Iran, later with Kurdish allies in the Caucasus.

Deutsch-Arabische Legion
Mixed German-Arabian membership, operated mainly in Tunisia.

1936 and becoming commander of the IInd Battalion of Infantry Regiment 56 on 12 October 1937. As a major he wrote *Schützenzug im Gefecht* (The Infantry Platoon in Battle) published by Mittler & Son in 1936 and in 1938 as a lieutenant-colonel *Gefechtstaktik des verstärkten Bataillons* (Battle Tactics of the strengthened Battalion).

Promoted colonel on 1 April 1939, he took command of Infantry Ersatz (training) Regiment 73 in October 1939, before moving to command IR55 (home station Würzburg) on 15 January 1940. After taking part in the assault on the west, Kühlwein moved to command IR133 — part of 45th Infantry Division — on 15 October 1940, a position he held until 27 February 1942 when he took command of the division itself. The division had moved from the west to the Eastern Front in June 1941 and opened its campaign in Russia by attacking the fortress of Brest-Litovsk. Promoted major-general on 1 April 1942, he led the division for over a year, the latter part of which it spent in the area of Voronezh. Promoted lieutenant-general on 1 January 1943, he left 45th Infantry on 29 April 1943, and was subsequently chosen to command the Brandenburg Division, taking up the role on 13 April 1944. During his time as CO the division became a Panzergrenadier Division, fighting in Serbia as part of Army Group F, and he left shortly afterwards in October 1944 (just at about the time that part of the division became Festung Division Rhodos (Fortress Division Rhodes). On 29 December 1944 he took over command of Training and Replacement Division 401 located in Wehrkreis I, garrisoned on Königsberg in East Prussia. In March 1945 he took command of Feld Ersatz Division 149 based in the Netherlands, before surrendering in May. In later years he lived in Bielefeld and died in 1976.

Below: Hermann Schulte-Heuthaus

HERMANN SCHULTE-HEUTHAUS (1898–1979)

The last commander of the Brandenburgers was born on 15 January 1898 at Klein Weissensee in East Prussia. Hermann Schulte-Heuthaus joined the Reichsheer as an officer candidate on 14 October 1914, and went on to be commissioned into 4th Guards Regiment serving from 10 March 1915 as a lieutenant. He fought bravely during World War I, winning the Iron Cross, First and Second Classes. The regiment survived the war but was disbanded on 30 April 1920, Schulte-Heuthaus along with it, and he had to wait until 15 September 1934 before he could resume his military career, rejoining the Reichswehr as a captain. On 1 October 1937 he took over command of the 4th Company of the NCO school at Potsdam, moving on to run the Potsdam Infantry School from 1 September 1939. He was promoted lieutenant-colonel on 1 August 1940, and on 1 May 1941 he finally got the chance to lead a unit in the field when he took over *Krad-Schütz-Bataillon* (Motorcycle Infantry Battalion) Nr 25, which he led until 28 February 1942. After the battles of the winter he was awarded the Knight's Cross on 23 January 1942.

On 25 March 1942 Schulte-Heuthaus joined Erwin Rommel's Panzerarmee Afrika staff as IIa — adjutant. He was promoted colonel on 1 April 1942 and from then on played an important role as a staff officer — together with Lt-Col Siegfried Westphal, Schulte-Heuthaus was involved in planning the great offensive east that began on 25 May 1942 and would take Rommel's troops to El Alamein. Briefly taking over command of 90th Light Division between 17 and 22 September 1942 — he continued on Rommel's staff when, on 1 October 1942, Panzerarmee Afrika became the Deutsch-Italienische Panzerarmee (German-Italian

BRANDENBURGER HOLDERS OF THE KNIGHT'S CROSS WITH OAK LEAVES

Name	Rank	Unit	Date
Siegfried Grabert	Capt	Lehr Regiment Brandenburg zbV 800	6 November 1943
Karl-Heinz Oesterwitz	Lt-Col	Panzergrenadier Regiment Brandenburg	10 February 1945
Max Wandery	Maj	Panzergrenadier Regiment Brandenburg	16 March 1945

BRANDENBURGER HOLDERS OF THE KNIGHT'S CROSS

Name	Rank	Unit	Date
Erhard Afheldt	Lt	Panzergrenadier Division Brandenburg	17 March 1945
Wilhelm Bröckerhoff	Maj	Panzergrenadier Division Brandenburg	7 May 1945
Erich von Bruckner	Col	Panzergrenadier Division Brandenburg	8 April 1945
Adrian von Foelkersam	2-Lt	Lehr Regiment Brandenburg zbV 800	14 September 1942
Siegfried Grabert (1)	Lt	Lehr Regiment Brandenburg zbV 800	10 June 1941
Hans-Wolfram Knaak (2)	Capt	Lehr Regiment Brandenburg zbV 800	3 November 1942
Friedrich von Koenen (3)	Capt	Brandenburg Division zbV 800	16 September 1943
Erhard Lange (4)	Lt	Lehr Regiment Brandenburg zbV 800	15 January 1943
Werner Lau	2-Lt	Lehr Regiment Brandenburg zbV 800	9 December 1942
Helmut von Leipzig (5)	2-Lt	Panzergrenadier Division Brandenburg	28 April 1945
Karl-Heinz Oesterwitz	Lt	Lehr Regiment Brandenburg zbV 800	30 April 1943
Alexander von Pfuhlstein (6)	Maj-Gen	154th Infantry Division	1942
Ernst Prohaska (7)	2-Lt	Lehr Regiment Brandenburg zbV 800	16 September 1942
Erich Röseke (8)	Lt	Panzergrenadier Division Brandenburg	14 April 1945
Konrad Steidl (9)	Capt	Brandenburg Division zbV 800	26 January 1944
Wilhelm Walther	Lt	Bau Lehr battalion Brandenburg zbV 800	24 June 1940
Max Wandery	Lt	Brandenburg Division zbV 800	9 January 1944

(1) Grabert was an early recruit to the Brandenburgers but was killed in July 1942 leading the 2nd Battalion's 8th Company, which suffered 87 casualties, in a successful attack to take bridges over the Don River near Bataisk for the 13th Panzer Division during the drive into the Caucasus.

(2) Acting commander of the 2nd Battalion's 8th Company, he was killed in action while defending the recently captured Dünaberg bridges over the Dvina River in Latvia on 26 June 1941, during the first days of Operation 'Barbarossa'.

(3) Nicknamed 'Fritz', Koenen came from a farming family in southwest Africa and was commander of the regiment's Tropical Company (later battalion) that served in North Africa from 1941.

(4) Gained the award for his leadership in Operation 'Shamil', a behind-the-lines mission to supply Muslims in the Caucasus with the arms and ammunition needed to revolt against the Soviet Union in 1942. 'Shamil' failed and only Lange and one other man, a Tartar, made it safely back to German lines.

(5) Commanded the Brandenburger detachment participating in Operation 'Dora', a reconnaissance into Niger and Chad to assess the feasibility of severing alleged Anglo-French supply routes in the area of Lake Chad in mid-1942.

(6) Pfuhlstein was removed from command of the Brandenburg Division in April 1944 for involvement in anti-Hitler conspiracies. He won his Knight's Cross in the Demjansk Pocket during 1942 while commander of a regular army unit.

(7) A Russian-speaking ethnic German who grew up along the Volga River, Prohaska led a platoon from the 2nd Battalion's 8th Company that captured a bridge over the Bjelaja River during the push on Maikop in the northern Caucasus during August 1942. The operation was successful but he was killed.

(8) Received for leading a group of men from the 6th Company of the 1st Regiment's 2nd Battalion to safety after spending 11 days behind Red Army lines in Poland, despite being wounded on several occasions.

(9) Received the award for commanding the division's 1st Battalion, 2nd Regiment, during successful operations against Tito's partisans in Bosnia.

Above: Otto Skorzeny was awarded the Iron Cross Ist Class on 12 September 1943; the Iron Cross 2nd Class on 26 August 1941; and the Knight's Cross to the Iron Cross on 13 September 1943. He was promoted SS-Sturmbannführer on 12 September 1943. He was awarded the Oak Leaves to the Knight's Cross on 9 April 1945 while an SS-Obersturmbannführer. He was also awarded German Cross in Gold at the end of 1944/early 1945. He was also awarded the *Totenkopfring der SS* ring. This was not a national decoration, it was rather a gift from the Reichsführer to reward those senior officers who showed outstanding achievement, devotion to duty, and loyalty to the Führer — something Skorzeny did during the July Bomb Plot. He ended the war as a SS-Standartenführer. *IWM HU 46178*

Above right: Lt-Col Wilhelm Walther won his Knight's cross on 24 June 1940 while leading the assault troops of the 4th Company of the Brandenburg Battalion. The story is recounted on pages 17–8. *Bundesarchiv*

Right: Siegfried Grabert was born on 11 January 1916 in Schorndorf an der Rems, Kreis Waiblingen, Württemberg. He was awarded the Iron Cross Ist Class on 2 June 1940; the Iron Cross 2nd Class on 12 May 1940; and the Knight's Cross to the Iron Cross on 10 June 1941 as a lieutenant in the 8th Company of Lehr Regiment Brandenburg then attached to XVIII Army Corps, Twelfth Army. He died on 25 July 1942 in area of Rostov, on the Eastern Front as a captain while commanding the 8th Company of the regiment. He was awarded the Oak Leaves to the Knight's Cross posthumously on 6 November 1943. He was also holder of the Infantry Assault Badge in silver. *Bundesarchiv*

Panzer Army), retreating back to Tunisia after Montgomery's victory at El Alamein. He escaped capture when German forces surrendered in Tunisia in early May 1943 and became commander of Panzerfüsilier Regiment Grossdeutschland on 7 July 1943 at a time when Grossdeutschland was involved in the battle of Kursk. (In October 1942, at the same time as similar renamings throughout the German Army, Infantry Regiment Grossdeutschland Nr 1 was retitled 'Grenadier Regiment Grossdeutschland' and Infantry Regiment GD 2 was renamed 'Füsilier Regiment Grossdeutschland.' This was done in homage to the units in the army of Frederick the Great, whom Hitler greatly admired. *Schützen* [infantry] regiments in Panzer divisions were at the same time renamed Panzergrenadier regiments. Rank titles for infantrymen were also renamed, *Schütze* [Private] becoming *Grenadier* or *Panzergrenadier*. For the Füsilier Regiment of Grossdeutschland, *Füsilier* also became the rank title for a private serving in the unit.)

Schulte-Heuthaus held the position in Füsilier Regiment Grossdeutschland for about two months — until 4 September 1943 — when he was wounded in action. After six months of recuperation, he then commanded the Ersatz (Reserve) Brigade in Cottbus from 27 March to 15 October 1944, before assuming command of the Panzergrenadier Division Brandenburg which he led until the end of the war. Brandenburg fought mainly on the Eastern Front, in the latter stages as part of the Grossdeutschland Panzer Corps which was finally destroyed by Soviet forces in Czechoslovakia in 1945.

After the war Schulte-Heuthaus returned to Berlin, living there until his death on 28 December 1979.

FRIEDRICH 'FRITZ' VON KOENEN (1916–44)

Born on 28 June 1916 in Danzig-Langfuhr, Friedrich von Koenan was the son of a South African farmer and was in South Africa when World War II started. He (and some 450 others) rushed back to Germany to join up. Many of these men — including Koenen — ended up in the Brandenburgers, 'Fritz' being promoted Oberleutnant and made commander of 13th Company — the regiment's training unit. On 28 October 1941 von Koenen and some 300 hand-picked men — the *Tropen-Kompanie* (Tropical Company) Brandenburg — left Germany for Africa. Rommel was not in favour of clandestine operations at first, and was not keen on the Brandenburgers' raison d'être — action behind the enemy's lines. However, as soon as the British Long Range Desert Group started operating, Rommel changed his view and it wasn't long before von Koenen's men had won Rommel over.

They proved to be excellent commandos and the desert proved an excellent battleground for such troops. Roger Bender and Richard Law's splendid book on the Afrika Korps (see Bibliography page 93) identifies a number of these desert missions by the Brandenburgers, designated *Abteilung* von Koenen in early 1943, including the one on which Capt von Koenen won his Knight's Cross. It took place on 26 December 1942 when he led a glider-borne unit that destroyed a railway bridge at Sidi bou Bakr. He was awarded the Knight's Cross on 16 September 1943.

Recalled from the desert he commanded the IIIrd Battalion of the 4th Regiment of the Brandenburgers in Greece and Yugoslavia, where he met his death. On 20 August 1944, as an lieutenant-colonel, he was ambushed by partisans in Visegrad, Herzegovina. Koenen, his driver and adjutant were all mortally wounded and the partisans looted his Knight's Cross as he lay dying.

The German Soldier's Ten Commandments
[in every German Soldier's Paybook]

1. While fighting for victory the German soldier will observe the rules of chivalrous warfare. Cruelties and senseless destruction are below his standard.
2. Combatants will be in uniform or will wear specially introduced and clearly distinguishable badges. Fighting in plain clothes or without such badges is prohibited.
3. No enemy who has surrendered will be killed, including partisans and spies. They will be duly punished by courts.
4. P.O.W. will not be ill-treated or insulted. While arms, maps, and records are to be taken away from them, their personal belongings will not be touched.
5. Dum-dum bullets are prohibited; also no other bullets may be transformed into dum-dum.
6. Red Cross Institutions are sacrosanct. Injured enemies are to be treated in a humane way. Medical personnel and army chaplains may not be hindered in the execution of their medical, or clerical activities.
7. The civilian population is sacrosanct. No looting nor wanton destruction is permitted to the soldier. Landmarks of historical value or buildings serving religious purposes, art, science, or charity are to be especially respected. Deliveries in kind made, as well as services rendered by the population, may only be claimed if ordered by superiors and only against compensation.
8. Neutral territory will never be entered nor passed over by planes, nor shot at; it will not be the object of warlike activities of any kind.
9. If a German soldier is made a prisoner of war he will tell his name and rank if he is asked for it. Under no circumstances will he reveal to which unit he belongs, nor will he give any information about German military, political, and economic conditions. Neither promises nor threats may induce him to do so.
10. Offenses against the a/m matters of duty will be punished. Enemy offences against the principles under 1 to 8 are to be reported. Reprisals are only permissible on order of higher commands.

ASSESSMENT

Below: Oberleutnant Siegfried Grabert. The most famous and engaging officer in the Brandenburg Regiment. In May 1940 he was the leader of a platoon of the 4th Company with the task of taking the bridges over the Juliana Canal intact and preventing the destruction of the locks at Nieuport. He was one of two Brandenburgers who removed the explosive charges from the Nieuport bridge. He then commanded the 8th Company and during the Yugoslavian campaign, seized the bridges over the Vardar on 6 April 1941. This success brought about the award of the Knight's Cross of the Iron Cross the following 10 June, the second in the regiment. Grabert fell the following year at the head of his company in Russia. *TRH Pictures*

The Brandenburgers conducted special operations from the invasion of Poland in 1939 until around mid-1943, when they increasingly took on more conventional roles and were effectively replaced by the SS's own special forces under Otto Skorzeny. Assessing the qualities and effectiveness of the Brandenburgers is fraught with difficulties not least because the unit's reports and combat diaries were mostly destroyed during the war. What evidence remains is fragmentary, anecdotal and often downright contradictory. Some of the claims made for the unit undoubtedly need to be treated with a good measure of scepticism, yet there is sufficient hard evidence to suggest that the Brandenburgers did make a significant contribution to the Nazi war effort, one out of all proportion to the size of the unit, particularly in the years of success between 1939 and 1942. In these years the Brandenburgers effectively spearheaded Germany's Blitzkrieg attacks, seizing key objectives such as intact bridges that allowed the momentum of the armoured thrusts to be maintained — a central plank of such offensives. That they did so often wearing the uniforms of the enemy or civilian clothes is a controversial topic and a matter of debate in respect of internationally accepted military law.

These tactical victories at the forefront of the Blitzkrieg were also matched by strategic triumphs, especially with regard to their missions in 1941 to keep the Danube River open and protect the Romanian oil fields that fuelled German's war effort. However, the enlargement of the unit, from battalion to regiment and then to division, was paralleled by a change in its character. Original recruits were chosen for qualities other than their knowledge of military skills, not least their expertise in foreign languages and customs. It was relatively straightforward to fill a battalion or regiment with such men and give them military training, but surely not a division. Equally important is the fact that Germany's Blitzkrieg attacks ended in late 1942 and with them went the need for a spearhead force like the Brandenburgers. The swift descent on Leros in late 1943 can be seen as their last classic operation. More and more from the latter part of 1942 the Brandenburgers began to undertake conventional operations and campaigned in large-scale sweeps against partisans. Neither were suitable employment for such a specialist force and it appears that, as losses mounted, morale deteriorated. Indeed, many of the first recruits, by this stage middle-ranking officers, chose to seek employment elsewhere, not least with the Waffen-SS and the SS's own special forces.

Ultimately the Brandenburgers fell victim to Nazi power politics, chiefly the struggle between the SS and the *Abwehr* that gathered pace in late autumn 1942. It is clear that the *Abwehr*'s senior figures, not least Canaris and Oster, were involved in anti-Nazi plots and their fate — and that of the organisation as a whole — was sealed when the much more ruthless intelligence and security services of the SS gathered firm evidence against them during 1943. As an integral part of the *Abwehr* the Brandenburgers were branded guilty by association and, although there appears to be little hard evidence that any were involved in the anti-Nazi resistance, the unit probably became seen by the Nazi hierarchy as politically unreliable. Consequently, if Hitler was to have special forces in the latter part of the war they had to be sourced elsewhere and preferably from among the ranks of clearly committed Nazis whose loyalty was unimpeachable. Otto Skorzeny, who had joined the Nazi Party in 1930 and the Waffen-SS in 1939, was the ideal candidate to lead such units as was amply demonstrated by his role in defeating the anti-Hitler plotters in Berlin during late July 1944.

Skorzeny's rise to prominence as head of Nazi special forces came at a time when the Third Reich's fortunes were declining fast. The string of sweeping victories of the first half of the war had given way to defeat after defeat between 1943 and 1945, a catalogue of disasters only infrequently punctuated by small-scale and temporary victories. Thus while the Brandenburgers fought to expand the Third Reich, Skorzeny's troops struggled to prevent its inevitable collapse. A second difference between the two forces was that the Brandenburgers received scant publicity for their exploits, possibly because of the significantly non-Aryan nature of the unit and certainly because the wider armed forces were also covering themselves in glory during their heyday. In contrast Skorzeny became a very well-known Nazi hero and recipient of many awards at a time when the regular German armed forces could provide little good news. His missions were used as a not insignificant propaganda weapon to boost the sagging morale of the German people at a time when bad news from the front was an almost daily event. The legend of Skorzeny grew after World War II, not least because the man himself was a great self-publicist and often made somewhat exaggerated claims. It is undoubtedly true that his rescue of Mussolini in 1943 and the Budapest mission the following year were brilliant coups, planned and carried out swiftly and surgically with little loss of life. They might also be regarded as much political as military operations that had not inconsiderable and wider implications — Mussolini was kept out of Allied hands and Hungary stayed within the Axis orbit — but they could not prevent Italy surrendering or Hungary being overrun by the Red Army. Skorzeny's role in the Ardennes offensive in late 1944 was ambitiously planned but little thought was given to the practicalities of raising and training such a specialist unit as the 150th Panzer Brigade. This was Hitler's fault and not Skorzeny's. In the event the brigade reverted to a conventional role within the first few days of Operation '*Wacht am Rhein*' and the teams of the English-speaking Stielau detachment had scant success, apart from making the Allies extremely jittery for a short time. Skorzeny was christened 'the most dangerous man in Europe' by his foes due to his early successes, but even the most dangerous man in Europe could not stave off Nazi Germany's ultimate defeat with a few thousand special forces, no matter how audacious his operations.

Above: Skorzeny's rescue of Mussolini did much to foster the commando's image. Postwar, as a brilliant self-publicist, his writings did the same. *Bundesarchiv*

REFERENCE

Comparatively little has been written about the Brandenburgers and the *Abwehr*, while Skorzeny's exploits, particularly Operation '*Greif*', have received somewhat greater coverage. However, a note of caution needs to be sounded, not least because of the convoluted histories of these special forces, which went through several transformations during the war. It is particularly true of the Brandenburgers that the scarce material available is often contradictory and confusing. Different references provide different information, disagree over the details of their operations, and even spell names differently and provide various dates for events that are known about. There is even some doubt that missions mentioned by some authors ever actually took place. The picture for Skorzeny's operations is somewhat clearer, most are recorded with a higher degree of accuracy, but Skorzeny, who produced several books on his wartime career, was prone to embellishing the facts, while skirting around the despicable aspects of Nazism. As a general rule the internet sites are interesting but often retread the same information but in truncated form. Many are little more than basic and some badly written, although a number do have interesting and unusual pictures depicting members and operations of these rarely photographed units.

WEBSITES

http://www.panzerworld.net/Pzdivs/PZB150.htm
A resume of the role of the 150th Panzer Brigade during Operation '*Wacht am Rhein*'. It comprises a short section on the unit's creation and performance and is linked to a useful order of battle.

http://www.joric.com/conspiracy/Oster.htm
This details the various anti-Nazi conspiracies instigated by or involving Hans Oster, Canaris's deputy in the *Abwehr*, that were to lead to both their downfalls and impact on the Brandenburgers. The site also includes pages on specific conspiracies, such as 'U-7', that directly implicated the *Abwehr* in treasonable acts.

http://www.skalman.nu/third-reich/heer-panzergr-div-brandenburg.htm
A useful order of battle for the Panzergrenadier Division *Brandenburg* that also includes brief details of its commanders and areas of operation. The same site has a similar list for the *Brandenburg* division.

http://www.forces70.freeserve.co.uk/Brandenberg/commanders.htm.
A site that runs through much the same information as the previous entry but in greater

detail. It also provides information on the Brandenburger regiment and in most cases names battalion and company commanders. The same site also includes pages on various Brandenburg missions, including Maikop and north Africa, as well as information on recruitment and training and holders of the Knight's Cross.

http://www.eliteforces.freewire.co.uk/Brandenburg/afghan.htm
This provides details of one of the Brandenburgers' least covered missions, that in Afghanistan during 1941. It is part of a much more extensive site that also provides information on Operations 'Sealion' and 'Felix', Bucharest in 1944 and Romania during 1941. Additional pages given brief information on uniforms and insignia. The same site provides similar coverage of the 500th SS Parachute Battalion that was part of Skorzeny's command during the war.

http:home.wxs.n1~graspol/frame 25 01.htm
A very basic and episodic account of the career of the Brandenburgers that also has brief passages on the *Abwehr* during the interwar years.

BIBLIOGRAPHY

Ailsby, Christopher: *SS: Roll of Infamy*; Brown Books, 1997.
An encyclopaedia of a bibliography of leading figures in the various branches of the SS. Among the hundreds of personalities covered are entries on those involved in the political struggle between the SS and *Abwehr* for control of Nazi intelligence-gathering operations.

Bender, Roger James, and Law, Richard D.: *Uniforms, Organisation and History of the Afrikakorps*, R. James Bender Publishing, 1973.
A terrific source book of information on Rommel's desert armies, well-illustrated, original and a mine of information.

Berthold, Will: *Brandenburg Division*; Mayflower Books Ltd, 1973.
Although of dubious accuracy and best treated as a work of fiction, Berthold recounts Brandenburg activities during the war, concentrating on the Eastern Front and the Balkans. It is a lively read and does include brief passages that seem to tally with known events and personalities.

Cooper, Matthew, and Lucas, James: *Panzer Grenadiers*; Macdonald and Jane's, 1977.
A general overview of the development of Germany's motorised infantry units that also includes a study of the Panzergrenadier Division Brandenburg's bitter struggle to hold the line of the Neisse River between Muskau and Görlitz in April 1945.

Foley, Charles: *Commando Extraordinary*; Arms and Armour Press, 1987.
First published in the 1950s it was written with help by the so-called 'most dangerous man in Europe' and remains one of the best — if exaggerated — accounts of the life and times of Skorzeny during World War II. It includes a section on the subject's trial at Nuremberg.

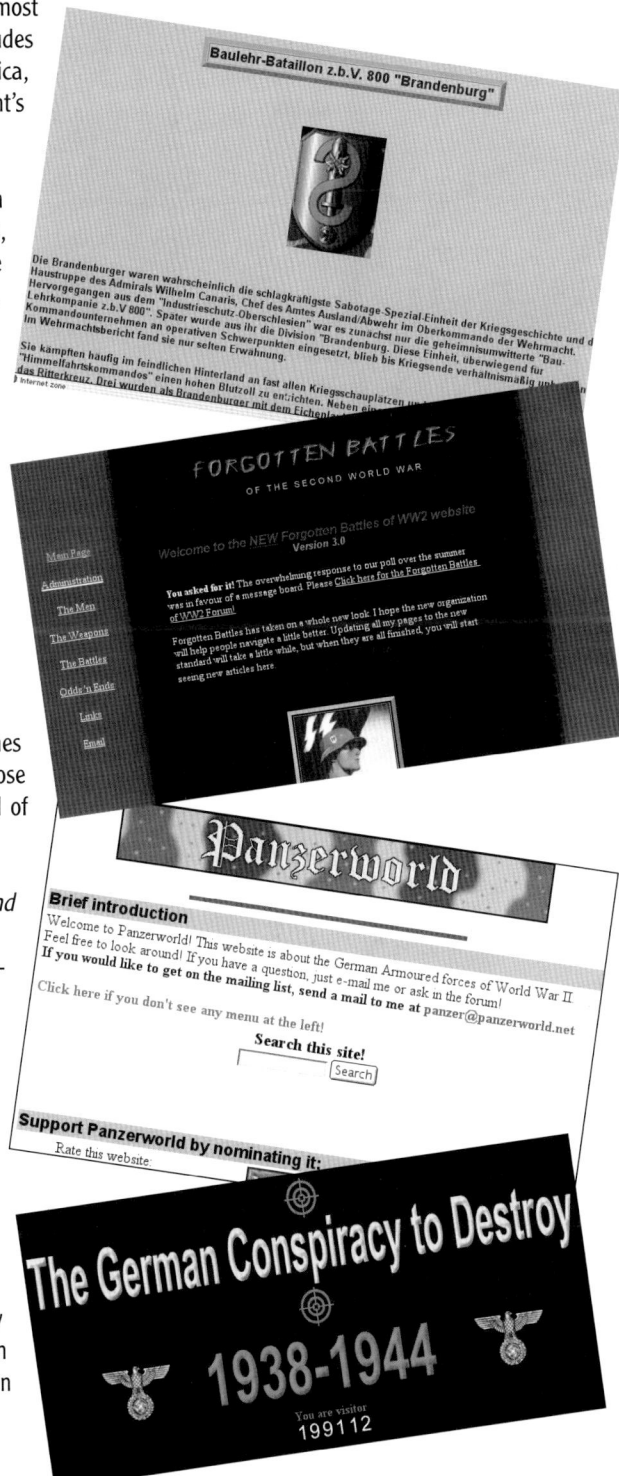

Höhne, H: *Canaris*; Bertelsmann, 1976.
A standard text on the head of the *Abwehr* that charts his rise and the fall of Germany's intelligence-gathering service

Kessler, Leo: *Kommando*; Leo Cooper, 1995.
Writing under his frequently used pseudonym, Charles Whiting recounts in lively style operations conducted by the Brandenburgers and Otto Skorzeny as well as the futile resistance efforts of the teenage Werewolves at the end of the war and the Nazi attempts to establish a National Redoubt in Bavaria at the end of the war. However, it suffers from poor editing and details of some events do not match those found in other sources.

Kurowski, Franz: *The Brandenburgers — Global Mission*; J. J. Fedorowicz, 1997.
A wide-ranging volume that recounts the history of the Brandenburgers and includes some interesting sections on the Brandenburgers most distant missions, including operations in Afghanistan Burma, India, Iran and Iraq that receive virtually no coverage elsewhere.

Lefevre, Eric (trans. Finel, Julia): *Brandenburg Division: Commandos of the Reich*; Histoire & Collections, 1999.
An excellent and detailed account of the Brandenburgers from their earliest days to their last battles as a panzergrenadier division. It also contains copious appendices that give details of the unit's changing organisation and commanders and there is a selection of rare photographs of operations and personalities. Of all the books on the subject, this appears the most measured and accurate.

Lucas, James: *Kommando — German Special Forces of World War II*; Arms and Armour Press, 1985.
A wide-ranging look at Nazi Germany's special forces on land, at sea and in the air. The greater part of the book concentrates on various land forces, particularly the major operations conducted by the Brandenburgers, specialist Luftwaffe paratrooper units and Otto Skorzeny. It also details the rivalry between the SD and *Abwehr*.

Lucas, James: *Storm Eagles — German Airborne Forces in World War II*; Arms and Armour Press, 1988.
Although it concentrates mainly on the Luftwaffe's parachute arm, this highly illustrated volume has chapters on the rescue of Mussolini in September 1943, the battle for Leros the following November and the Ardennes offensive in late 1944 that include reference to both the Brandenburgers and Otto Skorzeny. There is also a chapter that deals entirely with the 500th SS Parachute Battalion's attempt to kill or capture Tito in May 1944.

Lucas, James: *The Last Year of the Germany Army, May 1944–May 1945*; Arms and Armour Press, 1994.
Although wide-ranging in scope, it does include passages that look at the complex and confusing array of units that served under Otto Skorzeny and also gives a brief summary of Operation '*Panzerfaust*', his coup in Budapest in October 1944.

Lumsden, Robin: *A Collector's Guide to Third Reich Militaria*; Ian Allan Publishing Ltd, 2000.
Essential handy reference.

Pallud, Jean-Paul: *Ardennes, 1944: Peiper & Skorzeny*; Osprey Publishing Ltd, 1987.
One of the ever-popular Osprey series that recounts the story of two specialist units

during the Battle of the Bulge in late 1944, including Operation 'Greif' conducted by Skorzeny's 150th Panzer Brigade.

Parssinen, Terry M: *The Oster Conspiracy of 1938 — The Unknown Story of the Military Plot to Kill Hitler and Avert World War II*; HarperCollins, 2003.
An indepth look at the failed attempt by a circle of German officers, diplomats and others to halt the slide to war by assassination on the eve of the conflict. It includes details of the *Abwehr*'s involvement in the plot including the activities of Canaris's deputy, Hans Oster.

Ramsey, Winston (ed), et al: *After the Battle*, Battle of Britain Prints International.
This remarkable magazine and range of books provides a plethora of Brandenburg-related material, including: 'Gibraltar' in issue 21; 'Rescue of Mussolini' in issue 22; 'Operation Panzerfaust' in issue 40; 'The Battle for Leros' in issue 90; *Blitzkrieg in the West Then and Now* and *Battle of the Bulge Then and Now* (both by Jean-Paul Pallud). The level of research and meticulous detail make these publications hugely helpful.

Skorzeny, Otto (trans. David Johnston): M*y Commando Operations: The Memoirs of Hitler's Most Daring Commando*; Schiffer Publishing Limited, 1995.
Skorzeny tells his story in his own words and also recounts related matters such as the flight of Rudolph Hess, his assessment of German and Soviet military intelligence, and the massacre of US troops at Malmédy, Belgium, in late 1944.

Spaeter, Helmut: *The History of the Panzerkorps Grossdeutschland* (Vol. 3).
The final volume in the comprehensive account of undoubtedly the best of the non-Waffen-SS units in Nazi Germany's order of battle charts the history of the unit's latter battles as well as providing a history of the Brandenburgers as a commando unit, their development into the Panzergrenadier Division Brandenburg and the division's battles.

Schenk, Peter: *Invasion of England 1940: The Planning of Operation Sealion*; Conway Maritime Press Ltd, 1990
A detailed and extensive examination of the planning for the invasion of Britain.

Steffens, Hans von: *Salaam — Secret Commando to the Nile*; K. Vowinckel Verlag, 1960.
The memoirs of the *Abwehr* officer who planned the operation to infiltrate agents into Egypt during 1942.

Whiting, Charles: *Skorzeny*; Ballantine, 1972.
An highly illustrated account of the wartime career of the SS's most daring commander of special forces with details on his numerous operations.

Whiting, Charles: *Canaris*; New York, 1973.
An account of the career of Admiral Wilhelm Canaris, head of the *Abwehr*, Nazi Germany's intelligence service, from 19 January 1935 to February 1944 and who was subsequently executed for anti-Hitler activities.

Whiting, Charles: *Ardennes — The Secret War*; Century 1984.
The story behind the various clandestine operations planned and carried out during the Battle of the Bulge during late 1944.

Glossary

Abteilung	Similar to a battalion, a formation of combined units designed to be independent on the battlefield
ANZAC	Australian and New Zealand Army Corps
Aufklärungs	reconnaissance
Bergmütze	uniform mountain cap
Bergstiefel	puttees
Fallschirmjäger	airborne troops
Feldbluse	field tunic
Flak	*Fliegerabwehr-kanone* (AA guns)
Gamsbock	mountain goats
GebG	*Gebirgsgeschütz* (mountain gun)
Gebirgs	mountain
Gebirgsjäger	mountain soldier (infantryman)
Gebirgstruppen	mountain troops
Heer	army (not including SS units)
Heerestruppen	independent army units
Hochgebirgsjäger	high mountain troops
Kampfgruppe	battle group
Keilhose	mountain trousers
Landser	line infantry
leFH	*leichte Feldhaubitze* (light field howitzer)
Litzen	collar patch
OKH	*Oberkommando des Heeres* (Army High Command)
OKW	*Oberkommando der Wehrmacht* (Armed Forces High Command)
PAK	*Panzerabwehr-kanone* (anti-tank gun)
Panzerjäger	anti-tank units
Schirmmütze	peaked cap
Stahlhelm	steel helmet
Waffenfarben	colour on collars etc., denoting branch of service
Wehrkreis	war district
Wiesengrun	grass green, the *Waffenfarben* (branch of service colours) of the Alpine troops
Windjacke	windproof jacket/windcheater

Ranks

Jäger (private)

Gefreiter (corporal)

Unteroffizier (sergeant)

Feldwebel etc (warrant officer)

Leutnant (2nd lieutenant)

Oberleutnant (lieutenant)

Hauptmann (captain)

Major

Oberstleutnant (lieutenant colonel)

Oberst (colonel)

Generalmajor

Generalleutnant

General der Gebirgstruppen

Generaloberst

Generalfeldmarschall (field marshal)

INDEX

Abwehr 98–108, 116, 121, 122, 123, 127, 130, 172, 173, 174, 182, 185

Afheldt, E. 179

Allied units: Armies – First (Greek), 21; Second (Greek), 18, 21, 22; Second Shock (USSR), 42, 44, 45; Third (Yugoslav), 18; Fifth (US), 50, 55, 56, 58, 59, 60, 61, 62, 92; Fifth (Yugoslav), 18; Eighth (BR), 50, 53, 55, 56, 58, 59, 60, 62; Fourteenth (USSR), 48; 52nd (USSR), 45; 54th (USSR), 45; 59th (USSR), 45, 47. Army groups – Fifth 49; Fifteenth, 60, 61. Brigades – 5th (NZ), 29; 7th Tank (USSR), 45; 10th (NZ), 30; 19th (Australian), 30; 24th Rifle (USSR), 45; 58th Rifle (USSR), 45. Corps – I (Canadian), 55, 56; II (US), 50, 51, 53, 55, 59, 60; II (NZ), 52; II (Polish), 53, 55; IV (US), 55, 61; V (BR), 56; V (US), 53; VI (US), 50, 51, 55; VIII (BR), 53; X (BR), 51, 56; XII (BR), 56. Divisions – 3rd Algerian (FR), 51; 4th Guards Rifle (USSR), 45; 5th Armoured (Can), 56, 60; 6th (Australian), 18; 20th (Greek), 18; 24th Guards Rifle (USSR), 45; 27th (FR) Mountain, 62; 34th (US), 51; 36th (US), 51; 92nd (US), 61; 372nd Rifle (USSR), 45; Other – Desert Air Force (BR), 56. Regiments – 5th Rifle (FR), 51

Axis units: Armies – First Panzer, 18; Second, 15, 18; Tenth, 6, 48, 49, 54, 55, 56, 60; Eleventh, 60; Twelfth, 18, 22, 25, 89; Fourteenth, 52, 55, 60; Eighteenth, 15, 44, 48, 56, 60; 20th Mountain, 47; Ligurian, 56, 58, 60. Army Groups – B, 60; C, 15, 48, 55, 58, 60; Centre, 39, 40, 41, 42; North, 39, 40, 42, 44, 48, 60; South, 37, 38, 39, 40, 42. Corps – I, 44, 60; I (Para), 56; II, 47; X, 47; XIV (Panzer), 49, 50, 56, 60; XXVI, 60; XVIII (Mountain), 14, 60; 18, 20–3, 86; XXX, 18, 20, 21, 60; XL (Panzer), 18, 20, 21, 22, 24–5; L, 60; LI (Mountain), 49, 50, 56, 60; LIV, 48, 60; LXIX (Mountain), 52, 86; LXXV, 58, 60; LXXVI (Panzer), 56; Lombardy Corps, 58; Corps Ringel, 86. Divisions (other than 5th Gebirgs) — 1st Fallschirmjäger, 49, 52, 58; 1st Gebirgs, 6, 8, 37, 38; 1st SS Panzer (Leibstandarte), 22; 2nd (Italian) Grenadier 'Littorio', 61; 2nd Panzer, 21–5; 3rd Gebirgs, 16, 38, 86; 4th Gebirgsjäger 37, 38; 4th (Italian) Alpini 'Monte Rosa', 58, 61; 5th Panzer, 24, 25; 6th Gebirgs, 20, 21, 22, 23, 24, 25, 37, 38; 6th Gebirgs Nord, 6; 7th Flieger, 28, 30; 7th Gebirgs, 89; 9th Panzer, 22, 24; 10th, 6, 8, 88; 15th Panzergrenadier, 50; 16th Panzer, 49; 22nd, 28; 44th, 49; 71st, 50, 57; 73rd, 22; 90th Panzergrenadier, 60; 94th, 50; 98th, 60; 164th, 21; 254th, 44; SS Polizei (4th), 45. Kampfgruppen – Altman, 29; Krakau, 34, 35; Nord, 6; Schatte, 32; Utz, 33, 34, 35; Wittmann, 34, 35. Other – 3rd Austrian Mountain Division, 8; 3rd Jäger Regiment, 8; VIII Fliegerkorps, 27; XI Fliegerkorps, 26, 27, 28; Alpenkorps, 7, 8, 64; Bavarian State Police, 8; Chasseurs Alpins, 7, 58, 62; Goslarer Jäger, 7. Hungarian Third Army, 18; Italian Motor Group, 52; Luftflotte 4, 26, 27; Luftlande Sturmregiment, 28, 29, 30; Schlettstädter Jäger, 7; Schneeschuh battalions, 7. Regiments — 1st SS, 22, 24; 1st Fallschirmjäger, 31, 35; 2nd Fallschirmjäger, 31, 34, 35; 3rd Fallschirmjäger, 30; 8th Panzergrenadier, 51; 31st Panzer, 27; 71st, 57; 79th Gebirgs Artillery, 8; 85th Gebirgsjäger, 8, 19, 28, 32, 33, 35; 95th Gebirgs Artillery, 8, 19, 34, 78; 98th Gebirgsjäger, 8, 60; 99th Gebirgsjäger, 8; 100th Gebirgsjäger, 6, 8, 15, 19, 31, 32, 33, 34, 35, 51, 56, 57, 58, 62, 94; 100th Gebirgs Artillery, 8; 125th, 21; 141st Gebirgsjäger, 34; 179th, 51.

Alexander, Harold 52, 55, 56, 58, 59, 60

Antonescu, I. 116, 131, 135

Aretz, Lt 118

Bach-Zelewski, E. von dem 141

Belgium, attack on 109, 111, 112

Belgrade, 126, 138, 139

Billing, G. 153, 160

Bock, F. von 106, 109

Boehme, Franz, 18, 22, 23, 24

Bröckerhoff, W. 179
Broz, J. (Tito) 130, 134, 136, 137, 139, 141, 165, 174, 179, 186
Bruckner, E. von 179
Budapest 137, 141, 142

Canaris, W. 99, 100, 102, 103, 105, 106, 107, 111, 116, 122, 123, 127, 134, 1722, 173, 174, 182, 184, 185, 187
Carol, King of Hungary 135
Clark, Mark, 55, 56, 59, 60, 92
Cos, attack on 128, 130, 131, 177
Crete, 11, 25, 37, 38; battle of, 6, 15, 18, 26–36, 50, 52, 60, 72, 86, 88, 89, 90, 92

DFS 230 glider 121, 123, 125, 165, 168, 169
Dietl, Eduard, 13, 14, 16, 89, 118, 119
Dietrich, S. 142, 144

Eastern Front 116–121, 127, 131, 134, 137, 154, 162, 176, 177, 178, 180, 181, 185
Edelweiss, 16, 17, 64, 66, 69, 72
Einheit Stielau 141, 143, 144, 147, 153, 156, 158, 160, 164, 183, 185
Englandspiel (England Game) 100
Eppler, J. 121
Ernst, Richard, 58, 89

Fabian, Capt 107
Fallschirmjäger, 6, 11, 14, 30, 31, 34, 35, 49, 52, 58
Fieseler Fi156 Storch 126, 164, 169, 170
Foelkersam, A. von 119, 134, 137, 146, 147, 152, 172-173–1, 179
France, Campaign in 109–113
Franco, F. 115, 116, 172, 176
Frankworth, Maj 132

Freyberg, Bernard, 28, 29, 30, 33, 34, 35, 36, 52
Friedenthaler Jagdverbände 126, 176, 180

Gabcik, J. 122
Gamsbock, 6, 20, 64, 86
Gennep 109–111
Giskes, H. 100
Goliath 142, 165, 166–167
Gothic Line, 6, 15, 55–61, 92
Grabert, S. 109, 112, 113, 117, 179, 180, 182
Graziani, Rodolfo, 58
Gueli, G. 125
Gustav Line, 6, 15, 49–54, 90

Hardieck, W. 144, 145, 147, 154
Hartmann, Oblt 107
Heidrich, Richard, 34, 49, 103, 107, 122
Heinz, Maj 118
Herzner, H-A. 106, 107
Hettinger, Lt 118, 120
Himmler, H. 102, 103, 122, 127, 139
Hippel, T-G. von 100, 101, 102, 104, 107, 112, 116, 174–175
Hitler, Adolf, 15, 18, 26, 27, 36, 37, 38, 39, 40, 41, 47, 48, 53, 54, 59, 60, 62, 92, 93, 99, 100, 102, 105, 106, 107, 111, 112, 115, 116, 117, 122, 123, 127, 128, 130, 131, 134, 135, 137, 139, 144, 146, 156, 172, 173, 174, 175, 176, 179, 183, 185
Holland, attack on 109–111
Horthy, M. 137, 141
Horthy, N. 137, 141

Jacobi, P. 118
Jahn, Kurt, 58
Janovsky, Cpl 112
Jodl, Alfred, 36, 37, 143, 144

July Bomb Plot 173, 174, 176

Kaltenbrunner, E. 122
Keitel, Wilhelm, 36, 37, 106, 107
Kenyon, L. 130
Kesselring, Albert, 48, 49, 51, 54, 55, 56, 59, 60
Kleist, Paul von 18
Knaak, H-W. 179
Kniesche, Lt 105
Koenen, F. von 120, 121, 122, 132, 158, 177, 179, 181
Kubis, J. 122
Kübler, Ludwig, 8, 64
Kühlwein, F. 130, 177–178
Küstenjäger Abteilung (Coastal Raider Detachment) 129, 130, 132, 168
Kutschke, Oblt 107

Lahousen, E. 104
Lange, E. 179
Lau, W. 179
Lawrence, T. E. 100, 101
Leeb, Wilhelm von, 37
Leese, Oliver, 55, 56, 60
Leibstandarte Adolf Hitler, 1st SS Panzer Division 145, 153, 175
Leipzig, H. von 121, 129
Lemelsen, Joachim, 56, 60
Leningrad, 6, 38, 39, 40, 41, 44, 47, 48, 49, 60, 82, 86, 90
Leros, attack on 128–129, 130, 177, 182, 186, 187
Lettow-Vorbeck, P. 100, 101, 174
List, Wilhelm, 18, 20, 25, 92, 106
Löhr, Alexander, 26, 27
Luchs, 2-Lt 122

Maikop 118, 119, 173, 179, 185
Malmédy 143, 146, 148, 152, 155, 174, 176, 187

Mannerheim, Carl, 40
McCreery, Richard, 60
Meindl, Eugen 28
Meuse (Maas), River 109, 110, 142, 144, 145, 146, 152, 176
Meyer, Lt 126
Michael of Hungary 131, 135
Metaxas Line, 6, 19, 20–2, 90
Monte Cassino, 11, 15, 49–54, 58, 90, 92
Mors, Lt 123, 126
Müller, F-W. 129
Mussolini, 15, 122, 123, 125, 126, 127, 166, 168, 170–171, 186

Narvik, 13, 14, 16–7, 72
Naujocks, A. 107
North African campaign 121–122, 160, 179, 181, 185
Norwegian campaign 107–108, 111, 169

Oesterwitz, K-H. 179
Operations: Anvil-Dragoon 55, 58; Barbarossa 38, 115, 116–118, 178; Eisbär (Polar Bear) 130; Encore 63; Felix 113, 115, 116, 185; Greif (Gryphon) 142–156, 160, 162, 165, 184, 186; Iskra 47; Leopard 128–129; Marita 15, 18–20; Merkur 27–36; Olive 56, 59; Overlord 55; Panzerfaust 137–141, 160, 165, 184, 186, 187; Polar Star 47–8; Punishment 117; Rösselsprung (Knight's Move) 130, 134–137, 139, 174; Seelöwe (Sealion) 86, 109, 113–116, 169, 175, 177, 185, 187; Strafe 18; Taifun (Typhoon) 127–118; Tyr 36–8; Wacht am Rhein (Watch on the Rhine) 142–156, 160, 165, 183, 184; Wintergewitter 61
Oster, H. 99, 100, 102, 103, 111, 127, 173, 182, 184, 186, 187

Panzer Brigade 150 142, 143, 146, 147, 160, 162, 165, 174, 183, 184, 186

Patzig, K. 99, 102, 103
Peiper, J. 145, 146, 153, 155, 186
Pfeffer-Wildenbruch, K. 141
Pernass, M. 153, 160
Pfuhlstein, A. von 127, 130, 132, 176–177, 179
Pinkert, Capt 132
Polish campaign 105–107, 182
Priess, H. 144, 153
Prinz Eugen, 7th SS Mountain Division 136, 141
Prohaska, E. 119, 179
PzKpfw V Panther 141, 143, 142, 144, 148, 152, 162–163, 164, 186

Raeder, E. 103
Rappel, August, 58, 89
Reichenau, W. von 109
Reichssicherheitshauptamt (RSHA) 103, 122, 123, 175, 180
Reichswehr, 8, 64, 89
Rethymnon (Retimo), 6, 27–31, 34, 35
Ringel, Julius, 8, 14, 22, 28, 32, 33, 34, 35, 36, 37, 52, 86, 88, 89
Rommel, Erwin, 8, 18, 121, 178, 179, 185
Röseke, E. 179
Rote Kapelle (Red Orchestra) 100
Rudloff, H-J. 107, 109, 116
Rundstedt, Gerd von, 37, 60, 106
Rybka, Lt 42, 136

Sandstede, G. 121
Sas, G. 111
Schlemmer, Hans, 58
Schellenberg, W. 122, 123, 127, 175
Scherff, Capt. 144, 147
Schmidt, W. 153, 160
Schrank, Max, 49, 52, 53, 86

Schulte-Heuthaus, H. 131, 177, 178–181
Schüster, Karlgeorg, 27
Schwarze Kapelle (Black Orchestra) 100, 130, 177
Senger und Etterlin, Fridolin von, 50, 60
Skorzeny, O. 122, 123, 125, 126, 127, 130, 131, 133, 134, 137, 141, 142, 143, 144, 145, 146, 147, 148, 152, 153, 155, 156, 158, 160, 162, 164, 165, 168, 169, 174, 175–176, 180, 182, 183, 184, 185, 186, 187
Stalin, Joseph, 40, 41, 42, 44
Steets, Hans, 61, 62, 86, 88
Steidl, K. 179
Student, Kurt, 26, 28, 30, 31, 34, 36, 90, 123, 127
Stumme, Georg, 18, 21, 22, 24
Sturmgeschütz (StuG) III 133, 144, 147, 148, 162
Süssmann, Wilhelm, 28

Tilney, R. 129
Tito (Broz, J.) 130, 134, 136, 137, 139, 141, 165, 174, 179, 186
Trommsodorf, Lt 119, 120
Tropical Company 121, 132, 158, 177, 179, 180

Vietinghoff, von Heinrich-Gottfried, 48, 49, 56, 60, 61, 62
Vlasov, A.A., 42, 44, 45

Waffen-SS, 6, 74, 90
Walther, W. 107, 109, 113, 116, 175, 179, 180
Wandery, M. 179
Westphal, S. 143, 144, 178
Wilson, Henry, 18, 21, 22, 23, 25, 59, 60
Wüllberg, Capt 132